1839-1908 Ouida

**Strathmore**

A Romance

1839-1908 Ouida

**Strathmore**
*A Romance*

ISBN/EAN: 9783741142376

Manufactured in Europe, USA, Canada, Australia, Japa

Cover: Foto ©Andreas Hilbeck / pixelio.de

Manufactured and distributed by brebook publishing software
(www.brebook.com)

1839-1908 Ouida

**Strathmore**

COLLECTION
OF
BRITISH AUTHORS

TAUCHNITZ EDITION.

VOL. 1170.

STRATHMORE BY OUIDA.

IN TWO VOLUMES.
VOL. II.

## TAUCHNITZ EDITION.

### By the same Author,

| | |
|---|---|
| IDALIA | 2 vols. |
| TRICOTRIN | 2 vols. |
| PUCK | 2 vols. |
| CHANDOS | 2 vols. |
| UNDER TWO FLAGS | 2 vols. |
| FOLLE-FARINE | 2 vols. |
| A LEAF IN THE STORM, ETC. | 1 vol. |
| CECIL CASTLEMAINE'S GAGE | 1 vol. |
| MADAME LA MARQUISE | 1 vol. |
| PASCAREL | 2 vols. |
| HELD IN BONDAGE | 2 vols. |
| TWO LITTLE WOODEN SHOES | 1 vol. |
| SIGNA | 3 vols. |
| IN A WINTER CITY | 1 vol. |
| ARIADNÊ | 2 vols. |
| FRIENDSHIP | 2 vols. |
| MOTHS | 3 vols. |
| PIPISTRELLO | 1 vol. |
| A VILLAGE COMMUNE | 2 vols. |
| IN MAREMMA | 3 vols. |
| BIMBI | 1 vol. |

# STRATHMORE

A ROMANCE.

BY

OUIDA,

AUTHOR OF "IDALIA," "TRICOTRIN," ETC.

*COPYRIGHT EDITION.*

IN TWO VOLUMES.

VOL. II.

LEIPZIG
BERNHARD TAUCHNITZ
1871.

*The Right of Translation is reserved.*

# CONTENTS

## OF VOLUME II.

| | | Page |
|---|---|---|
| CHAPTER I. | Requiescat in Pace | 7 |
| — II. | After long Years | 13 |
| — III. | The Pilgrimage of Expiation | 18 |
| — IV. | The Cabinet Minister | 28 |
| — V. | Among the Lilies of the Valley | 37 |
| — VI. | One of the Legion of the Lost | 51 |
| — VII. | The Shadow of the Future | 59 |
| — VIII. | "Seized, in the Name of the Emperor" | 81 |
| — IX. | "Roses my Secret Keep" | 87 |
| — X. | The Night Whisper of the Past | 110 |
| — XI. | Under the Aisle of the Palms | 119 |
| — XII. | Can Oblivion be Bought? | 136 |
| — XIII. | "Morituri te Salutant!" | 150 |
| — XIV. | Lost in the Hour of Redemption | 167 |
| — XV. | "And Retribution arose" | 175 |
| — XVI. | The Choice that was left | 185 |
| — XVII. | In the Cabin by the Sea | 199 |
| — XVIII. | "Ist auch Dies ein Irrthum, so schont mich, ihr klügeren Götter" | 215 |
| — XIX. | "And Unforgiving, Unforgiven" | 222 |
| — XX. | Evil done that Good may come | 230 |

## CONTENTS OF VOLUME II.

| | | | Page |
|---|---|---|---|
| CHAPTER XXI. | The Roses of the Spring | . . . . | 247 |
| — | XXII. | "Sur l'Avenir Insensé qui se Fie?" . . . | 257 |
| — | XXIII. | "Dios Consiente, pero no para Siempre" . . | 267 |
| — | XXIV. | The Symbol of the Dying Flower . . . | 279 |
| — | XXV. | Quæstores Parricidii . . . . . | 287 |
| — | XXVI. | The Outcast by the Gates . . . . | 293 |
| — | XXVII. | Thalassa! Thalassa! . . . . . | 305 |
| — | XXVIII. | Under the Wings of the Angel . . . | 310 |
| — | XXIX. | "The Bows of the Mighty are Broken" . . | 317 |
| — | XXX. | "In the Silence of the Night" . . . | 324 |
| — | XXXI. | "E poi Uscimmo a Riveder' le Stelle" . . | 340 |

# STRATHMORE.

## CHAPTER I.
### Requiescat in Pace.

OVER that grave the twilight shadows stole, the evening dews gathered in the spring violets which clustered round the marble, the birds went to roost in the boughs which swayed above, and the first faint light of the young moon fell across the letters of the inscription, carved deep into the stone as though to stand there, in their recorded crime, through all change of season and all wear of time, eternal as the sin of which they told. She—his murderess—had gone some hours past; and by the grave, unconscious that she had been there before him, and there sworn a vow of vengeance ruthless as his own, stood the companion and the avenger of her guilt. Always thus in solitude and in the stillness of the night Strathmore came hither; often, very often, for his nature was too brave and too proud to spare itself one tittle of its chastisement, and the love which he had borne the man whom he had slaughtered, seemed to well up in deeper tenderness as everything else in him grew harder, colder, and more merciless. A command he could not resist seemed to impel him to come there as men go to the scene of their past crimes, and to stand beside the record of his guilt, beside the tomb where the life his hand had slain in all its glory and its youth, lay rotting to decay in the womb of the black, dank earth.

There, with his head bowed on the cold marble, and his hands clenched on the wet grass that already covered the ground, he often lay through many hours of long, lonely nights; in what remorse God alone saw. He would have poured out his own life like water, to bring back the life that he had slain.

He stood there now, gazing down upon the white shining stone and the dark leaves which swayed against it; he felt as though some atonement had been wrought to Erroll by the vengeance which the day just passed had crowned. Had his arm ever paused in the blow he had struck to the assassin of one, and the betrayer of both, it would have been nerved and steeled afresh by the memory of the dead. Beneath the polished ice, the courtly worldliness of Strathmore's character, lay the fierce, untamable nature of the Barbarian, or the untutored Southern, their passions, their love, their vengeance; to him there was not alone revenge in that which he had wrought on the traitress who had stained his hands in blood; there was a wild justice done, there was a duty expiated to the dead in the retribution which had pursued the murderess.

As he stood there in the shadowy light, while the moon streamed upon the sepulchre lying at his feet, the solitude, which reigned unbroken about Erroll's grave, for the first time was shared, and on his ear fell the low, mellow, chanting voice of Redempta the gipsy.

"English lord, I have given you your vengeance! Is it sweet in your teeth, or has it turned to ashes as you ate?"

He started as her form suddenly rose from the depths of the woodland gloom and stood before him by the grave; but the chill smile which had so much of cruelty came on his lips as he glanced at her.

"Redempta, the only thing in life whose sweetness never palls, and cannot die, is vengeance."

Her deep, lustrous eyes, which were now heavy and weary, gleamed for the moment with the evil which glittered in his own, as at the touch of fresh flame dying embers leap to life.

"Ay, ay, she has suffered! I have seen misery gather in her eyes, and shame bowing her head to the dust, I have watched her shiver under the scorn of laughter, and I have heard her moan with pain like a hopeless, fallen thing. She has suffered! *That* cannot escape me!—*that* cannot be undone! I have avenged him, and now——"

Her voice dropped, and she was silent, while over the lurid light of her eyes a humid softness gathered, and her lips trembled with a voiceless movement—her thoughts were with the dead. For the heart of the woman was in pain, and sickened with the futility of a revenge which could not yield her back what she had loved; it knew not the exultant and pitiless lust of the man, which rioted in vengeance, and fed on its knowledge, and its memory, insatiate and unpalled. For there was this wide difference between the passions of their lives: hers sprang from love which still lived and was deathless, his from love which had become hatred, and in that hatred lost all other sense.

Strathmore glanced at her in the gloaming; he owed this woman much, since he owed her the first secret of his power over the life which he had pursued and hunted down; and the sole price which the Bohemian had asked or taken had been that which she had first named: "to see her suffer."

He stretched out his hand with some louis d'or:

"Redempta, you are ill-clad and in want; take these now, and in the future let me serve you?"

She signed aside the proffered gift with a proud gesture of denial, and on her face came a strange smile, derisive yet melancholy:

"My lord! I told you long ago that Redempta the Vagrant took no price for that which she brought you—no wage for her vengeance. Since his hand lay in mine, no man's gold has soiled it; and with the future I have no share; my work is done. The future is for you: it lies before you; go where it beckons!"

As the Czechen words were uttered in the monotonous, chanting recitative in which she spoke, to the memory of each recurred the spring night far away in Bohemia, when the ruddy gleam of the gipsy-fires had shone through the aisles of the pine woods, and when from the slumbering passions written on his brow she had made sure prophecy of all which, when they should awaken, would scorch and devastate his life. Her hand closed on his arm in a grasp which he could not have shaken from him without violence, while her eyes dwelt on him where he stood in the gloom, and studied his face with the same fixed, dreamy gaze with which she had looked on him then: a look which had much of compassion.

"I have no future, but one waits for you; you must reap as you have sown; you must gather the harvest, and eat of the fruit of your past. It is the inexorable law! The past has been wrought by your own hand; but the future will escape you. You will seek to build anew, and lo! the curse of the dead sin will rest on your work, and the structure will crumble, falling to ashes as it reaches its fairest. The sin of the guilty has been avenged, but the sin to the innocent will never be washed away. You will be great and powerful, and success will go with you, and fame; but the bloodstain will be on your hand for ever, and when you have made atonement, behold it will be seized in your grasp, and through you will the guiltless be menaced!"

The words in her Czechen tongue fell slowly and melodiously in the silence in her mournful and monotonous recitation, while her eyes dwelt on his face with their vague, fathomless gaze. Her hand dropped from his arm and left him free.

"In the future you will remember the words of Redempta. We shall meet no more. Farewell!"

She turned from him, and, with the swift, noiseless movement peculiar to her tribe, was lost in the veiling shadows of the night. He stood motionless where she had left him, in the dull, grey light as the moon passed behind the clouds of the east. Again at her words ran a ghastly chill, as at the touch of steel in a vital wound; less from their prophecy than from their truth; the future stretched before him, darkened for all time, by the shadow of remembered guilt. His hand might pioneer his road to power, and reap him honour in the sight of men, but there for ever on it must rest the stain of innocent blood. His life might pass onwards in the fulness of years and the ripeness of triumph, but there for ever at its core must lie the curse of an inexpiable act.

Never to lose it, ever to bear it through all the years to come, that burden of life taken, never to be restored; of sin wrought, never to be undone! Veiled in the mist of hidden years, who knew what guiltless life that guilt might strike? who knew what retribution might be coiled and waiting to take its vengeance for the unforgotten crime? who knew where the after-harvest of his passions might be reaped and garnered?

The future! the future! He had said in his soul, "vengeance to the living, but to the dead, atonement." Standing there beside the grave of him whom he had slain, while the words of the prophecy echoed in his ear, the phantoms of the years to come seemed to rise and swarm about him, and rend, and tear, and shatter from his hands the work of Expiation.

That night the Seine wound slowly and darkly through the open country and under the pale, clear stars, and among the rich glades of woodland, towards the city, there to grow black and sullen beneath the arches of dim-lit bridges, and to wash the low walls of the dreary Morgue, and to see the yellow candle faintly burning above the iron cradle of the Enfans Trouvés, and the thousand lights gleaming bright along the palace façade of the Tuileries.

And where the river was still clear, and cool, and fresh, ere it had reached the evil heat and brooding shadows of the city, where green leaves still swayed in its water, and in its depths the starlight gleamed, where its darkness was still repose, and its silence holy, a human form hovered on its brink, bending wearily towards the tranquil gliding waters, where the water-lily floated, and the hush of night seemed visibly to rest.

It was so cool, so serene, so peaceful: to lie there lulled to dreamy death by the cadence of its ebb and flow, and know no more the passionate pain, the breathless tumult, the vain despair, and the unending bitterness of life, were this not wisdom, oh you who suffer?

It looked so to her; for her soul was weary of its travail, and her heart was fain to be at rest. She looked far across the dark and silent country, where no living thing stirred, and upward to the stars, whose white light fell upon her deep and melancholy eyes; her hands were pressed upon her bosom and her lips moved in faint, broken words:

"I have avenged thee. What have I more to do with life?"

Her head drooped upon her breast, and she leaned nearer and nearer towards the waters, where the quiet stars were shining, and the pale lilies slowly floating in their shroud of leaves, where were oblivion, and peace, and death; and in the silence she listened to the tranquil murmuring of the tide. And as she thus leaned nearer and nearer yet towards that cool and restful place, in her weary eyes shone the gleam of unshed tears, and in her face a new light came as on the face of one who, having been long imprisoned in the loneliness of exile, beholds escape at last, and liberty and rest.

From her parted lips a whisper stole, broken and yearning, on the hush of night:

"My love! my love! I come!"

And in the silence there was the dull moan of severed waters, and the troubled lilies trembled on the river's breast: then, with a sighing sound, the wind swept over them, and all was still.

The waters flowed upon their changeless course.

Through the summer night the river wound its way under the radiance of the stars, and bore her with it more gently than life, more tenderly than human hands. The waters rippled on with liquid murmur, and the dead body of the Bohemian floated down the stream in its serene and solemn rest, finding repose at last after the heat and travail, the passion and the pain, of many years. To her untaught, unfettered soul, love had been God, and vengeance, Duty; and death was ransom justly won, after a mission justly wrought; death in her wild, instinctive, barbaric creed was sure reunion with him for whom she had suffered and been sacrificed, and to whom her life had been unceasingly consecrated even to the last, if erring in its revenge, yet heroic in its martyrdom.

The waters bore her onwards slowly, softly, as merciful hands bear the bier of the dead; now in the cool shadow of the leaves, now in the clear sheen of midnight planets, while on her upturned brow and her closed eyes the moonlight shone with fair and peaceful gleam, and in her dark, floating hair the stainless lilies wound, and through the hush of night the winds gently breathed over the surface of the waters, which murmured low about her as though in pitying whisper:

"Rest in peace, O human soul! And judge her not for sin which had its root in love, you great and countless criminals upon earth, whose lust is avarice, and whose god is self."

## CHAPTER II.
### After long Years.

A SULTRY night brooded over London, close and stifling in the dusty, crowded streets, fair and pure above-head, where the stars shone over the leaden roofs and the fretted pinnacles of the great Abbey, over the thronging carriages rolling through the midnight, and the black river, with its spectral mists rising against the sky. It was a hot, oppressive night, with heavy storm-clouds drifting to the westward, and every now and then a far-off roll of thunder faintly echoing; and outside the walls of St. Stephen's men thronged, talking eagerly, and avaricious of news, and waiting to learn the fate of the existent Cabinet; for in the political horizon, as in the summer skies, a storm threatened darkly, and the kingdom had thrilled with the first ominous echoes. And they surged and swayed and filled all the crooked streets round about, and were newly fed by fresh arrivals, and talked thirstily in busy groups, some anxious-eyed and with pale eager faces; for the Ministry was unpopular, and on the issue of the night there rested not alone the question of resignation, but the question of war or peace, in whose balance the God of Gold hung trembling.

Within the walls the heat was heavier, the crowd more dense, for many peers had come down to their seats beneath the clock, and the galleries were crammed; the import of the night was widely known, and the attack upon the Ministry from the most distinguished leader of the Opposition carried with it all the aspirations of his great party, and was keenly dreaded by his adversaries then in office.

For he was essentially a great Statesman. His genius was emphatically the genius of Power. In classic ages he would have been either a tyrant as Pisistratus, or an intriguer as Themistocles; a ruler as Cæsar, or a conspirator as Catiline; what he grasped, how he grasped, mattered nothing to him, so that he had his hand on iron reins, so that he had his foot on bended necks. The subtle ruses, the unscrupulous finesse, the imperious command, the absolute dominance of power, these were what he loved; and what he wielded, for his mind was one of those which are formed to *rule*, and before which the mass of minds involuntarily stoops suppliant. In his age and in his country, his ambition was perforce chained within bounds, and he could not be that which he would have been in a nation or a century where such governance might have been grasped—an irresponsible and despotic ruler, recognising no limits to his sway, and reigning by the sheer strength of a will of steel, and of an intellect which would have raised his people into greatness and dominance abroad, and would have permitted no rebellious hint against his *fiat lux*. This, circumstance and nationality forbade to him; but the character and the genius which could have made him this, made him in the highest sense a great and successful politician. A profound master of statecraft, an astute reader of men, a skilled orator as well by the closeness of his logic as by mere rhetorical grace, comprehending to the uttermost the truth of the trite byword *ars est celare artem;* never for one instant irritated into abandonment of the suave courtly dignity which did much to fascinate men to his will, and with that proud disdain of wealth, of empty place, of childish honours, which gave to his career a lofty and unsullied renown—he who in his youth had desired Age and Power, now, approaching to the one, and having attained to the other, found ambition richly ripened to fruition, and exercised over the minds of men a sway wide and acknowledged, a fascination resistless and dominant.

As he rose at midnight in the hot, close stillness, all eyes turned on him, and the cheers which thundered his welcome echoed loud and long, then died away, leaving a silence in which the fall of a pin would have been heard, had one dropped from the lattice-work, behind which were seated the fairest and proudest women of the two great political parties. The dead hush reigned through the Lower Chamber, so that no syllable of the opening words should be lost, as upon the air fell the first clear, chill, melodious tones of his voice, which in invective was ever tranquil, in command ever calm, in denunciation ever courtly, but whose wrath scathed keen as steel, whose mockery pitilessly withered all it touched, and whose dreaded sneer spared neither friend nor foe.

He stood in the full light, one hand in his breast, the other slightly outstretched; on his face a certain melancholy repose, a tranquil and haughty power; in his eyes the swift light, which swept the House like an eagle's glance; on his lips the slight smile that his opponents dreaded; while the lucid, classic, resistless flow of his oratory rolled on, calm, polished, subdued, as suited an audience he had long studied, never losing its dignity, while it rose to denunciation, holding in passion, while it lashed with scorn, fascinating the ear by the melodious music of voice, while it scathed with delicate irony, or rose to stately and measured rebuke.

He spoke long and with a masterly eloquence; his speech was an analysis and attack of a measure of the existing Government, obnoxious at home and pregnant with offence abroad. Loud and repeated cheers thundered through the Chamber as his keen logic mercilessly dissected the weak and wavering policies of the Ministry, and his brilliant argument cleft down their barriers of defence, and rent asunder their sophistries of rhetoric, as the sword of Saladin cut its way alike through iron casque and veil of gauze.

When he resumed his seat the victory of his party was virtually won, and one of the most marked triumphs which had attended a continuously successful career had been achieved: a tottering government, already jeopardised by its own imprudence, and unpopular with press and people, had been shaken by an attack to which it could oppose but feeble reply and futile defence, and it was widely whispered that the Ministry must resign on the morrow.

Since the great speeches of Sheridan and Canning, few had created so keen an excitement, few weighted so markedly the balance of parties, few thrilled the House so profoundly with the breathlessness of a gladiatorial contest, the heat of a close struggle, the grandeur of a great conquest. As he left the Lobby afterwards his name was on every tongue, and while the proud tranquillity of his features and of his manners was unruffled, and he passed from the scene of a supreme conflict with the easy negligence of his habitual air, unmoved to excitement or to exultation, in his eyes gleamed an imperious rejoicing light under their drooping lids, and they glittered dark with a grand triumph; for this man's god was Power, the essence of his life, the goal of his ambition, the idol of his creed.

As he passed out from the Commons to his night brougham, the multitudes gathered outside (amongst whom had been spread swiftly as wild-fire the news that the Ministry had been defeated on their unpopular measure, and the country been saved from the risk of a needless war by the issue of that great Field-night) recognised in the gaslights the grace of carriage and the haughty features of the well-known member, and pressing forwards by one impulse to view him more closely, broke by one impulse also, into a long, loud shout of salutation, which rang through the sultry air of the late night, quelling in its own thunder the distant roll of the rising storm.

It was Titan homage, rendered with the spontaneity of academic applause, and the hoarse roar with which the masses hurl out their gratitude and welcome, grim, wild, half barbaric, yet grand in its deafening echo and intoxicating in its enthusiasm, like every proclamation of the people, which in the Leader of the Hour recognises the virtual Sovereign of the Land.

He whom they thus saluted passed through them, bowing slightly on either side in acknowledgment, with dignity and courtesy; he held the imperious patrician code of his Norman race, he was an Optimate to the core, and the plaudits of the Populares were almost as indifferent to him, almost as disdained by him, as their censure; he had much of the despot, he had nothing of the demagogue. But in those cheers echoed the homage which multitudes yield to a single dominant intellect; in that welcome rang the acclamations which greet and confirm command; in that human thunder, which outpealed the thunder of the skies, his sway was ratified by the nation; and as his glance swept over the people, and he passed down the narrow path, left him, lined by eager crowds, the Statesman's pulse quickened and beat higher and the lustre of his eyes gleamed darker with their scornful triumph; Strathmore tasted to its full sweetness the one lust of his soul—POWER.

O strange unequal portioner called Life! unjust are its awards and inscrutable its decrees.

The murdered man, who when the summer sun had sunk to rest, had been hurled into his grave, guiltless of all crime save of a too loyal friendship, lay rotting in a foreign land, forgotten from the day when the seal had been set on his sepulchre, by a world which has no time to count its lost.

And his destroyer lived, high in honour amidst men.

## CHAPTER III.

### The Pilgrimage of Expiation.

A SOFT, serene, richly-tinted picture, fairer than a thought of Lancret's, more golden and tranquil than a dream of Claude's, since one hour of sunlight on one stretch of moss, one fruit-laden bough, one changeful brook, outshines and baffles the best that we, vain painters of nature, can ever catch of her glorious loveliness on canvas or palette. Who knows this better than the Masters of the Art?

The setting sun shone on the oriel casements of an antique ivy-covered Elizabethan mansion, and streaming through the unclosed door of an old stone wall, ripened to gold the fruit of an orchard, whose branches nodded through the opening. Far away to the west, wide, calm, limitless, stretched the great ocean, the gleam of the light falling on the white sail of some fisher boat in the offing. Beyond the tangled leaves of trees, shone the glisten of wet sands and the red boulders of the rocks. In the silence there was no sound but of the birds' last nest-songs, and of the murmuring seas; and under the shelter of dense boughs, shutting out the sun, was a shadowy solitude, where nothing came save the fragrance of countless flowers, and nothing was seen save the silent sunlit bay, when the arching branches parted to show the sheen of sand and sea. It was a home fit for Undine, here in the shadow of the leaves, the earth covered with the delicate bells of heath, the foliage filled with the soft movement and music of young birds, the blue waters gleaming through the spaces of the boughs, the silence but the more serene for the lulling cadence of the seas; and she to whom it was consecrated might well have been sketched as Undine, where she sat, with her head slightly drooped and her lips slightly parted. For she was in the earliest years of opening youth, and of a loveliness ethereal, poetic, such as Dante may have prefigured amidst the angel shadows of the Paradiso, or Guido Reni have beheld flit through the heaven of his visionary thoughts, too pure, too fair, for the artist to transfer to grosser colouring.

Both poet and painter would have loved that face, but neither could have made it imperishable on written vellum or on tinted canvas; it could no more have been imprisoned to such transcript than the blush on the heath-bells, than the smile on the seas, than the fugitive play of the sunlight. It had a beauty beyond words, beyond Art.

The brow was low and broad, the skin delicate as a white rose-leaf, with the faint flush on the cheeks beautifully fitful; the eyes large, dark, shadowed by their lashes till their violet depths looked black. But what lay beyond poet to phrase, or artist to produce, were not these, but were the spirituality of the whole face vaguely suggestive of too early death, utterly above all grosser passion, all meaner thought of earth, and the touching and nameless contrast of the sunny joyous smile upon the lips with the fathomless sadness of the eyes, of the grace and radiance of childhood with the ethereal melancholy of the features in repose. It was a loveliness like that of the delicate tropic flower which blooms but to perish in all its early beauty; too fragile for the storms and darkness of night, too soilless to wither on earth. She sat there, with the shadow of the thick leaves above her, and around her the melody of the ocean, the music of the birds, and the dreamy hum of bees deep down in the chalice of flowers.

And one unseen, as he stood and watched her, was never weary of gazing on that delicate picture, though it had been familiar to him from his childhood. He was a youth of two-and-twenty, tall, lithe, of a thorough Saxon beauty, with his bright fearless face, his bold blue eyes, his tawny hair, yet he did not suit that scene; he was out of harmony with it, and he broke its spell, even as he broke that of her thoughts, as he put aside the boughs and bent towards her very gently:

"Lucille! where are your dreams?"

She started a little, and looked up at him with a glad smile.

"Nello! I banished you; is this the way you obey? Look! how you frighten the birds and trample the heath."

Lionel Caryll looked sad and repentant as the singers flew from him with a rapid whirr of their wings, and he glanced down on the trodden bells.

"Oh, Lucille, I am sorry! But surely you love me something better than you do those birds and those flowers? *They* feel no pain!"

"I think they do," she said, musingly. "Look how birds' eyes grow wild and piteous when you go near their nests, and how they droop and pine if they lose the one they love; and look how the flowers fade when they are taken from the sun, and wither slowly when they are torn away to die under the pressure of your hand. Ah! I cannot bear to see a flower crushed or broken, Nello. We cannot tell what it may suffer."

Her eyes grew humid and earnest in their dark depths, for the ruling power of her nature, as its fatal danger, was a deep and infinite tenderness, a too keen and too early susceptibility. Young Caryll did not understand her, he did not even follow the thread of her thoughts; in the long years they had spent together, the poetic and profound mind of the child had always been above and beyond the boy's comprehension; they were so now, but now, as then, he felt for all she did and said a tender and reverent love, as for something at once too holy and too fragile for his rougher hands.

"Who could hurt what you plead for, Lucille?" he said fondly. "But if you give so much compassion to your flowers and birds, give a little to me."

She laughed joyously:

"Pity *you*, Nello! What pity do you want? You are as happy as I am! Why, Nello, you are sunshine itself!"

The young man's bright face laughed sunnily in answer: it was the truth, his nature and his life were both shadowless.

"Yes, but pity me for seeing that the song-birds and the heaths are both dearer to you than I! True they suit you better, Lucille; they are poetic and delicate, and I am neither; but they cannot love you so well!"

In the half-laughing words, in the half-boyish appeal, there was, almost unknown to himself, an inflection of jealous pain, of touching humility, which struck on his listener's ear with some vague sense that she unwittingly had wounded him, though how she knew not. With caressing grace she stooped towards him, where he lay at her feet, and pushed back the tangled hair from his forehead.

"My own dear Nello, I know that! Could you think I rank those things before you? For shame! I thought you knew better how I loved you!"

For the playmate and companion of her childhood was very dear to her, and it was an impulse with her to soothe all pain, from the flutter of a frightened bird to the sorrow of a human heart; and Lionel Caryll gazed upward with an eager pleasure in his eyes, while his lips were mute: it was the reverent and breathless gaze of the young devotee at the beauty of a Madonna or a Vivia Perpetua, the beauty which is too sacred in his sight to waken passion, or be profaned by aught save a holy worship.

He rose with a smothered sigh as he recollected the object of his errand, for he would gladly have stayed here till the moon rose, with murmur of the sea in his ear and the hand of Lucille softly playing with his hair, in the familiar affection which from her infancy she had shown to, and received from, one whom she called her brother.

"Lucille, Lord Cecil is here—I came to tell you."

"Here!"

"Yes, he has come down for part of the Easter recess; only a day or two, for he is going to Osborne. He bade me fetch you to him."

Ere the words were spoken she had sprung to her feet, dropping the Vita Nuova she was reading, and the feathery seaweeds which had lain on her lap, to the ground, and had left him, lightly and swiftly as the flight of a wild bird.

Lionel Caryll stood in the shadow of the leaves, looking

after her. From his earliest years, when the young child, orphaned and desolate and unconscious in her glad infancy of her own fate, had first come to Silver-rest, he had been careful of her every step, jealous of her every smile; he had followed her like a spaniel and tended her like a woman, and risked his life and limb many a time to bring her down some sea-bird's egg, some flower from the cliffs, some treasure from the waves.

Lucille loved him very fondly, for this child's whole life and nature were tenderness; but the boy had always felt what he felt now, that two stood before him in her heart— the dead, whose name she cherished with a reverence which was almost a religion, and the one whom she and the world knew as her guardian.

In the deep embrasure of one of the windows sat a man, with a staghound at his feet, and his face in shadow, as Rembrandt or Velasquez painted the faces of the statesmen and conspirators who sought their canvas, to whose portraits, indeed, he bore a strange and striking resemblance, for Strathmore with the flight of years had altered little. The darker traits were more traceable, the better less so; for in the human face, as in the picture, with time the shadows deepen and the lights grow fainter. The eyes were more searching, the brow more powerful, the features colder and more inscrutable still. Otherwise there was but little change save this, that whereas before, the character of his face had been suggestive of evil passions, dormant and not yet called into play, it now bore the shadow of them from the past, the trace of fires which had burned to ashes, scorching as they died.

Strathmore, who was God and Law unto himself, had moulded his life with an iron hand, although on that hand was the stain of crime. Submerged for a while under the surge of passion, the ambition which had been drowned under a woman's love had returned to him; a diplomatic career he had abandoned for public life at home, and he had reared himself from the fires of past crimes to follow one road—Power. Eminence in statecraft, his astute, subtle, and masterly intellect was formed to attain and wield. Under his chill and withering eloquence parties writhed; before his courtly and poignant wit opponents cowered; beneath the dominance of his will, wavering adherents bowed; and before the silent and profound mind of the successful politician men felt abashed, discomfited, yet governed despite themselves.

Strathmore was great in many things—in his genius, in his endurance, in his power, in his arrogance; and he had that veiled yet astute will which bends that of all others to its bidding, and governs the minds of men by a resistless, though not seldom an evil, fascination to its sway. To trample out the memories of the past by dissipation was impossible to the man whose intellect was masterly, and who had rioted in the drunkenness of guilt; the revel of orgies was distasteful, the pursuit of licentiousness was contemptible to him. Forgetfulness he sought otherwise, under the iron tramp of mailed ambitions; or rather, to speak more truly, forgetfulness he did not court, as weaker men would do; but as he had kept the mad love which had betrayed him before him, to be avenged brutally and ruthlessly, so he kept the crime which had stained his soul, to be atoned for as though destiny lay in his hands, so he kept the blood-stain on the statue of his Life, to be wrought out by his own hand in after work. For Strathmore, though the pride of his nature had been smitten to the dust, and though he had reeled and fallen under passion, had refused to gather warning from the past, but held it still his to mete out fate to himself and others, as though he were not man but deity.

The sunlight played without, among the leaves while the ocean broke upon the sunny sands, and he sat there in the shadow: on his face was the look of a weary and hopeless melancholy, which never wholly passed away, for the soul of this man, if merciless to others, was not less so to himself; in spirit he scourged himself for the lives which rested on his, as loathingly as ever Carmelite or Benedictine scourged the body for its sins, and whilst before men's sight his life was cold, unruffled, brilliant, and his "path strewn with the purples" of fame and of power, there were dark hours in his solitude, of remorse, of anguish, of unutterable horror, when the great and fallen nature wrestled with itself, and struggled in its agony nearer to God's light. For *repentance* is a word by a thousand-fold too faint to utter that with which Strathmore looked back upon the past—looked back upon the homicide guiltier than Cain's.

Suddenly, where he sat in the embrasure, a shadow fell athwart the sunshine without, and raising his eyes he saw the young life which was freighted with his venture of atonement. She stood there in the full golden light, which fell on her fair and shining hair; on her eyes, dark as the violet skies of night, and full of their mournful earnestness; on her lips, which wore the sunny and tender smile of the long-dead, radiant with welcoming joy while words were mute; words could not have spoken half so well!

"Lucille!"

He rose, and she sprang towards him, lifting her fair young face to his gaze, while he stooped and kissed her brow with his accustomed caress, which she received as a child her father's. Her hands closed on his softly and caressingly, her lips were tremulous, her eyes, loving in their earnestness, looked up to his winningly, beseechingly:

"Ah! you are come at last; you have been so long away!"

"'So long!' You have watched for me, then?"

"My heart watches for you always!"

He smiled; her answer gave him pleasure. Long years before he had set his will to fasten the love and gratitude of this young life upon himself, and every assurance of them was dear to him, for they were the assurance of his fulfilment of Erroll's trust, of his atonement through the living to the dead.

"And you are happy, Lucille?" he asked her.

She laughed the soft, low laugh of her still lingering

childhood, in which pain had been a thing unknown, to which sorrow had been a mystery ever veiled.

"You ask me that so often? 'Happy?' All my life is happiness. I cannot even fancy grief. I try sometimes, and I cannot."

"Thank God!"

The words were spoken low and heartfelt, and he shaded his eyes with his hand as he gazed down on her, while over the coldness of his face stole a warmth and a softness which never came there save when he looked on her. Her singular and poetic loveliness, as she stood before him in the mellow sunlight, with her dark eyes uplifted in their beseeching beauty, struck on him; he saw for the first time that she was passing out of childhood.

"You are changed, Lucille," he said, as she threw herself at his feet, where he sat, in that graceful and trustful abandon which was as natural to her now as when she had first come caressingly to his side on the sea-shore; for this opening life had been left free, pure, untrammelled by art or bondage, as any of the white-winged birds which spent their summer days above the waves.

She looked up incredulous and amused:

"Changed? How can I be in six months?"

"Six months is six years at your age: the passage from childhood to womanhood is very brief; crossed sometimes in a night, sometimes in an hour!"

"Is it? But *I* have not crossed it."

"No, and I do not wish that you should."

She lifted her eyes to his, full of that appealing earnestness which gave them so strange a sadness, so touching a beauty.

"No more do I. When time rolls on, the shadows deepen across the dial in the orchard, and the sands of the shore; so they say they do in life. Is it true, Lord Cecil?"

"Fatally true, my child."

She shuddered slightly:

"Ah! and that is why I wish mine could rest for ever

where it is. I am so happy, and I dread the shadow! In shade the flowers die, you know, killed by the darkness and thirsting for the sun; so should I."

"Hush, hush, Lucille!" he said, passionately, as he drew her towards him, where she sat at his feet. "'Dread!' 'Darkness?' What have they to do with you? Neither shall ever touch you. Your future is my care; think of it as what it will be, *shall* be, as fair and cloudless as your past and present. No shadow shall ever fall on you!"

"Not under your shelter!"

And as she spoke gratefully and caressingly, the smile was on her face which still smote him as with steel, and she bent towards him with that tender and trustful grace natural to her from her earliest infancy: she loved the hand which fostered her—the hand stained with her father's blood.

The human life which the last words of the man he loved had bequeathed to him in trust, was dear to Strathmore as the dead had once been; and when remorse had struck prostrate the granite of his nature, in the chasm left, this single softness had been sown and taken root; even as on the chill and isolated mountains ice-covered and inaccessible, deep down in some cleft and hidden rent, lives some delicate blue alpine flower. Begotten of remorse, born of a thirst for atonement, and fostered by a passionate, almost a morbid, craving to fulfil to the uttermost Erroll's latest bidding, his tenderness for Lucille had become the one holy and unselfish thing in a heart to which the gentler and purer feelings of human nature and of human ties were by nature alien.

Strathmore's haughty and sin-stained soul hung on this young and fragile girlhood for its single chance and power of atonement. It was not *she* for whom he cared; it was the dead. Had the last words of the man he had wronged and hurled from earth, condemned him to endless self-chastisement, or self-sacrifice, he would have obeyed them equally, nor spared himself one iota of their enjoined torture. Pitiless to others, I say he was not less pitiless to himself; his life, stained with great crimes, was riven with a great remorse;

his nature was like those lofty and darkened ones which first filled the cells of Clairvaux and the ranks of Loyola; natures passion-stained and crime-steeped, but which, even as they had spared none in their guilt, spared not themselves in their expiation.

The trust bequeathed him, and bound upon him, by the weight of the two lives which his act had struck from earth, he fulfilled sacredly. His hand had orphaned her, but his hand sheltered her, and was prodigal in the wealth, and care, and luxury with which it surrounded her; it seemed to Strathmore as though thus, and thus alone, could he atone to him who had given her life. In his mother's home she had grown from infancy to early youth, fondly nurtured, and trained to know that it was from him as her guardian that she received all which made her young years so joyous. Those to whom her education was entrusted he forbade to use any laws with her save those of gentleness, and directed to surround her with all tenderness, to shield her from every touch of pain or harshness, and to indulge her in all things. He was scrupulously obeyed, and the result might have been to many natures dangerous; with Lucille, the inherent character was too loving and too sweet to be thus harmed, to do aught but expand to all its richest luxuriance, its purest delicacy, in the constant sunlight in which it grew, though, as the hot-house flower is rendered unfit for the cold winds without by the warmth which surrounds it, so might this nature be for the harsh conflicts of life. But, then, these she was never to know—from these she would be sheltered, as the exotic is, through the whole of its brief and radiant life.

In pursuance of Erroll's desire, he trained himself to speak to this child often and calmly of her father, as of one lost and dear to him as to herself, until Lucille held, inseparably interwoven and beloved in her memory, the dead, and the living to whom the dead had bequeathed her, and who filled his place. It had been hard to say which were the dearer to her, the ideal of her father which she cherished, or the love for Strathmore which grew with her growth. No instinct had made her shrink in infancy from the hand which was stained with her father's blood; no prescience now warned her that he who fostered her was her father's foe. All her joy, all her gifts, came from him; for her, his eyes were ever softened, his voice was ever gentle; the distant visits he paid her were sealed with gold in her life, radiating every day they graced with a glory ever missed in his absence. And thus Erroll's young child grew up in her graceful loveliness, her happy innocence, with no shadow allowed to fall on her from the dark tragedy which had orphaned her almost from her birth, but with a deep and reverent love for him, between whom and herself, had she known the truth hid from her, there would have yawned a hideous and impassable gulf, there would have stretched a fell abyss of crime which would have made her shrink from every touch of his hand, shudder from every caress of his lips.

## CHAPTER IV.

#### The Cabinet Minister.

A KNOT of lords and gentlemen, diplomatists and ministers, were grouped together in the ante-room at St. James's, after attending a Levee—the last of the season—chatting while awaiting a chance of getting to their carriages through the crowd, where torn shoulder-knots, trampled epaulettes, the débris of gold lace, fragments of bullion, broken plumes, or shreds of order ribbons, bore witness to the severity of the conflict, which is a portion of the ceremonial attendant on the Germanised Court of England.

"But V—— gained so much by the Schönbrunn Treaty; he is far too exigeant," said the French Ambassador, alluding to the subject under discussion, which was the aggression of a petty Duke, who might chance to embroil Western Europe; European tempests not seldom being brewed in a Liliputian teacup.

"But others gained, too, by the treaty," suggested an

English Minister, "and grapes shared are poisoned to most gatherers. With a whole bunch to ourselves, we grudge the broken stalk that we leave behind."

"*Hein! c'est vrai!*" laughed a Prussian Statesman, applying himself to his tabatière. "Still if he were decently wise he would be content."

"Is it wise to be content?" smiled the English Minister; and his smile was cold and ironic. "What duller atmosphere possible than Contentment? A satisfied man has nothing to desire, gain, or contest; he is a mould-grown carp in stagnant waters——"

"Which are the quietest," added the Prussian, who had too much slow Teuton blood in him not to relish "stagnant waters." "I suppose V—— thinks with you, or he would never thrust forth such claims; he knows the Federation will never acknowledge them."

"But they will foment disturbance; they will draw the eyes of Europe on him for half a dozen months, and many would rather be decorated like Midas, than move unnoticed and unknown in

secretum iter et fallentis semita vitæ,"

said the English Statesman, with a contemptuous laugh, cold, slight, and clear.

"Et puis," said the Ambassador, with a slight shrug; "the opportunity was tempting. Man was created a dishonest animal, and policy and civilisation have raised the instinct to a science."

"And what he seeks now is for 'Patriotism.' Let none of us forget that. 'Pro Patria' is so admirable a plunder-cry; I don't know a better, unless it be 'Pro Deo,'" smiled the Englishman, whose own *cri de guerre* was, with but little disguise, "Pro Ego."

Standing at a little distance, wedged in by the titled and decorated mob, a man looked at him as he spoke; the words were inaudible where the other stood, but the smile he saw and knew of old, he had seen it on his lips when the sun sank down beyond the purple shroud of mist, seen it as the duellist stooped to watch the dark blood slowly trailing through the grasses, with the passionate and cruel lust which branded him assassin. Raoul de Valdor had long forgot that hour, from the indifference of custom to a life so taken, and by long years passed in a fashionable whirl. At the time it had chilled and revolted him from the man who, with deliberate purpose, had slain his friend with the unerring aim and greed with which a tiger darts upon his prey, insatiate to destroy and indifferent to destruction. But their intercourse had remained the same, and the remembrance had drifted into the mist of long past things. It rarely recurred to him, yet it did so now, standing in the thronged ante-chamber of the palace, when glancing at the successful Statesman, with the ribbon crossed on his breast, and the cold courtly smile on his lips, there arose before him, sudden and distinct, the memory of that summer night, with the hooting of the shrill cicala, and the sullen surge of the noisome waters as the reptiles stirred amongst their reeds, and the last rays of the evening sun gleaming above the storm-cloud as the dying man reeled and fell.

He looked at Strathmore as he stood among his peers; and, strange, dissimilar, unbidden, the scene rose up before the memory of the inconsequent and thoughtless Frenchman, as he stood among the court crowd of St. James's. Yet he had been present at many such scenes, and the value of life taken had never weighed on him, nor its memory ever remained with him, before. In his creed of honour duels were blameless; in his country's custom they were habitual. What long ago had revolted the dashing and daring spirit (which with many faults and many follies had something of the old code of the gallant gentlemen who had fought and died for the White Lilies) had been the pitiless *purpose* which he had read ere the shot had been fired, and which had borne in his sight the fixed and treacherous intent of the murderer. It was this which he remembered now.

The throng parted, the knot of ministers separated,

Strathmore came forward to go to his carriage, and Valdor moved also; they met, as they had done a hundred times, since that night by the Deer-pond of the old Bois.

"Ah! you Valdor! Charmed to see you. I had no idea you were in England, much less at the Levee. Insufferably warm, isn't it? Such a press!" said Strathmore, giving his hand to the man who, sixteen years before, had whispered in his ear, "*Fuyez! il est mort,*" unheeded, as he stooped to sever the gold flake of the hair which trailed among the dark dew-laden grasses.

"Such wretched rooms!" laughed Valdor, as he glanced contemptuously through the reception-chambers, unaltered since Queen Anne. "I only arrived yesterday. I have come to town on family matters—a disputed inheritance affair. But permit me, mon ami, to offer my congratulations on your recent honours; never was a finer political victory won. Your coup d'état was supreme!"

Strathmore smiled.

"You give me and my party too much distinction; we only effected, dully and slowly, by speeches and leaders, what you over the water would have done in a week by a few cannon-balls and closed barrières. But the British mind refuses the quick argument of a fusillade—as if it were not as wise to be convinced by a bullet as by a newspaper! Will you do me the pleasure to drive home with me?"

They pioneered their way through the arristocratic mob, and reaching the air at last, after the heated atmosphere of the densely-packed palace, passed to Strathmore's carriage, while the crowds without, waiting to see the courtiers leave the Levee, crushed themselves close to the wheels, and rushed under the horses' heads, and pushed and jostled, and trampled each other, in eager curious haste to see the favourite Minister—he who, could he have had his way, would have ruled them with a rod of iron, and swept his path clear from all who dared dispute his power, by the curt Cæsarean argument of armed hosts!

"Have you any engagements for to-night, Valdor?" he asked, as the carriage moved.

"None. I was going to dine at the Guards' club, and look in at the Opera."

"Give me the pleasure of your society, then. I have a State dinner this evening; the cruellest penalty of Place! Though truly it is selfish, perhaps, to ask you to throw over that most graceful of all sylphs, La Catarina, for ministerial proprieties."

"The egotism, at least, does me much honour. I shall be most happy. Your season is pretty well over, Strathmore; you eat your farewell whitebait soon?"

"To-morrow. I shall leave town in a week or two; the session will virtually close then."

"Where are you going, après? White Ladies?"

"Not yet. I shall be there the last days in August, when I hope you will join us. Völms and plenty of people will be down; and by all they send me word, the broods are very abundant and the young deer in fine condition. No; I go from town into Devon to see my mother, stay there three or four days, and then start for Baden, give a week coming back to Fontainebleau with His Majesty, your execration, and to White Ladies by the First."

"You go into Devon next week?"

"Or the week after. Why?"

"Because I am bound there. Perhaps you remember I have English blood in me by the distaff side? and there is a property down there which ought, I think, to be mine by rights, at least it needs looking into; *pas grand' chose*, but valuable to a poor wretch a million or two of francs in debt. I must make investigations at your Will Office ('Doctors' Commons,' n'est ce pas? 'Doctors',' because it has the testaments of those the doctors have killed; and 'Commons,' because it is common to nobody who hasn't the money to pay the fees. You English have a grim humour!). We can go down to the south together, Strathmore?"

"Certainly." (Valdor did not note that the answer was

slightly constrained, and halted a moment.) "Where is this property you name?"

"Bon Dieu! I don't know! The place is—peste! it is in my papers but it is out of my head!—wait a moment—is—is —Torlynne, surely, or some such title."

"Indeed! That is close to my mother's jointure house of Silver-rest. I remember it is a disputed title, an old moated priory with fine timber, but wholly neglected."

Valdor twisted his scented moustaches with a yawn of ennui:

"Vous me faites frémir! What on earth should I do with a 'moated priory?' It sounds like a ghost-story! However, I shall go down and prove my title if I can; for I suppose it will sell for something?"

"Undoubtedly. Since you will require to be on the spot, I am sure I need not say that Lady Castlemere will be most happy to see you at Silver-rest, if you like to stay with us."

Valdor thanked the kindly Fates which thus, by a fortunate chance, preserved him from the horrors of Devonian hotels, and accepted Strathmore's invitation, proffered from a cause he little guessed. Strathmore had heard of his intended visit to the south with annoyance, almost for the instant, with apprehension; it was this which made him hesitate, and but coldly consent to the suggestion that they should travel together. He knew that Valdor had heard those last words breathed with a broken sigh, "Lucille! Lucille!" and he dreaded to see the child of Erroll in the presence of one who had been with him in that hour. But as instantly he remembered that do what he would, Valdor, compelled to visit Torlynne, would certainly pay a visit of compliment to Lady Castlemere, and, living on the same solitary shore with Silver-rest, could not fail to meet Lucille. Therefore, with that policy which he used in trivial as in great matters, he disarmed all danger by meeting it d'avance; any act unusual on his part might have wakened Valdor's curiosity or wonder concerning the lovely child whom he would find there as his ward; to invite him at once beneath the same roof with her was to avoid, entirely, exciting that piqued interest which, though no link remained to guide him by any possibility towards the truth, might yet have induced him to inquire much that would have been difficult to satisfy.

The foresight was wise, the reasoning just, the inference and expectation both rightly founded; yet—woe for us, mes frères!—the surest barriers raised by men's prevision are but as houses builded on the sands, which one blast of shifting winds, one sweep of veering waves, may hurl down into dust.

"What spell have you about you, mon cher?" said Valdor, two hours later, in the drawing-rooms of Strathmore's residence, as he threw himself into a dormeuse. Time had passed lightly over Valdor, and left him much the same—a gay, débonnaire, brilliant, French noble, whose fortunes were not equal to his fashion, in whom a transparent impetuosity mingled in odd anomaly with the languor of the world, in whom the fire of the South outlived the indifferentism of habit, and who, with many follies and some errors, had honour in his heart and truth in his tongue. He looked younger than he was, with his delicate brune tint, his soft, black eyes, his careless and chivalrous grace; and the man in whose society he now was looked on him disdainfully as "bon enfant," because his hot passions were short-lived, and the nonchalance of his nature made him candid as a child.

Strathmore raised his eyebrows:

"'Spell!' What a romantic word! How do you mean it?"

Valdor laughed, throwing back the dark waves of his hair; he was a little vain of his personal beauty.

"I mean to account for your perpetual success. You command success as if you had all the genii of fable to back you. Men censure you, oppose you, hate you, inveigh against you, and you have a strong party of foes, but they never contrive to defeat you."

"Well, I am not very tolerant of defeat."

"Pardieu! who is? But most of us have to swallow it sometimes. What I want to know is how you succeed in perpetually compelling your enemies to drink it, and avoiding one drop of the amari aliquid yourself!"

Strathmore smiled; the frank expression of curiosity and opinion amused him; he had himself the trained reticence of the school of Machiavelli, and years had of necessity polished his skill in the knowledge "how to hold truth and how to withhold it," once laid down by him as the first law of wisdom and of success.

"You ask for a précis of my policy! You know I invariably contended that what men choose to accomplish they may compass sooner or later, if they use just discernment, and do not permit themselves to be run away with by Utopian fancies or paradoxical motives. Let every one make up his mind to be baffled in what he undertakes nineteen times, but to succeed on the twentieth; I would warrant him success before he has reached half the score."

"That tells me nothing!" said Valdor, petulantly, though, in truth, it was this very inflexible and long-enduring patience, which nothing could dissuade or daunt, that was the key of Strathmore's rise to power. "Well! you must keep your secret, mon ami, and I dare say it has too much science and subtlety in it to lie in a nutshell. But as for your theory, which makes one think of the Bruce Spider-tale—peste!—it won't answer always. Look at *us;* we persevere for ever, and never succeed!"

Strathmore smiled slightly; he knew Valdor referred to the efforts of his own French party, and the loyal Utopia of a Quixotic and chivalric clique, found little sympathy with a statesman the distinguishing and most popular characteristic of whose politics was their entire freedom from all idealogy or vagueness.

"Mon cher! I spoke of a man who pursued a certain definite goal and power for himself, not of those leagued together for the chase of a shadowy chimera. To seek a palpable aim and a palpable ascendency is one thing; to embrace a visionary crusade and an ideal flock of theories is another. *I* mean blasting a rock with rational materials and science; *you* mean climbing the clouds with ropes of sand!"

"Then," said Valdor, impatiently, with a dash of envy and a dash of intolerance—"then it would appear that the wise man consecrates his labours and his ambitions to the advancement of himself; it is only the fool who wastes both on mankind!"

"Certainly," smiled Strathmore. "Who ever doubted it?"

At that moment the doors of the vestibule were thrown open, and the first of the guests bidden to his State dinner was announced: further tête-à-tête was ended.

Strathmore was not popular among his colleagues; his personal coldness and his consummate indifference to how he wounded, repelled men, the generosity of feeling and the cordiality which in earlier years had been very strong to the few whom he liked, were gone. Although his liberality was as extensive, it seemed rather to proceed from disdain of wealth than any kindlier feeling, and though at times great and even noble deeds were traced to him done in privacy, they appeared rather to come from some rigid law set to himself than from any warmer feeling toward humanity. But his ascendency was indisputable, his intellect priceless to his party, and the brilliancy of his career without a rival; and men rallied about him, and confessed his influence as the most prominent politician of his day, and the assured leader of the future.

Valdor looked at him as he sat that night at the head of the table entertaining many of the most distinguished men of his country and time, fellow-Ministers and foreign Ambassadors, while the light from the chandeliers above, flashing off the gold and silver plate, the many-hued exotics, the snowy Parian statuettes, and the bright-bloomed fruits, fell upon his face with its peculiar Vandyke type, in which were blent the haughty melancholy of Charles Stuart with the statesmanlike power of Strafford, the serenity of a fathomless repose with the darkness of passions untameable if aroused.

Valdor looked at him as Strathmore drank his Red Hermitage and exchanged light witticisms with the French Representative, and again, unbidden and unwelcome before the thoughtless mercurial mind of the dashing and languid *lion*, rose the memory of that night in the Bois de Boulogne, and of the tiger-lust with which the death spasm had been watched to slacken and grow still.

"*He* has forgotten!" thought Valdor, with marvel, admiration, revulsion, loathing, all commingled. "He slew without pity; he lives without remorse."

So rashly do men judge who draw inferences from the surface; so erringly do they condemn who see not the solitude wherein the soul is laid bare!

## CHAPTER V.
### Among the Lilies of the Valley.

THE afternoon sun was warm on land and sea, and a light amber haze was lying on the soft outline of the hills, the stretches of golden gorse, and the glisten of the moistened sands, as a steam-yacht which had come down channel from the Solent, and rounded the coast, anchored in the little bay of Silver-rest, where nothing was ever seen save the fishing-smacks and tiny craft of the scattered population, whose few rough-hewn shingle cottages nestled under one of the bluffs.

"There is your Torlynne, Valdor," said Strathmore, pointing to some gable-ends which arose some mile or two off in the distance above masses of woodland, as they walked up from the shore. They were expected at Silver-rest, but the day of their arrival had been left uncertain, as he had not known when he might get finally free. Strathmore allowed himself little leisure in office; he never appeared either hurried or occupied, but he burnt the candle of his life at both ends, as most of us do in this age, and must do, if we would be of any note in it.

"Ah, pardieu! I wish it were an hotel in the Rue de Grammont instead!" laughed Valdor, as he glanced across. "Not but that, I dare say I shall never get it, unless I languish through your Chancery till I am eighty. I shall hear the verdict is given in my favour, just when I am receiving the Viaticum!"

"I hope better things; it is a vast pity it should moulder unowned. Meanwhile, the litigation befriends me with a most agreeable companion during my exile at Lady Castlemere's. I fear you will be terribly bored, Valdor; my mother lives in strict retirement."

"Another instance of those who once ruled the world abjuring it in advancing life. What years it is since I had the honour of seeing her. I was a little fellow—a court-page, proud of my blue and silver! Does she live alone, then?"

"Oh, no; merely away from the world. She has a grandson with her, a lad at college; and also a ward of hers and of mine, little more than a child as yet, Lucille de Vocqsal."

"De Vocqsal! An Austrian name, isn't it!"

"No, Hungarian; it may be Austrian, too, however—*is*, indeed, I think, now you name it. You must expect to find Silver-rest dull—it has nothing to boast of but its sea-board."

"And its country," added Valdor, as they passed through the lodge gates.

Strathmore glanced carelessly over the magnificent expanse of woodland and moorland, hill and ocean, which stretched around.

"Yes; but that has not much compensative attraction for either you or me, I fancy."

They went on in silence, smoking, through the grounds, which were purposely left in much of the wildness and luxuriance of their natural formation, with here and there great boulders of red rock bedded in the moss, and covered with heaths and creepers, and Strathmore looked up in surprise as a sudden exclamation from Valdor fell on his ear.

"Bon Dieu! Look there. How lovely!"

Strathmore glanced to where Valdor pointed, marvelling that the landscape should rouse him to so much admiration, for the fashionable French Noble was not likely to be astonished into any enthusiastic adoration of the pastoral beauty of nature, or the sun-given smile on the seas.

What he saw was this.

A rock of dark sandstone overhung the turf below, forming a natural chamber, whose walls were the dense screen of tangled creepers and foliage pendent from its ledges, or the great ferns which reared to meet them, and whose carpet was the moss covered with lilies of the valley, which grew profusely where the tempered sun rays fell through cool leaves and twisted boughs, flickering and parted. And under its shelter from the heat, half buried in the flowers, lying in the graceful abandon of a child's repose, resting her head upon her hand in the attitude of Guido's "Leggiatura," her eyes veiled as they rested on her book, one sunbeam streaming through the fan-like ferns above, touching her hair to gold and shining on the open page she read, was Lucille.

The steps of both were involuntarily arrested as they came upon her in her solitude; there was something of sanctity in that early loveliness,

> Soft, as the memory of buried love;
> Pure, as the prayer which childhood wafts above—

that silenced both him to whom it was familiar, and him to whom it was unknown. Then Strathmore turned to move onward through the grounds; he felt repugnance to break in on her repose, or to meet her in the presence of the one who had heard the dying lips faintly whisper the name she bore, in their last farewell to her lost mother.

But Valdor put his hand upon his shoulder.

"Wait for Heaven's sake! Who is she?"

"A lovely child, but no more than that as yet. My ward, Lucille de Vocqsal."

"Mort de Dieu! She is the most beautiful poem, picture

—Heaven knows what—that ever I beheld. Make her lift those eyes; what must the face be when they are raised?"

"You will see her later on," answered Strathmore, coldly. "I shall not disturb her now; she is very young, and would not understand our having pryed on her in her haunt. And pray do not use that flowery language to her; youth flattered into vanity is ruined, and you would talk in an unknown tongue there."

He moved away, and Valdor, something surprised and something annoyed, prepared to follow him with a lingering backward gaze. But it was too late; a squirrel swinging downward from the boughs above made Lucille raise her eyes. She saw Strathmore, and, with a low cry, wild in its gladness, sprang from her couch among the lilies, and flew to meet him. Midway, she saw, too, that he was not alone; and paused, hesitating, with the colour, delicate as the rose flush on a sea shell, deepening in her cheek. She knew by instinct that Strathmore was haughtily reticent before all auditors, and although too highly bred and nurtured to know embarrassment, she had something of the beautiful wild shyness of the young fawn with those who were strange to her.

A shudder ran through Strathmore's veins as he perceived her standing before them there in the sultry mellow haze; while the eyes of his companion rested on her—the eyes which had watched with him the shadows steal over the face, and the convulsion shiver through the limbs of her father, in the summer-night of years long gone.

Then he moved forward and greeted her with all his accustomed gentleness, less tenderly than when they were alone —but to that she had long been used when any other was present at their meeting—and led her towards Valdor.

"Lucille, allow me to introduce to you one of my oldest and most valued friends."

"Pardieu!" thought the Frenchman; as after a graceful acknowledgment of his salutation, none the less graceful, but the more, from that delicate proud shyness which was like the coy gaze of the deer, Lucille turned to Strathmore with low, breathless words of joyous welcome, and the radiance of that smile at which the sadness fled from off her face, as though banished by a spell. "Pardieu! when was anything more exquisite ever born; it is not mortal; it is the face of an angel. I have seen something like it, too, somewhere; now she smiles it looks familiar. Perhaps it is some head of Guido, some fantasy of Carlo Dolci, that she makes me remember. She seems to love her guardian; is she the only thing on earth he does not ice? The last man living, I should have supposed, that would have taken such an office; however, it may be done from generosity here. Strathmore would ruin his friend without mercy if he stood in his way, or awoke his passions; but he would give royally to his deadliest enemy who asked him in need. A bad man sometimes; a dangerous man always; but a mean man, or a false man, never!"

Which fugitive thoughts flitting through the volatile and reckless mind of Valdor, which seldom stayed to sift or criticize, were just enough in their deduction, drawing one of those haphazard truths by instinct, for which patient and shrewd observation often toil half a lifetime in vain.

"What were you reading there among the lilies of the valley, Lucille?" asked Strathmore, as they passed onward through the grounds, while her head was ever turning with a graceful, upward movement to look on him, and her eyes were ever seeking his with their loving, reverent regard, as though she could scarcely believe in the actual joy of his presence. They were but few and rapid visits which he paid her, but they were remembered passionately from time to time. The fairest summer lost its beauty if he never came with its golden promise; the dreariest winter was glad and bright with all the warmth of spring in her sight if it brought her but a few hours of his presence. From the moment when as a little child on the sea-shore she had asked him his name that she might say it in her prayers, Lucille had clung to the memory of Strathmore with a strange and deepened fondness far beyond her years.

"I had taken Æschylus and Euripides."

"You can read them in the original then, mademoiselle?" asked Valdor, in surprise.

"Lucille learns very rapidly, I believe," answered Strathmore for her. "She has been taught chiefly what she fancied to study, and one of those fairy fancies was Greek. I believe merely because she had heard how the sea she loves was loved in Hellas—was it not, Lucille?"

She smiled, and looked over to the sunny waters.

"Well! I can fancy how the Ten Thousand clashed their bucklers for wild joy, and shouted 'Thalassa! Thalassa!' to the beautiful dancing waves. I love the ocean! It is a music that is never silent, a poem that is never exhausted. When I die I should like my grave to be beside the sea."

"Death for you, mademoiselle!" broke in Valdor, while his eloquent southern eyes dwelt on her with admiration. "The gods have lavished on you every fairest gift, but they will be too merciful to those who look on you, to show their love towards so bright a life, in the way the Greek poets deemed the gentlest."

Lucille raised her eyes to his with something of surprise; she was unused to the suave subtleties of flattery, while a shadow stole over her face, such as an artist would let steal over the young face of Proserpine or of Procris whilst yet they lived their virginal life amongst the flowers, the shadow of that unknown future which lay awaiting them coiled in the folded leaves of yet unopened years.

"I wonder they chose early death as the gentlest fate," she said, softly; "to die in youth, to leave all the warmth of life for the loneliness of the grave, to grow blind to the light of the sun, and deaf to the voices we love, and to lie alone there, dead, while the birds are waking, and the wind is blowing over the flowers, and the day has dawned for all but us! Oh, who could choose it?"

The words, spoken with the unconsciousness of childhood, yet with the utterance of a poet, were very touching, and silenced both who heard her; one they smote with the memory of that dawn when the birds had sung under the leaves, and the rejoicing earth had waked to gladness, and alone amidst that waking life had lain in rigid stillness the brother he had slain.

"She knows nothing of that past story, or she would not speak thus of death to him," thought Valdor, moved and impressed by this beautiful child, whom he had seen among the lilies: she was a study so new to him.

"Æschylus and Euripides have saddened you, Lucille," said Strathmore, as he moved a wild rose-bough from her path. "Those tragedies of curse and crime are far too gloomy for you."

"Oh no, I love them!" she answered him, with the ardent eloquence natural to her, and cultured, not fettered, by education; "they are grand, they are like a sea-storm by night! And they are so human through their grandeur too; the Eumenides may be fable, metaphor, spirit-allegory, what it will, but while *one* man sins, Orestes will be mortal, and will live? That guilt wrought in a moment's vengeance; that burden bound upon the murder for ever; those ghastly shapes which follow him, though to all other sight he is alone; they surely are true for all time while crime is still on earth!"

"And there is a crime yet more accursed than Orestes'— Orestes' victim was *guilty!*"

Her thoughts had been uttered from an imagination freshly steeped in the solemn verse of the tragic poet; his answer broke, beyond all check of will or power, from the sleepless remorse of conscience, stung into one momentary bitter Meâ Culpa.

Past the ear of the young girl it drifted harmless, revealing nothing, and like an utterance of an unknown tongue: his companion knew whence the words sprang, and thought,

"I did him wrong: *that* was remorse."

Strathmore caught his look, and his proud and disdainful nature shrank in wrath from its generous compassion. After long years of constant intimacy, through whose whole tenour this man had never seen deeper than the rest of the world saw, nor probed his silken social vest to the iron cross worn beneath, Strathmore knew that he had betrayed his secret to him. Sensitive, and intolerant of intrusion, he resented pity yet more than insult.

The clear, silvered moonlight fell on Lucille's face that evening where she sat beside the open window in the twilight, which at her entreaty had not yet been banished from the chamber, though in the inner drawing-room beyond the chandeliers were lit, and Valdor and Strathmore's private secretary were playing closely contested écarté.

The stillness was unbroken. Lady Castlemere sat silent, a stately and noble woman, who bore her seventy years with dignity, though attenuated by bodily infirmity; in whose glance was still the fire, and in whose features the arrogance of earlier years, though both were tempered now by a touching and chastened gentleness. Her grandson, Lionel Caryll, was silent also; though bold and careless enough ordinarily, he feared his uncle; to him as to all youths Strathmore had always been cold and negligent; in the presence of the profound man of the world, the able and subtle statesman, the chill and brilliant courtier, he felt abashed, shy, ill at ease, and the polished ice of tone and manner froze the boy's frank young heart. The stillness was unbroken, save by the sound of the waves from without, or the noise of a grasshopper under the leaves, whilst the moon shone on the silvered sea, calm and phosphor-lighted; and Strathmore where he sat looked at Lucille, as, with her head bowed slightly, and her dark wistful eyes gazing out on the night, the starry radiance fell about her.

With much that was dissimilar, she had all the brightness and delicacy of her father's beauty, though upon it was a vague, intangible shadow of sadness, as though the tragedy of his fate had left an unconscious melancholy on the life which took its existence from him. Strathmore saw and noted this; he had done so often, and it always smote him with keen dread; for every touch of sorrow which could have fallen on her he would have held as a breach in his fulfilment of her father's trust. His eyes rested on her, and his thoughts filled with the thronging shapes and memories of the past. Forbidden intrusion in the press of the world, trodden down in the path of power, dashed aside by the mailed hand of a successful and unscrupulous ambition, they coiled about him *here*, and would not be appeased. While she smiled up into his face; while he spoke to her calmly of her father; while he bent his will to rivet her affection and her gratitude, a vain remorse was on him. As in monkish times, those whose lives were fair in the sight of men, and who wielded the sword as the sceptre of sway over the world, came to the dark sepulchre and the blood-steeped scourge for their chastisement, so he came for his into the fair and innocent presence of this young life.

He sat long silent, looking on her where she gazed out to the moonlit sea, his thoughts in the travail of the past; and he slightly started as his mother, who was near him, spoke:

"Lucille will soon cease to be a child!"

"Not yet—not yet!" he answered hastily, and almost with pain. "In Heaven's name, let her guard her childhood over all the years she can!"

"Surely, but it will flee of itself beyond our arrest. One touch will soon scare it for ever."

"Accursed be the touch that does!"

Lionel Caryll heard, and looked at him, and the young man shuddered as he caught the look on Strathmore's face; he did not know that the sole feeling which prompted Strathmore's words was a passionate wish that the childhood—so easy to gladden, so easy to shield—could be prolonged for ever; a passionate fear, which crossed him for the moment, lest, when she should be no longer child but woman, others beyond his control should make shipwreck of the life in whose innocence, peace, and protection his atonement lay.

Their words did not reach her ear, but the sound of them roused her from her reverie, and she came and knelt before him with her hands crossed on his.

"Lord Cecil, I have something to beg of you."

He looked down into her large soft eyes.

"Of me, Lucille? You know you never ask in vain."

She laughed with a child's gay joy.

"Ah, how good you are! I want you to let me come and see White Ladies?"

"White Ladies! Why there?"

"Because it is your home. It is not far away, and I should so love to see it. It must be such a grand and stately place, with its cloisters and its forests? I have read of it in the archives, and chronicles, and legends. I know them all by heart! And they frighten me, some of them—that one, its terrible burden:

> Swift silent Strathmore's eyes
> Are fathomless and darkly wise,
> No wife nor leman sees them smile,
> Save at bright steel or statecraft wile,
> And when they lighten foes are 'ware,
> The shrive is short the shroud is there!

It is not true of the name either now. Your eyes are not cruel, and your hand never harmed any!"

The innocent, half-laughing words struck him like a dagger's thrust;—the legend on *her* lips which had been on Marion Vavasour's, prophetic of the guilt into which his passion and a woman's lie would hurl him! The sickly memory of the Domino Blanc passed over him; more horrible in all its remembered brilliance and beguiling, than any scenes of misery and torture. He heard the very ring of the masker's laugh, so mockingly sweet, so luringly fatal! He lived in that hour again fresh as though it had been but yesterday! He shuddered, and in the moonlight the pale bronze of his cheek grew whiter; but Strathmore, a courtier and a statesman, had not now to learn the lesson of self-control, of calm impassibility. He smiled:

"Why take pleasure in those dark legends of a benighted age, Lucille?—they have nothing in common with you, you fair child! What I have brought you befit you much better. Come, let us see how you like them!"

He stretched out his hand, and took from the table, where

he had lain them earlier in the evening, some cases of pink pearls as costly in their value as they were delicate in setting and in hue; he was prodigal of all that could either amuse or adorn her, but, from her age, these were the first jewels he had brought her, and, stooping, he clasped their bands of gold upon her arms, throat, and hair. The white moonlight fell about her where she knelt before him, on the graceful abandon of her attitude, on her face, upraised as a child lifts it in prayer, and he watched the flush on her cheeks, the breathless pleasure on her lips. Every time he saw her glance lighten, and her lips laugh, *through him*, he felt that so far the trust of Erroll was fulfilled, that so far his atonement was wrought out, that so far his expiation might claim to wash out the sin.

"Ah! how beautiful they are, and how kind of you to bring them!" she whispered him, rapidly and caressingly. "You have always some new thought for me. Look how they gleam and glisten in the moonlight! What jewels are they? They have the blush of a wild-rose——"

"And of your cheek," said Strathmore, with a smile.

She laughed: reared in innocence and seclusion, she was wholly unaware of her own loveliness, and flattery had never polluted her ear nor profaned her heart. She had the fairest charm of youth—unconsciousness. Then her eyes, uplifted to his, grew earnest; she leaned slightly forward towards him, and her voice changed from its breathless pleasure to a tender and almost saddened earnestness:

"Ah! how good and generous you are to always give me pleasure; and yet, do you know—do you know—I sometimes wish you did not give me half so much, that I might show you better how Lucille loves you! I sometimes wish that you were not rich and great, but poor, so that you might know how little it is *these* I care for; a lily of the valley, a heron's feather, a forest squirrel from WhiteLadies, would be as dear to me if from *your* hand. It is so little to love those who give us joy; the proof of love is to endure in pain!"

"God forbid that you should prove yours so!"

Her words moved him; any evidence of her affection was welcome for the sake of the dead, yet every evidence of it struck him with a pang of remorse. This child, who caressed his hand as the one from which she received all joy and blessing, would have shuddered in horror from its touch had she known the life it had blasted from earth!

"Do not wish that, Lucille," he added, gently. "I need no proof of what I know. Remember, I read your heart like an open book, and can see all that is written there."

She smiled, a sweet and trustful smile.

"Yes! I forgot; only sometimes I wish that I could *prove* it to you. While you make me so happy, what value is there in gratitude! The very dogs love the hand that feeds them! But, Lord Cecil, you have not told me—may I come to White Ladies?"

"Some day, perhaps."

But as Strathmore put her tenderly aside, and rose to approach his mother, he thought, with a shudder, of the dark shadow which lay athwart that threshold, making it impure for her fair and innocent youth to cross. White Ladies!—where a fatal love had trampled aside all laws of hospitality and honour; where the beginning of that ghastly tragedy had opened, only to close when the sun went down upon his wrath, and the dying sigh trembled through the silence; where her father's memory filled every chamber, haunted every familiar place, and peopled the vacant air, with the thronging phantoms of a vain remorse!

As he had entered the room from that beyond, having finished his game, Valdor had overheard her request, and had noted the manner in which it was received.

"She has never seen White Ladies, and he will not have her there! It is strange!" thought the Parisian, struck by the circumstance, as he might never have been but that the fair face which he had beheld first among the lilies, had wakened a new and deepening interest in him. Lucille was so unlike all he had ever seen.

"Your ward is very lovely, Strathmore," he said that

night, as they walked up and down the lawn under the limes smoking. "She reminds me of some one, I cannot for the life of me think whom. Can you help me?"

"Not at all. It is rather an uncommon style of beauty," answered Strathmore, indifferently, while swift to his own memory swept the recollection of that sunset hour when Valdor had watched the death-spasm convulse the face whose features she took, and the death film gather over the eyes from which her own had their smile.

"True. But I have seen some one like her," persisted Valdor. "Did I ever know her parents?"

"Very possibly. But both died so many years ago that it is not likely, I fancy, that you would recall them."

The answer was negligently given, as in a matter of small moment, yet in no way as though he avoided the inquiry; for though his earlier regard for truth had not worn away, the profound and acute mind of the politician had dealt too long in finesses not to deem them legitimate under private or public necessity.

"De Vocqsal," repeated Valdor, musingly. "She was of Hungarian birth, I think you said? May one ask, without intruding, anything more?"

"Of course, my dear Valdor!" said Strathmore, surprisedly, with his slight, cold smile. "You speak as though Lucille were some enchanted princess! But there is little to learn. Her name you know; she lost her parents in her infancy; I and my mother are her guardians. What remains? She is still a child!"

"But a lovely one, pardieu!" laughed Valdor, thinking to himself that he had been a fool building up a mare's-nest. "Do you know that I have actually been bête enough to suspect you of a nearer tie to her. I fancied she might be your daughter."

Strathmore smiled:

"Mon cher! your imagination has run riot! That my mother's home is hers might have assured you of the legitimacy of her birth."

The Comte laughed gaily:

"Of course!—and *I* should be the last to wonder at a generosity in you. But—one question more! Why will you not let her go to White Ladies? I could hardly help echoing her prayer myself."

"She may go, certainly, but she is almost too young to be brought out at present; and White Ladies, whenever I am down, is as completely 'the world' as the London season; seen there, she might as well be presented at once. However, she must very soon be both; but the question of when, is more for my mother's adjustment than mine. I do not think it is for a young girl's happiness to begin womanhood, coquetry, heart-burnings, and late hours too soon; but most likely women differ from me."

He spoke negligently, with easy indifference, as men speak of a trifle which, turn whatever way it may, will have no import to them, and Valdor dismissed his supposed secret as a chimera. But as they parted that night, Strathmore's eyes followed him with their dangerous and merciless light lit in them; the mere interrogations had aroused his wrath, and aroused with it insecurity and suspicion. "He meant no more than he said. He is as transparent as glass!" he thought, with the disdain which a reserved and self-contained mind entertains for a frank and unreserved one. "It is impossible he can fancy the truth; the likeness in her is not strong enough to suggest it; even if it did it could never go *beyond* fancy. There would be nothing to support it, nothing to corroborate it. Yet—if I thought there were a fear, I would find some means to stop his babble."

The thought did not travel further, and did not take definite shape or meaning; it was only the vague shadowing of an impalpable dread, but it was coloured by that inexorable pitilessness which swept from his path all that obstructed it, the pitilessness which made at once the force of his career and the evil of his character. His yearning to work out expiation through the living to the dead was holy in its remorse; such may well claim to wash away and to atone for the dead·

liest sin that can rest upon the soul of any man. But—this is the greatest evil which lies *in* evil,—the ashes of past guilt are too often the larvæ of fresh guilt, and ONE crime begets a brood, which, brought to birth, will strangle the life in which they were conceived.

That night, after her attendant had left her, Lucille, who felt wakeful, she knew not why, threw open one of the casements of her bed-chamber and leaned out, resting her cheek on her hand, and her eyes on the moonlit seas, lying wide and bright in the stillness of the summer night, with here and there, against the starry skies, the dark sail of a coasting vessel gliding slowly and silently. A child in years, she had the heart of a poet; and that vast limitless ocean in serenity and storm, in the tempest of black midnights, and the calm of holy dawns, had been a living poem to her from her infancy;—indeed the beautiful myths, and the idyllic dreams she drew from it, had much to do with deepening the susceptibility of a nature already too poetic and too ethereal for its own peace and its own welfare.

She leaned out, under the leaves and clematis-flowers, clustering about her window, while her hair, flung backward, fell unbound over her shoulders, and her deep wistful eyes travelled over the starlit Atlantic, whose ceaseless melody swelled upward from the beating surge, through the quiet of the night. As she rested there, two shadows passed before her sight; one crossing the sward under the limes below, another passing before the lighted casements of a chamber in a wing, built out, so that divided by a lawn, it stood opposite to her. The first was Lionel Caryll, smoking, and walking backwards and forwards there, with all a youth's romance, to watch the light which shone from her window, through the clematis-clusters, while he mused vaguely, timidly, of what he loved this fair child too reverently, to dare draw out from the golden haze of an immature dream which could not call itself a hope. The second was Strathmore, who, in this brief break upon his life of feverish power and unceasing conflict, could not wholly abandon the habits of his accustomed sphere, nor cease wholly to work the wheels within wheels of a keen ambition and a ruthless statecraft, but who, pacing to and fro his chamber, dictated to his secretary the verbal subtleties of a foreign correspondence. The two shadows crossed her sight; the moon-rays fell on young Caryll's face, lending it much of delicacy and sadness, as his steps sounded slowly one by one upon the stillness; and the strong waxlight within showed Strathmore's profile distinct, as though cut on an intaglio, as he passed swiftly up and down before the open windows, the countenance full of haughty intellect and lofty power, like the face of the man, whose iron brain framed, and whose iron hand would have carved out the blood-system of "Thorough"—master of all men, save of himself!

On the two the innocent eyes of the young girl fell, as she looked into the night, and away across the starlit ocean; and on the one they scarcely glanced, but on the other they lingered long. It was not on the youth as he paced under the windows, keeping fond yet holy watch on the light of her casement, and dreaming over thoughts hardly less guileless than her own, that Lucille looked, but on the worn and unrevealing face of the statesman, cold in its power, dark in its written record of spent passions, as he consumed the sleepless hours of the gentle night in the exercise of a restless and dominant ambition. She lingered there long, and wistfully, hidden in the shroud of fragrant clematis, and her eyes never wandered from that resting place; then she gently closed the window, and over her face was a deep and loving tenderness, a hush of sweet unutterable joy that smiled on her lips and filled her eyes with unshed tears.

"How great he is—and how good!" she whispered softly to herself. And then she knelt down beside her bed, with her hands crossed on her heart, and her young face upraised, and, even as she had done from infancy, prayed to God for Strathmore.

## CHAPTER VI.
### One of the Legion of the Lost.

IN a bed-chamber au deuxième, in a house in the Rue Beaujon, Champs Elysées, sat a woman, while in the street below rattled the wheels of passing carriages, and through the windows little was seen save leaden roofs, and dripping water-pipes, and dreary skies, for the day was wet and cheerless. The chamber was luxurious to a certain extent, if something too glittering and meretricious; the hangings were of *rose tendre;* ormolu, buhl, rosewood, marqueterie, porcelaine de Sèvres, were not wanting; and cachemires, sables, flowers, *objets d'art*, were scattered over it, the offerings of those young *lions* who were anxious to have their names associated with one who had been the most notorious and dazzling star of the demi-monde years ago, and who, even yet, by a resistless spell of fascination, was as costly to them as the Baccarat, and the Lansquenet, and the Rouge et Noir, which drew thousands of francs from their pockets in the midnight privacy of her salon. Out of the bed-chamber opened the drawing-room and the supper-room, both furnished in the same style; with warm nuances of colour, which struck the eye pleasantly; with carefully-shaded light, which cast its own twilight here upon everything; with an ensemble which looked glowing and illusive when the apartments were lit, and scented with dreamy odours of pastilles, and redolent of the bouquets of rich wines and the smoke of chillum from eastern hookahs. On the dressing-table of the bed-chamber lay many jewels, chiefly inimitable counterfeits, for the originals of most had been parted with for two-thirds their value as soon as received, and the paste was all which glittered there in company with the cases of rouge, cosmetiques, pearl-powders—all the dreary pitiful paraphernalia of the life which masks the youth it has lost, and dares not, or cannot, wear the dignity of coming age, but only hideously masks the tread of time, and wreathes a death's-head in an unreal smile! And by the table sat a woman. It was but noon, and she was alone; the pigments and powders of the toilette-table had not yet been used, and they were sorely needed. Needed—to lend their bloom to the hot, parched lips, their lie to the haggard and faded brow, their blush to the hollowed cheek, their lustre to the heavy eyes. Needed—for in this face there was such still splendid remnant of bygone loveliness as will linger in the discoloured petals of a flower which has been trodden and trampled in the mud—such trace of a brilliant and matchless beauty too great for any age to utterly sear out, as only served to make the wreck more bitter—such straying rays still lingering of the gracious glory with which Nature had once dowered her peerless work, as only made the souls of young and virginal women, who passed her in the crowd, vaguely shudder at all which had been thus lost, thus sullied, thus debased. And this was Marion Vavasour!

Where had fled the dazzling radiance which had seemed of old to fill her face and form with light? Where had fled the haughty grace with which she had swept through the presence chambers of Courts, bending monarchs to her will? —the superb triumph which had wantoned on her lips, and sat throned upon her brow?—the lovely youth which had beamed from her antelope eyes, and smiled in her sparkling wit?—the resistless sorcery with which she had bought the souls of men at her will, when the night-luminance streamed on the diamonds flashing in her glittering hair, or the gladness of the morning fell about her where she stood, wreathed in the fragrant clusters of her summer roses? *Where?* Where all things fall!—into the grave of Time, which, ever full, yet ever yawns for more—into the abyss which waits for the Womanhood that is sullied, and sin-steeped, and gives its glorious dawn and noon to sowing broadcast seeds of evil whose deadly harvest ever ripens, and is reaped by its sower in the dark vale of waning years.

*Facilis descensus Averni.* Down—down—even as one slips down a shelving and glassy slope the Discrowned had fallen, slowly yet surely, for there are no resting-places on that road; once launched, there is no refuge, save in the chasm below. The fate to which an inexorable vengeance had doomed her had been hers, and would be hers until the uttermost letter of its pitiless Mosaic law had been fulfilled. Dethroned, disgraced, exposed, mocked, reviled, stripped of her power, and stricken into poverty and shame, there was but one fate for this wanton, merciless, beautiful, evil woman —the sorceress in angel guise, the destroyer veiled in lovely youth, the *bella demonia con angelico riso*.

Not for her the purging bitterness of shame, the purifying fires of remorse, the acrid yet holy tears of the Magdalen, whose heart whilst crime-riven is contrite. Not for her: she knew humiliation, but she knew nothing of repentance; she only knew revenge. She suffered: but not with the suffering which on the ashes of guilt raises the sanctuary of expiation. Perhaps, had mercy been yielded to her prayer in the hour of her extremity, had she been humbled to the earth with the god-like forgiveness which would have *spared her*, and bade her "go, and sin no more," the faint rays of purer light which here and there strayed across her soul might have dawned clearer and stronger, and have saved her. Perhaps! Few are so deeply lost that an infinite mercy cannot do something to restore them. It had been denied her, and Marion Vavasour from that hour gave herself up to dazzling evil, and steeped herself recklessly in that gilded degradation which ere then she had shrunk from, and drank to the lips of guilty pleasure, and used her beauty with fearful and pitiless power to accurse her own soul and all others that she drew into the Circean tempting.

And therefore was she thus now, fifteen long years after. For the riches of sin flee swiftly, scattered in a mad extravagance; and as her beauty stole away before the step of time, so stole her power with it; so she sank downward in that decline whence there is no ascent; so she drifted swiftly and surely over the passage of years from brilliance and sovereignty and evil sway, towards that dark and lonely end which he who drove her forth to her fate ordained to her in words which needed no prophet's prescience to give them their prediction. And therefore she was thus now.

She sat alone, whilst over the stove the chocolate simmered, and without the ceaseless pouring of the rain dripped wearily. Where were her thoughts? Away in that glad omnipotent time when she had reigned wheresoever she moved, commanded wheresoever her brilliant glance fell; when the riches of empires and the mines of both hemispheres had been rifled to adorn that marvellous loveliness which kings adored; when she had listened to the nightingales among the fragrant aisles of her rose-gardens with that soft poetry which made her deadliest spell, her most seductive veil; when she had seen princes bending to her feet, and royal women outshone by the glory of her face, while Europe babbled of her fame? Surely: they wandered far back over the past as she sat there, with no companion in her solitude, save the drip, drip, drip of the unceasing rain from the black leaden roofs without: wandered far, while in the columns of the *Patria*, which she was wearily glancing through, her eyes rested on one name:

"STRATHMORE."

And that name was associated with dignity, with honour, with a wide renown, with the great policies of Europe, with all which encircles the career of a dominant and successful statesman. What weakness was there in this patrician power, what crevice in this blade-proof mail, what flaw in this haughty and inaccessible life, through which the bolt of a woman's retaliation could speed its way to the quick?

None!—none!

It had baffled her hopelessly through all these years, which to her had been a gradual descent from empire into impoverishment, which to him had been a gradual ascent from ambition up to power. Yet she had held it in close sight persistently. For there is nothing at once so hopeless and so persistent as a vague, shapeless, impotent, yet undying, desire for Revenge. All these years she had had watch kept on him, and through them all she had failed to discover one aperture through which the adder of retaliation could worm its way and leave its venom. Yet she had never given up hope; she had never surrendered her search; for I have said that in the nature of this woman there was much of the panther, its cowardice, its velvet softness, its cruelty, its wanton love of destruction; and, like the panther, she lay in wait.

Her eyes rested now on the word "Strathmore;" honour, dignity, power, sway, these were what she beheld ever paid to him, gathered by him, become alike the mistress and the ministers of the man who had once been the abject slave of her caress and her word. Their parts had changed; he had hurled his tyrant down into the dust, and stood afar off—afar as though their lives had never touched—where her passionate hatred, her burning bitterness, could no more assail him than the fever of fretting breakers the icy summits of mountains above them. And a hopeless sickness, a faint despair came over her, as her eyes gazed upon his name. Should she *never* reach him, should she *never* gather up from the wreck of the past, sufficient of the force, the power, the will of Marion Vavasour to smite that steel-clad life, that soul of bronze, even as he had smitten hers, to make him reel and stagger beneath her blow, even though to compass his destruction she herself might perish?

With a passionate gesture, she crushed the journal in her hand, and threw it from her; her lips set, her eyes gleamed, her hands, so fair and delicate still, clenched with convulsive force, and in her teeth she muttered thirstily, dreamily:

"It must come, it *shall!* 'Tout vient à point à qui sait attendre!'"

And then she arose and went before her toilette-mirror, and leaning her head upon her hands, sighed, whilst a hot, arid mist gathered in her eyes: far more cruel to her than death or shame, or privation, was the loss of her glad and glorious loveliness.

"Oh! woman, woman, you miserable insect-thing!" she said, bitterly, while her old mocking smile came about her lips, but now derisive and now joyless. "Only born to pander to men's pleasure—only created to intoxicate their senses and to damn their souls—what are you worth—what are you worth? A butterfly of less value than a dead leaf, when one short summer has stolen your beauty! You reign by the brightness of the eyes, the bloom of the cheek, the whiteness of the bosom, and when those are gone you may lie in a kennel and die. What are your victories? Only such as drink, or dice, or the Turf win as completely! What are your slaves? Only those who are the slaves not of you, but of their own passions: Impotent, wretched, ephemeral thing! —only loved for the vice you gratify, only of worth while there is youth on your lips!"

The mocking, scorning words broke out with the pride and the eloquence of long-past years; to her heart she felt their truth.

"And yet—and yet," she muttered, "it *is* power—while it lasts. To see them, as I have seen, thirst for a glance and hang on a smile, and love a sneer, a rebuff, a cruelty rather than no word! To make them, as I have made, kneel and pray, and grovel in the dust to kiss one's feet; and bend their proud necks to the yoke, and break their stern souls down to a spaniel's humility; and deal out anguish and despair, heaven and hell, at will. Ah! it is Power! None wider, none surer on earth, while it lasts!"

The words were passionate now and triumphant; for the instant she lived again in the rich and royal Past, and tasted all its glories. Then her head sank, and the salt tears filled her eyes, and her hot pale lips quivered, and a piteous wailing cry broke from her:

"Oh, my lost beauty—my lost beauty!"

And then after a while she took up the rouge, and the powders, and the paint, and sought wearily and futilely to counterfeit all which had fled for ever; and when she arose after that ghastly task, through all, despite all, there was something beautiful still; the haughty grace, the antelope eyes, the sovereign glance, the perfect form, these naught could wholly destroy save death; but it was only such fugitive, sullied, faintly-lingering beauty as made the history it told more bitter and heart-sickening; as would linger about the golden cup which had been bruised, and polluted, and burned in the fire, as would remain to the glorious statue which had been defaced and overthrown in ruins in the dust, as would be given by the painter of the Purgatorio to the faces of the fallen and accursed as they bear their doom.

## CHAPTER VII.
### The Shadow of the Future.

THE summer morning broke warm and clear over the western coast, and Strathmore, as he rose and dressed, bade his servant set the windows open. The ocean sparkled in the light, the birds sang among the leaves, the golden gorse blossomed far and wide over the bluffs and moors; but in his youth he had had little sight or heed for these things: he had none now; the fairness of the opening day he barely noticed. But beneath his windows rose another song than that of the thrushes, as sweet as they and as joyous; the song of a young heart and a young voice rising up to heaven with the early day, with the fragrance of the flowers, with the freshness of the dew, with the odour of the grasses, with all things fair and pure. It was the invocation of the Spirits to the Hours, from Shelley's "Prometheus:"

> The pine-boughs are singing
> Old songs with new gladness,
> The billows and fountains
> Fresh music are playing,
> Like the notes of a spirit from land and from sea.

And the words, with the improvised music, uprose on the air as a lark rises into the clouds.

He heard it, and approached the window; in the sunlight

Lucille was bending down among the flowers like Milton's Proserpine,

*Herself the fairest flower;*

filling her hands with their fragrant wealth, with golden laburnums, snow-white lilies, roses dew-laden, buds nestled in their dark wet leaves, and drooping coils of scarlet creepers. He stood and watched her where she moved in all the gladness of her youth and the brightness of the morning, among the boughs and blossoms, while the burden of her song echoed upon the air, and the sunny warmth of light fell on the fairness of her face. He watched her, and over the world-worn coldness of his face a strange softness trembled, and into his calm pitiless eyes came a yearning pain—he thought of the dead. He had loved him, he had been loved by him so well! and across the dreary stretch of years no cry of a vain agony could reach, to pierce the tomb where he had been hurled in all his glad and gracious manhood. The life lay rotted to ashes in the grave: what avail the passionate throes of a remorse, impotent, tardy, powerless with God or man? Remorse could not bring back the dead! Yet remorse ate into his soul as the brand burned into the brow of Cain; with him by night and day, beside him in the glitter of courts, lying in wait for him in his solitude, consuming his peace under the purples of power, it burned ever in him; this remorse, hidden under an armour of steel, veiled from men's sight beneath a powerful, successful, impenetrable career. And into his eyes now, there came a weary, passionate, yearning grief, as he gazed down upon the young life which had sprung from that of the lost, where she stood among the flowers with the joyous echo of her song floating softly down the air; and his lips moved in an unconscious, broken prayer, as though that prayer could reach the grave.

"My friend, my brother! I will guard her without shade or soil, her life shall be before my own. Oh God! may not *that* suffice?"

"Lucille will soon be a child no longer."

His mother spoke again the same words as she had spoken the night before, where she stood in the embrasure of one of the oriel windows, a woman aged, but of noble presence still, in carriage and in feature not unlike to Marie Antoinette, with her silvered hair turned back from a haughty brow, and the sweeping folds of her black robes draping a form bowed but full of dignity; for Lady Castlemere had been the proudest woman of her day until the steel of her will had been bent and softened in the fires of calamity and the crucible of age. Strathmore stood opposite to her, leaning against the casement; it was near sunset, and they were alone. He looked up from what he was reading:

"Unhappily, yes."

"And she has great loveliness, Cecil?"

"Very great; she has had from childhood."

"Then we must not always imprison it here! In a year or so at latest she should see some other world than that of a solitary sea-shore, some other society than that of her birds, and dogs, and flowers. Your wish, of course, decides all concerning her, but neither your duty nor mine would be fulfilled if we denied her for ever any other sphere than this."

Strathmore was silent some moments; he felt an invincible reluctance to realise the truth that Lucille was growing out of childhood; a yet greater to give the signal for the flight of all that made her as glad and as innocent as a child, by her introduction into a world where she would learn her own loveliness, be sullied by flattery, see hollowness, artifice, frivolity, all of which she never dreamt now, and be taught either joy from other hands than his own, or the pain from which he would have no power to shield her.

"Some time—yes," he answered, slowly; "though she will learn nothing by wider freedom save what is best unlearnt. She must be introduced, and presented, and all the rest, of course; but there is no haste for that. She is so young yet; and whilst she is happy here, she is better here."

His mother was silent too for a while. I have said that

Strathmore had at no time given her more than a chill regard and a courteous respect; he was not a man to be bound by or to feel any of these ties, but she loved him—loved him better since she had shuddered at his crime and aided his atonement. She was silent; then she moved towards him, and laid her hand lightly on his shoulder, a hand like his own—long, fair, delicate to the touch, yet never to be shaken from its grasp, the hand which seems instinctively formed to hold Power.

"Strathmore, forgive me if what I say pains you; you know how deeply I should grieve to do so; but as Lucille grows older, a question occurs to me which I never remembered during her infancy. All those who see her, believe her parentage foreign, and never dream of looking beyond the fact that she is an orphan, and a ward of yours and of mine. But—if men meet her who learn to love her, they may look closer, and to whosoever becomes her husband in the future you must tell the history of her true name and fate."

Strathmore almost started, and a look of distaste and repugnance passed over his face: the young life which had been to him like a child-angel of atonement looked to him too sacred for the sensual thoughts of love to approach, or the touch of a lover's kiss to profane.

"Love! Marriage! They are desecration to associate with that young innocent child," he said, impatiently. "Let her love, as she does, the waves and the birds and the flowers; they are the only things pure enough for her. *Our* brute passions have nothing in common with her."

"Still—unless she were consigned to conventual seclusion—it will be impossible to prevent the love of men from fastening on her by-and-by?"

"True: but it will be time enough to speak of that whenever her own heart is touched."

There was the look in his eyes which ever came there when his will was crossed; but Lady Castlemere's will was as resolute as his own. She pursued the subject:

"But in the event I name, to one to whom Lucille may be

betrothed in the future, her parentage must be made known. Has this never struck you?"

"I see what you mean; but it shall never be so."

The reply was calm, but it was inflexible. In his heart he swore that none should ever learn that fatal secret, none ever glean the power to unfold to her that he whom she caressed and revered, and honoured and prayed for as the guardian and giver of her every joy, had been the destroyer of her father.

"But how can it be avoided?"

In his cold fathomless eyes she saw the evil look glitter darker and darker, which would have been restrained to none save herself, and he answered her chillily:

"With that I will deal whenever the time comes. Suffice it, I shall never permit any to learn a secret which is buried for ever, as much by *his* will as by mine."

She mused a moment over his words:

"Then," she said, slowly, "then—Lucille must wed with some one who must love her too well to ask her descent; there are few who love thus, Strathmore."

He looked at her in impatience, in surprise, in curiosity:

"Why talk of love at all? To think of marriage for her looks to me as premature, as it seems pollution! In the seclusion in which you live here you select all her acquaintance, and she meets none who can whisper to her of what she does not herself dream."

"Perhaps not; but there is one here who may do so."

"*Here?*"

"Yes; my grandson loves her: he scarce knows it himself, they have been so long together, from her infancy; but I know it; and some hour or other, unpremeditated and involuntarily, he may discover his own secret and utter it to her."

"A boy's puling fancy! a lad's moonstruck sickness! Why have him here if he must taint the air she breathes with the miserable maundering of sentiment?"

He spoke with intolerant, contemptuous impatience, his slight, bitter smile upon his lips, chill and disdainful; it incensed him more than he showed, that this youth should have dared to dream of love in association with Lucille, should have dared to desecrate with his amorous follies the opening life which seemed too pure for any coarser touch of earth.

"My home is Lionel's," answered Lady Castlemere, briefly and coldly, for her grandson was as dear to her as Lucille—in truth, more so. "What he feels for her would not merit the harsh and scornful words you give to it; his love is like much first love, timid, shrinking, delicate, most reverential. He would breathe no word in her ear he would not speak in my presence, and he holds her in most perfect tenderness. It is an affection which has grown with his growth; he is not conscious yet of its force; but a word, a moment, may reveal his own heart to him, and then—I cannot answer for his silence."

"Secure it then. Send him on the Continent, or to Egypt, till the Oxford Term. I forbid a boy's maudlin sentimentality to desecrate her ear."

"Nello's love is purer than most older men's!" said his mother, with a sigh. "And I do not see the necessity to banish it wholly until we know that she would not respond to it——"

"Respond to it!"

Strathmore echoed the words half in derision, half in incredulity, wholly with anger; around Lucille the only holy feeling which his nature had ever known had gathered so much that was hallowed, pure, and of profound sadness, that, for any passion to approach her seemed like profanation, and for any other hand to attempt to wrest her from his guardianship looked sacrilegious theft.

"Why should she not? Though a boy to you, he is not so to her. She feels for him a loving affection, born with infancy, which may well deepen into what would be the safest and happiest love which she can know. His character is known to me as no other's can be; it is one to which her peace might be securely trusted; and with him the impediment which would surely arise with any other man could not occur; he would never dream of inquiring more deeply into her history. There are many reasons that induce me to think Nello's love—if she can feel any for him—would be the calmest haven we could secure for her. I leave the matter in your hands, you are her guardian; but I know that her happiness and peace are too paramount with you for you not to weigh them well. Pardon me if I suggest, Cecil, that it would be well neither to fetter her until she is old enough to know her own heart, and has had larger experience, nor, on the other hand, to banish wholly either him from her, or hope from him, lest thus you should shipwreck what else would be a tranquil and shadowless love? These matters seem beneath you, but they are not so, since you have made that young child's peace your care."

"Nothing is beneath me which can bestow on her a moment's joy, or spare her a moment's pang."

The brief words were the truth; to screen or to gladden the life which he felt to hold in wardship from the Dead, he would have given his own; for in this man's heart as there were "depths which sank to lowest hell," so there were also "heights which reached to highest heaven." He spoke no more, but stood silent, revolving many thoughts—thoughts which had but one centre and one goal: Lucille's future peace.

As he went to his own chamber, half an hour afterwards, he met her on the wide staircase; she was dressed for the evening, and about her hair was wreathed a chain of delicate shells of a rare kind and opal hue: they formed a graceful ornament, and he noticed them as he paused.

"Oh, they are Nello's shells!" she answered, laughing. "Are they not pretty? He brought them from the cliffs to-day, and risked his life to get them. He said so sadly that he could not give me costly pearls like yours, that I told Babette to string them on a Trichinopoly chain, and fasten back my hair with them. I knew he would be pleased."

The words struck him as they would not have done but for others he had lately heard. He looked down into her fair eyes, now glad and laughing, yet in whose depths a sadness ever lay, deep, yet undefinable:

"You love this boy, Lucille?"

"Oh, dearly!"

She spoke warmly, earnestly, for the companion of her childhood was, indeed, very dear to her; and of "love," in men's and women's sense, Lucille knew nothing, scarce its name, save as it was written to her—vague, mysterious, solemn, glorious—in the pages of Dante and his brother poets. Strathmore passed his hand over her brow with a gentle caress, and went onward in deep thought. It was strange how this single holy feeling, which had grown out of his trust from Erroll, penetrated and intertwined a life which seemed, in all other respects, chill as ice, impenetrable as steel, and filled to the brim with insatiate ambition, worldly wisdom, and power which was not seldom as unscrupulously sought as it was imperiously wielded. It was singular how in the cold yet restless, successful yet insatiate, callous yet embittered, career of the Statesman, this solitary, pure, and chastened tenderness had been sown and rooted. Lucille was the sole living thing he loved, Lucille the sole living thing he would not have trampled down in his path unheeding; and a sickly sense of *loss* came over him as he thought that, however he had thus far fulfilled her father's trust, her future must pass into the care of others whom it would be beyond his power to control; that, with whatever gratitude, reverence, and love she now regarded him, the time must come when her guardian must surrender her to her husband, and the joy of her life be given from other hands, and other lips, than his.

"Caryll, I need a few words with you. Will you come hither?"

Strathmore stood outside one of the dining-room windows smoking on the lawn without, while his secretary and his nephew lingered over the olives. Valdor was away on some legality connected with Torlynne. The young man rose and went to him instantly, where he stood in the moonlight; Strathmore held him at a distance, and Caryll feared, almost disliked him—all youths of his age did. The graceful negligence, the haughty courtesies, more cold in their suavity than their omission could ever have been, the subtle bitter sneer, the profound knowledge, felt rather than ever shown —all these awed and repulsed them, apart from the lofty and glittering fame which surrounded the successful and inscrutable Minister.

"Walk away from the windows, if you please," said Strathmore, as he moved across the grass. At the bottom of the lawn he turned and glanced at his nephew. "So, Caryll, I hear you love my young ward—is it true?"

At the suddenness of the personal and merciless question, spoken, moreover, in that soft, harmonious voice of which every inflection could cut as coldly as an ice wind, Nello was speechless; he coloured to the temples, and his eyes dropped shyly as a girl's; his love was sacred to him, and he dreaded his inquisitor. In the light of the moon Strathmore's eyes studied him searchingly, and the politician, accustomed to read men's thoughts at a glance, read the youth's heart to its depths. He smiled, unconsciously, contemptuously: his nature was unsympathetic, and for the timidity and poetry of young love he had no compassion—he had never known them himself—and here, as well as a foolery, they looked a profanity.

"*Chi arrossisce e se tacen, parla assai,*"

he said, with the derisive coldness which was as terrible as a knife-thrust to the ardent, sensitive, unveiled heart of the boy, who shrank under the glance and the tone, as a prisoner under the cold steel of the inquisitor. "And may I ask on what grounds you have upbuilt your romance, or what right you have to presume to build it at all?"

The hot blush died off young Caryll's face, leaving it very pale: he had scarce known his love himself, until these abrupt and merciless questions threw their light upon it.

"Right!" he said, hesitatingly and hurriedly. "I have no right, sir—scarcely hope."

"'Scarcely!' Then you cherish some?"

His eyes, with a chill disdain slumbering in their depths, fastened in relentless watch upon his nephew's face, till the painful flush and pallor kept changing there like a woman's. It was a terrible ordeal to Lionel Caryll to have his heart probed and bared by this negligent, callous, pitiless, polished man of the world!

"Who does not, sir, who loves?" he murmured, almost indistinctly.

"Then you think that Lucille gives you hope?"

The questions were put coldly, carelessly, but with an authority which seemed to the youth to wrench answers from him whether he would or not.

"Yes—no—I cannot tell—I dare not say," he muttered, hurriedly. "She is very gentle to me, but that she is to all things; she loves me, I know, but it may be only as a brother. Still—still—with time, I fancy—and she wore my shells in her hair to-night——"

His cold smile played a moment about Strathmore's lips. To this man, whose soul had been drunk long ago with the madness of passion, and was now steeped in the intoxication of power, the shyness and the romance of a first love seemed puling puerile sentiment.

"You consider you *have* hope," he said, chillily. "Whether founded or unfounded, time will show. And now, how much of this 'love' have you presumed to whisper to my ward without my permission?"

"Not a syllable!" said the young man, eagerly. The interrogation roused his pride, and made him shake off the awe which he felt for the man who stood there, smoking in the moonlight, with his searching glance fixed on him, and his point-blank questions dealing, without sympathy or compassion, with what was to him the very core and goal of his life. "Not a syllable, I swear, Sir! I have never let her dream of any other feeling than that with which we played

together in her infancy. I would not—I dare not—she is too
sacred in my eyes. To speak of love to her would seem
profanation; to think of it, does almost!——"

He spoke hurriedly but earnestly, and with all the delicacy
and tenderness which characterised a love that his own temperament, and Lucille's early years, had both tended to make
rather reverential than impetuous, rather poetic than passionate, such as the young knights of Arthur's Code felt for
some holy and lofty love, their guiding-star from afar off,
but beyond the reach of grosser desire.

His answer found favour with Strathmore, and softened
the haughty and scornful intolerance with which he had
hitherto regarded the young man's attachment; he perceived
at a glance that here there would be no maudlin romance,
no sickly sentiment to brush the bloom off the fair opening
leaves of Lucille's young heart. He was silent, and paced
up and down for a few moments, musing on his nephew's
reply; then he paused, and looked on the young frank face
in the moonlight, while Caryll's eyes met his, fearlessly now,
though a boyish flush was hot on his temples.

"You are perfectly right," he said, briefly. "I am glad
you have so much perception and so much reticence. To
have taken advantage of your position and opportunities to
usurp her ear, without having received my permission, I
should have considered very unwarrantable, and should have
resented proportionately. As it is, you consider that you
have some grounds for hope, and I am aware myself that
Lucille holds you in sincere affection; whether it may ever
ripen to more, neither you nor I can tell, and I distinctly
forbid any attempt to force it prematurely to do so."

Young Caryll bent his head silently; he felt powerless
against this serene, inflexible will, and he knew that Strathmore, as her guardian, had a right to speak as he would.

"You understand? Now listen further. For two years I
forbid any attempt to speak of love to her, or to secure her
own. I do not interdict to you such means as may warrant-
ably foster her affection for you; to do so would be unjust,

but you must neither rouse nor fetter her heart in any way. At the end of that time she will be old enough to make her own choice, and she will have seen a wider world than this; you can then say to her what you will. If it prove that the hope you now cherish is legitimate, and if she find that you are dearer than any one has, or could, become to her—if, in a word, her happiness depend on you—I will sanction your suit. Give me your word to keep the silence I exact?"

Nello hesitated a moment. Two years! It looked an eternity! But an influence was upon him he could not resist. He had feared Strathmore before, now he felt his power; he saw, moreover, that the words were gentle and were just, and he bowed his head and gave the pledge.

Strathmore paused a brief time, looking at him keenly, and taking gauge of his character—a gauge which satisfied him that Lady Castlemere had been right in her estimate of her grandson.

"Very well," he continued. "Meanwhile, I will assist your career, so that should you ultimately be united to Lucille, your position may be honourable for her. You leave Oriel in the spring? My mother's wealth is so tied that she can give you little or nothing, and you must make your own way in life. But I will return you for a seat in the House, and I will allow you such an income as will give you your independence, and leave you unshackled. It will rest with yourself then to become worthy of Lucille, and such as I should trust with the care of her future."

Young Caryll looked at him, bewildered, incredulous, distrusting his own senses. He had heard of Strathmore's ascetic indifference to wealth, and the generosity with which he gave it to others, but for himself he had had scarcely passing notice from him, and he listened dreamily, marvelling whether his dread had been error, and if beneath the chill and satiric suavity of manner there lay compassion and warmth. Words broke from him, full of the gratitude he felt, eager, breathless, fervid, eloquent from their simple truth and depth, and tremulous both with surprise and emotion,

To the sanguine and dauntless heart of youth what luminous glory streamed over all his future with Strathmore's words! For youth knows and fears nothing of two barriers in Life's path, which men call Death and Failure.

Strathmore arrested him in the midst of his warm protest of deathless gratitude, for the nature of the man was too true to assume a virtue it had not.

"No thanks," he said, coldly. "I in no way merit them from you. It is not any feeling towards yourself for which you need be grateful, it is simply for her sake, not yours. You deem it possible that Lucille may love you; I desire that her love should be shadowless. I should have said the same to any other man of your youth, and of your hopes; what she may prize, I desire to make worthy of her."

The words fell on the young man's warm, eager heart, just lain bare in all its agitated gratitude, like an ice-touch; and it closed, shrinking and troubled. Yet a certain tone in Strathmore's voice, even and tranquil though it was, struck on him; he fancied that in it, with all its chillness, all its calmness, there was something as of *repressed pain*. He was silent, hesitating, and embarrassed; but his nature was candid, and he spoke on his impulse.

"Lord Cecil, may I ask you one question?"

Strathmore turned as he was moving away.

"Certainly."

"Then—then—in my love for Lucille I have your full sanction, your cordial wishes?"

"On the conditions I have named—yes. I have told you so. Why ask?"

"Because—because," murmured Caryll, indistinctly and impulsively—"because I have sometimes fancied, sir—forgive me if I offend you—that your solicitude for her, your kindness towards her were so great, that you might have other views for her womanhood——"

"Other views! I do not comprehend you."

The languid coldness of tone froze the boy's heart, as if it were gripped by an iron hand; but the impulse which impelled him was stronger than even embarrassment, timidity, or awe, and his words broke out involuntarily:

"I thought, my lord, that—that—perhaps you brought her up to wed her yourself when she should be of age? She is so lovely; and guardians have married their wards——"

He paused, terror-struck at the effect of his words. Strathmore started, as though a shot had hit him; and in the summer moonlight his face grew death-white, as with the spasm of some ungovernable horror.

"*I* wed her—*I*! Good God! you do not know what you say——"

For the first time in his life Lionel Caryll saw the veil rent asunder, the steel armour pierced—for the first time he saw the equable tranquillity of Strathmore's habitual manner broken down, and shattered into passionate feeling. And he marvelled, wonder-stricken and aghast at what his simple words had caused;—caused only for an instant; the next, Strathmore regained self-control.

"Your fears are very idle," he said, calmly. "I have no taste for marriage; and the great disparity between Lucille's years and my own is sufficient to show you the groundlessness of your supposition. Fulfil your share of my conditions honourably, I shall fulfil mine towards you. And now go back to Curtis and the olives; we have said enough on this matter."

Caryll obeyed him, going slowly across the lawn, dissatisfied and troubled, despite the hope which was warm at his heart, and the future which beckoned before him; he saw that there was some mystery here which he had never before suspected, and which seemed to him hopeless to wrest from the granite soul of a man in whose hands he felt like an impotent child. The horror which had rung through Strathmore's words—"*I* wed her—*I*!"—thrilled through his memory, too real for the doubt which had tortured to longer pursue him; yet the fear could not wholly be banished. By the side of the accomplished and courtly Statesman he felt his own inferiority and insignificance, and he felt, too, with a lover's instinct, that Strathmore, despite of, ay! even increased through the years which he had named, had all which most fatally fascinates women to love, where they meet no pity and no response. The words he had heard, the look he had seen, had declared his dread not alone improbable, but impossible; yet that dread he could not wholly abandon, it clung to him heavily, wearily, as he re-entered the lighted rooms. And yet it was not for one moment that he doubted that his uncle had spoken the truth.

For some moments Strathmore walked to and fro in the still night. His nephew's question had struck on his ear with horror, almost in loathing. His hand stained with her father's blood, touch her own with a husband's caress! Her fair innocence learn to rest in its holy sleep on the heart which imprisoned so dark a secret! He seek her, wed her—*he!* the assassin of both the lives from which had sprung her own! He recoiled from the thought thus suddenly and unwittingly bidden before him, recoiled, sickened and horror-stricken. It looked to him abhorred as crime, accursed as incest! He thrust it from him in its mere harmless suggestion as men thrust the first dawn of some hateful guilt.

Not that it had temptation for him; it had none. Lionel Caryll's doubt was groundless. Strathmore's feeling for Lucille, while it was the only tender, was also the only pure, feeling he had ever known; her father's could not have been more completely unsullied than his, and the profound melancholy which mingled with it served but to make it more hallowed. The repressed pain which his nephew had detected beneath the cold tranquillity of his tones was not due to the spring to which Nello traced it, but simply to that sense of reluctance that any other should have the moulding or marring of her fate, that sense of loss at the knowledge that hereafter others would usurp alike her affections and her guardianship, which had come upon him after the words of his mother.

He had spoken to young Caryll in the manner he had done, from his belief in the possibility that Lucille might centre her peace in the youth's love, and his intention that nothing which his own foresight could provide for or against should ever bar the way to her happiness. But it had cost him some effort, for his sense of atonement to Erroll lay in his knowledge that he made her life bright and pure as sunlight, and to surrender it to other keeping was to imperil, perchance to shipwreck, what alone could give him power to say when he lay upon his death-bed, "I have atoned!"

It had been this pain which had been carefully repressed throughout his interview with his young nephew, it was this dread which weighed on him where he paced the lawn in the moonlight alone. Strathmore was a man of action and of power, a ruler amongst men, who crushed mercilessly all which opposed him, and bent all who came beneath his influence with an unerring and resistless hand; who deified Will, and believed that every man as he is devil, so he may be also God unto himself. And yet for the first time, as he paced in his solitary walk through the fresh summer night, with the sounding of the sea in the silence, a vague foreboding passed over him that he might be powerless to control the mystical ebb and flow of fate, that to the craving agony of a vain remorse, expiation might be denied and shattered at the last!

Lucille was alone when Strathmore entered the drawing-room, half lying on a low couch with that restful grace with which a young fawn throws itself down to repose when tired by its play. He paused a moment, looking at her as the silvery light of the candelabra fell on her where she lay, her head resting on her arm, her lashes shadowing her cheeks, which were slightly flushed—this dawning fragile life, with its bloom delicate as the bloom of a rose-leaf, and its strength slight as the frailness of the harebell which one rude touch withers, how easily it might be wrecked, how easily crushed! It was a frail argosy in which to place and peril the expiation of a crime, heavy, blood-stained, bitter as the fratricide which slew Smerdis in the dark days of olden Egypt.

He approached, and bent over her.

"My darling, are you not well?"

Her eyes unclosed, and the touching sadness ever on her face in repose, beamed away in the sunlight of her father's smile.

"Oh yes. I am never ill, you know. I feel a little tired sometimes, that is all. Do come and sit by me, will you, and not go away?"

"Surely. But you should not feel this tire, Lucille, at your age; lassitude is weakness."

She laughed brightly.

"Not with me. When have I had a day's ill health? Who could have, by the side of the free, strong, beautiful sea? I am only tired, and I was lying thinking, Lord Cecil——"

"And of what?"

Her eyes dwelt on him lovingly, reverently in their dark and mournful beauty, and her voice was hushed in its earnestness.

"I was thinking of how great you are, and how good; and how you who sway men with your word, and empires with your will, yet have so much care, and thought, and love for me."

"Good!" He echoed the word with the bitterness of anguish; he had trained himself to bear all these things from her lips, and had sedulously fostered the reverence and gratitude she felt for him, but none the less did they cut him to the soul; and now and then, even his will of steel and his long-worn visor could not conceal the spasm of a struck wound, of a wakened conscience. His voice had a thrill of mingled pain and tenderness in it now as he stooped towards her:

"Never give that word to anything which I do, Lucille, least of all to what I do for you. You know that you are dear to me for—your father's sake."

"I know; but I cannot love you less, but more, because you loved him so well," she said, softly, while her hand nestled into his, and drew it caressingly closer to her. At the clinging touch and the gentle words, the brand of crime, seared on the soul of the murderer quivered, as the brand of fire quivers in the living flesh of the doomed.

Yet he sat there, calm still, letting his hand lie in hers, and his lips wear the words with which he ever spoke of the dead; for his strength was great to endure.

"True, I loved him well," he said, gently; "and so would you have done; Lucille, you do not forget him; you think of him fondly, sometimes, as though you had known him—as though he were living now?"

"Ah, yes," she murmured, softly. "I think of you both, think of you together; you have told me of him until I know him so well, and when I kneel down I often pray to God to let me see his face, and hear his voice, in my dreams, as well as yours. And He does."

Strathmore sat silent; his hand lying in hers, his heart smitten by those innocent and childlike words as by the stroke of the avenging angel.

"Your dreams are more merciful to you than the life which robbed you of him," he said, calmly and gently, for he suffered without allowing one sign to escape, or one blow to be spared him. "Love your father's name better than mine, Lucille. He is more worthy it than I."

"Lucille could not love anything *better* than you," she said, musingly, while her earnest, wistful eyes fondly studied his face with that regard which he had noticed as too mournful and too deeply contemplative for her years, when, as a little child, she had asked why he suffered, on the sea-shore. "Where was it that he died, Lord Cecil, and how? You have never told me that."

"He died abroad."

"And were you with him?"

"Yes."

"Did he suffer?"

A slight quiver shook his voice:

"I hope to God, no."

"He died happily, then?"

"He died at peace with all, even with those who injured him. Not happy, since—since he left your mother scarce older than you are now."

Lucille sighed, a hushed, broken sigh.

"No—and his death was hers. I think *I* should die of a great grief, as my tame curlew did when his sister-bird was killed by the eagle. He could not live; why should he? There was no joy in the air, or the sea, or the sky, when what he loved was taken."

She was silent, her hand clinging caressingly to Strathmore's, as her eyes grew wistful with thoughts too poetic and too deep for her years. He rose involuntarily:

"Hush, Lucille! No grief shall ever touch you! Why think of what cannot, what *shall* not, come nigh you? Are those letters? Is the evening mail come?"

"Oh yes; those are yours. But come and sit by me to read them. Do!"

He obeyed her: inflexible as bronze to any other, a wish of Lucille was sacred to him. As her guardian, he had commanded that her desire should never be disputed nor disappointed, and to himself, when with her, he allowed it to be law. A nature less pure, less loving, less incapable of being warped to egotism or tyranny than hers, might have been ruined by this limitless indulgence; with Lucille it had no effect, save that of rendering her affections more clinging and deeply rooted, and her character more tender and dependent; the very luxuriance of its beauty was fostered by the warmth it basked in, if it were more certain to be blighted at the first sweep of frost or storm. She lay still watching him, while he sat beside her breaking the seals of his correspondence. His face wore no evil traits to her; she only saw its power, its intellect, its profound melancholy; she only saw that the eyes so cold, the lips so mocking to others, for her ever wore gentle smiles and generous words. "Je n'en puis rien faire —ces traits ont toutes les plus grandes qualités et tous les plus grands vices," a French sculptor had once said, casting down his calliope and chisel before a bust of Strathmore. But

Lucille only saw the nobler, and saw none of the darker meaning, and she lay looking at him lovingly, reverently, silently: she was never more truly happy than thus. And as he sat thus, beside her couch, Valdor, who had that moment returned and entered the drawing-room, looked at them unperceived, and wondered afresh, as he had done before, what secret this could be which united Strathmore to this young girl, and which made a man ordinarily negligent in manner, indifferent to all human affections, and solely devoted to ambition and power, be tender towards her as a woman, submit to all her gentle caprices, forestall her lightest wish, and watch with pleasure for her slightest smile. It was a mystery which he could not fathom. Strathmore, glancing upward, read his thoughts. Valdor looked keenly at him, to note if he resented having thus been seen; he might as well have sought to note the marble features of the Parian bust near him move and speak!

Strathmore was never betrayed into an unspoken expression of what he felt; he was calmly and impassively impenetrable. He did not move now, but smiled a courteous welcome to his friend, and spoke of some political news which the day mail had brought.

But he remembered the look with which the frank Henri Cinquiste had gazed at himself and Lucille, and the words he had spoken the night before, of surprise at her having never visited White Ladies; and he acted on both.

"Lucille, White Ladies will be full next month," he said with a slight smile, the next morning, looking up from his letters where they sat at breakfast, the sunlight flickering through the screen of foliage and roses which overhung the Elizabethan windows.

She looked up eagerly, a flush on her cheeks, and her lips parted.

"Would you like to be with us?"

He spoke still with a slight smile, as of a man listlessly amused with the bright caprices and easily-bestowed pleasures of a child.

"Oh, Lord Cecil!——"

She did not say more; Valdor and his own secretary were strangers to her, and indulgence had never made her exacting.

"Very well, then. Plead with my mother, if she have no objection, to do me the honour to come there, and bring you with her."

"What a fool I was to suppose he did not wish her to visit White Ladies! My brain must be going, to dream such nonsense. That lovely child bewitches me!" thought Valdor, as he listened.

Two days afterwards, Strathmore left for the Continent. These brief visits were all he, a Foreign Minister, spared to Silver-rest; he was seldom fatigued—never alone; he was absorbed in the keen contest for power, and lived, with scarce a week's retirement, in the fulness of the world.

Valdor remained; all that he needed to see or do at Torlynne could have been seen and done in a week's time, but he stretched it over almost to the time at which Strathmore would be at White Ladies, and he should go thither with the rest of the autumn guests. The French noble had no pastoral tastes; "*Hors de Paris, hors du monde,*" was most essentially his creed; the sounding of the seas and the soft wild beauty of the western coast had no music and no charm for him; a *viveur*, a state-conspirator, a man of fashion, he was customarily wearied and impatient at a day's detention in any other world than his own. Yet he stayed on, in, or near the solitudes of Silver-rest.

He was captivated by the child-beauty, the spiritual, unconscious loveliness, which he had first seen among the lilies of the valley, flowers whose grace and fragility were like her own. He was at once enchained and held in check by it; to Lucille he could not speak of love, or even of compliment, as he would have done to others, they seemed profanation; yet he began to feel for her a far holier and more enduring tenderness than he, a wit and a voluptuary, had before known. She was silent with him; except with those whom she knew well, she had something of the soft shyness of the half-tamed fawn, and her nature was one of those, poetic, introspective, deeply thoughtful, and meditative far beyond their years, which speak but to few, and only find utterance when moved by the voice that they respond to, as the Æolian chords only echo to the touch of certain winds. But it was this which was newest to him; it gave him much to conquer, and he saw that whoever would win her heart must never startle it rudely from its innocent rest, but wind his way gently and slowly. He felt as both Strathmore, a cold and negligent Statesman, and Caryll, a romantic and unworn youth, had equally done, that "love" was no word to whisper to Lucille, and that, grasped too quickly or too boldly, the sensitive plant would surely close and recoil.

But Valdor had never failed, and his nature was sanguine; therefore he stayed on near Silver-rest, and learned a purer passion than he had ever known, while he listened to the young girl's voice, that was low and sweet as the lulling of the seas; or watched her, himself unseen, where she sat gazing on the changing face of the waters, with the deep shadow of ivy-hung rocks above, and sunlit sands stretching before her; or heard her songs rising in mellow evening air, with some sad, wild German legend or rich cathedral chant for their burden; or won her to speak to him of the things in which her eyes and her heart—those at once of a poet and a child, an artist and a dreamer—found beauty and delight: the silvery flash of a seagull's wing, a bird resting on a heather spray, a crested wave leaping in the light, a trailing coil of forest-leaves.

Strathmore had made provision for the early, guileless, hesitating love of the boy Nello; he had made none—could have made none—against the more subtle, more eloquent, and more tutored tenderness of the man who had been beside him when he had slain her father, while in the west the sun had set, in the dead years long gone.

## CHAPTER VIII.
### "Seized, in the Name of the Emperor."

IT was past midnight, in the salon *au deuxième*, in the Rue Beaujon.

The lights were many, and in their dazzle the warm nuances, the rose-tendre hues, the ormolu, the mirrors, the smoking-couches, made an enticing *forberia della scena* in its own florid, demi-monde style. The air was heavy with the odours of wine from the supper-room, whose folding-doors stood open, and with the perfume of that chillum which was a speciality of the Rue Beaujon, and which some who smoked it averred to be delirious as Monte Christo's hatchis. Two or three tables stood about the room, and round each were grouped some half-dozen men, young attachés, soldiers, bankers, Englishmen, or nouveaux riches, few if any of them over thirty, some wanting ten years of it, and all flush of money, or they would have found no entrance there. At one table they were playing Trente-et-Un, at the other Trente-et-Quarante, at a higher maximum than is permitted at Baden, *gros jeu*, where the colours revolved and the gold heaps changed, swift as thought in a dizzy whirl, and swifter than the thought of many could follow them. For the gaming which is forbade publicly will, like every other dangerous instinct, be indulged in secresy; and the play in the Rue Beaujon was greedily sought after suppers that left the pulse heated with fiery wines, and the reason little able to baffle the intricacies of hazard. It had made many a career beggared and ruined, ending in the Faubourg d'Enfer with crossing-sweeper's rags, where it had begun in the Boulevard des Capucines with a thousand-franc breakfast; and it caused not a few lives to cease by a pistol-shot in de Bois de Vincennes, or an overdose of morphine in the grey early dawn.

The play was at its highest, the stakes enormous, the gold on the tables flashed and glittered under the light which was thrown back from the rose hangings and the gilded walls;

the heavy odours of the wines filled the air with an intoxicating aroma, and the wreaths of smoke still curled in spirituous vapour, though the hookahs had been left, while now and then the hazard went on in a dead silence, only broken by the formula of the cards; and oftener was played in a mad whirl, a reckless rotation, in the noise of wild jests and riotous laughter and unbridled licence of words from brains half drunk.

And she who was the evil Circe of this evil Avernus, with a glance would turn attention from the cards, till—too late—the stake was lost; or with a smile would daze and dazzle some novice till his gold poured in showers into the bank; or with some gay mot, which still rang with something of the old moqueur, bewitching wit, would raise a laugh at the right moment, till her confederate—who played croupier for the nonce—raked in by rouleaux the money of the tyro. "Men who tempt, and women who are tempted!" So runs the old hackneyed, maudlin, threadbare dictum, much akin to the time-worn opticism which runs, "the Pagans who persecuted, and the Christians who were martyred;"—as if there were not six of the one and six of the other! Pshaw! leave formularies aside, good world, and open your eyes. Women, from Eve downwards, have been First Tempters, and the tempters among them make up half the ranks of their sex, subtle wooers and destroyers of their hundreds.

In the light, with the bloom of art upon her face and the lustre of art lent to her eyes, with mock diamonds glittering where once the costly sapphires of a peeress had lain, with the enamel covering the deep haggard lines, and a smile haunting the lips with the mocking shadow of its old resistless witchery, there was some loveliness still: though ghastly—without its youth; though wrecked most piteously—to those who had known her in the years of her glory; though fearful in the story which it told—to those who paused to read it. There was loveliness still, though a wretched travesty of that which once had been; though justly and truly looking on it she had cried out in her bitterness, "O, my lost beauty! my lost beauty!" since none who remembered what Marion Vavasour once had been, and despised the wreck, remembered and despised as utterly as she. For this woman, who was without remorse for her work or conscience for her crimes, had a ceaseless misery for the social degradation which denied her Pride, and for the encroaching years which left her without Power, since these had been her gods, omnipotent and beloved, and were now drifted from her reach for ever, never again to be recovered.

The Mistress of Paris, who had beheld Greece rise in arms at the havoc of her loveliness, flung to the ribald, brutal crowds of the common soldiery, would not more bitterly have felt her degradation than did this woman. For, though sensual, merciless, frail, and fatal as She who, in the verse of Æschylus, comes with Death and Havoc following on her loveliness, she had loved to reign with imperious will, she had loved to veil her infidelities in poetic grace, she had loved to have her foot on the bent neck of a prostrate world; and now—*now*—she sickened at herself; not for her guilt, but for her humiliation; not for the deep stain upon her soul, but for her broken sceptre, her jeered crown, her rent and trampled purples.

Is it not this, and no better than this, which now and again passes for Remorse? yet which is no more Remorse than its twin-brother, trembling Fear, is true Repentance.

Remorse Marion Vavasour never knew, and never could know; but anguish for her own lost omnipotence she did. She knew it now; to-night, while the noisy laughs echoed about her, and the reeking fumes filled the air of her salon. Oh! bitterness of bitterness! she, into whose presence sovereigns had humbly sued to come, could not resent the coarsest word that was uttered in her presence; she, at whose feet princes had vainly knelt, while statesmen paled before the beauty of her smile, must tempt, and court, and seek these unfledged youths, these nameless idlers; their witless profanities fouled the ear which had once listened to the graceful wit and delicate flattery of monarchs, their slighting glance contemptuously leered upon the face whose beauty once had been the theme of courts, the hymned of prince and poet, the torch which lit whatever it passed, to love, and feud, and madness. She who had ruled the rulers of the earth, could now be slighted by the lowliest!—deadlier than sackcloth and ashes, than hempen cord and sheet of penitence, were the rouge upon her cheek, the laughter upon her lips, the mock gem upon her breast, to this woman whose fastidious pride, whose victorious sway, whose aristocratic grace, whose capricious imperious will had been as haughty and dear to her as those of any anointed queen.

It was long past midnight; the play was fast and furious; the stakes of frightful enormity; the gamesters now and then drank down fiery draughts of fierce Roussillon, or above-proof cognac, or poisonous absinthe, and went, madder than before, to the wild whirl; the light flashed back from the rose hangings and gilded ornaments on to the faces of the cards and the heaps of gold; and now the game went on in a riotous chorus of jest and laughter, and now in the dead silence of high-strung excitement, while here and there fell a muttered oath, or twitching lips turned pale, as a million of francs was swept away on the turn of a colour or the hazard of a card.

Suddenly on the panels of the door, came a loud summons as at the gates of a barricade, thundering, impatient:—many of the gamblers, their brains besotted and their reason whirling with the delirium of play, scarce heard and did not note it, but he who played as croupier grew pale, and with a rapid sign began to sweep away the piles of Naps, while the Priestess of the Pandemonium, who ere this had slaughtered human lives with her skilled lie, and sent a murderer out to work her vengeance with cruel, unfaltering falsehood, stood in the gaslight with the unreal smile arrested upon her lips, and her cheek quivering slightly under its rouge.

She knew that the Rouge-et-Noir of the Rue Beaujon was discovered beyond concealment at last.

"Au nom de la Loi!"

Sharp and swift upon the summons for admittance, the door was burst open by instruments which wrenched and splintered all the intricate locks and bolts for those little scrupulous of ceremony or tolerant of delay; the gaudy rose portière was thrust aside by rough hands, which dashed down all the barricades erected behind it; the salon and its privacy were invaded, the police filled the chambers.

"*De la part de l'Empereur!*" said a voice, serene, inflexible, as bland as though it gave a welcome salutation, as frigid as though it pronounced a sentence of death. Confusion, riot, tumult, execration arose pêle-mêle; the stakes were seized, the doors were closed so that no egress was possible; the tables were overturned, the croupiers dashed wildly here and there, trying to get to covert like a fox run close by the pack; some of the gamblers, their brains dizzy with the chillum and the wine, stared stupidly and helplessly at the seizure; others, cursing and blaspheming, sprang at the gold and cards, swore they were but playing at Boc with three francs as their maximum, and offered bribes, at any rates, with insane eagerness to have the thing kept dark. And while his subordinates secured the croupiers and the stakes, and other officials quietly took down the names and addresses of all present, the Inspecteur approached the mistress of the salon, and, with the same tranquil and inflexible courtesy, arrested her in the name of the Emperor.

For the moment, losing her self-possession, her presence of mind, her swift invention, and her ready diplomacy, the hideous contrast of her present and her past smote on her through the darkness of evil years and the callousness of a soul unsexed; she writhed from under the official's touch as from beneath that of an adder, and gazed at him with the wild stare of a hunted animal hard pressed, and, wringing her white and delicate hands, laughed a shrill, terrible, mocking laugh:

"The Emperor—the Emperor! 'In the name of the Emperor!' What! are the years come back when I was his guest and he mine? Does he remember how often he sat at

my table, that he summons me now to his Court? To the
Tuileries! To the Tuileries! Of course! these diamonds are
fit for the Tuileries!"

Rending the false jewels from her bosom and her hair,
she cast them on the floor and trod upon them with her foot,
those miserable symbols and insignia of her fall, crushing
them to powdered glass, and laughing all the while, with
bitter delirious mockery of herself.

In that brief instant of passionate misery, of ghastly irony,
something of her old resistless grace, of her old imperious
pride, returned as she wrested herself back from the official's grasp, and stamped into shining dust the worthless
gems, while above the uproar round the gaming-table, above
the clash of the gold as the police swept the stakes away,
above the oaths of the startled, half-drunk gamesters, rang
that laugh, once silvery as music, now jarred and dissonant:

"To the Tuileries! Of course!—To the Tuileries! My
diamonds are fit for a Court!"

The Inspecteur, smiling slightly, took no note or heed of
this delirious despair, and seemed neither to have seen nor
heard it, but, proceeding without pause or hesitance with
his errand, arrested her. For what she said had not even a
meaning to him; he had heard of her but under her last
alias and *nom de guerre;* he knew her but as a prisoner who
had transgressed the law, and Marion Vavasour had no
power now—not even to make the world, which is swift to
forget, remember her past.

And this is the last step into the abyss of oblivion, when
none even pause to recall *what we were.*

As a voiture dormise bore her, in close escort, from the
doors of the house in the Rue Beaujon, apprehended on the
proven charge of having a private gambling-hell every night
in her salon, the vehicle was stopped in its progress a little
farther down the street by carriages which blocked the way.
The blind of the window nearest her was but half drawn, and
she, who had now recovered her composure, her finesse, and

her dissimulation, leaned forward as though to show how little moved she was by the charge against her by watching the night with idle amusement. The carriages which entangled the dormise stood before the residence of a French Prince, not enclosed by a court-yard, the doors standing wide open, as the guests dispersed after a State entertainment of more than ordinary magnificence. Descending the broad flight of steps, which was lined on either side by lacqueys, and lighted to the brightness of noon, came the English Minister for whom the equipage waited, the gas shining on the riband which crossed his breast and the orders and stars which glittered there, and falling on his face—a face of pride, of dominance, of successful and imperious power.

Marion Vavasour, looking on him thus, shivered with the thirst of an impotent vengeance, and drooped her head upon her hands with a bitter moan of chained and baffled hatred.

He lived in riches, in dignity, in honour, with his name on the lips of the world, and the cup of his ambition filled to the brim and crowned; while she——!

"Oh, Heaven!" she whispered, passionately, through her clenched teeth, "will the hour *never* come when I can strike him in his power and his arrogance? Will the day *never* dawn when I shall say back in his ear, 'Such mercy as you gave, I give to you!'"

And in the warm summer night in the Paris street they passed each other thus as the carriages rolled on: the Minister who went from a State-gathering, and the Arrested who was taken to Judgment.

## CHAPTER IX.
### "Roses my Secret keep."

WHITE LADIES was filled.

In the great court-yard, troops of saddle-horses, or carriages with their postilions and outriders splashed and tired, came home in the grey twilight while the dressing-bell rang;

in the King's Hall covers were laid for half a hundred guests; in the preserves a thousand head of game were bagged each day, yet no ground beaten twice; in the stately galleries trailed the sweeping dresses of peeresses; and under the roof of the Abbey were gathered not a few of those whose playthings are the policies and destinies of nations. For the master of White Ladies was in Office; and, while the dictum of the world never swerved him from his own course, he was a man who knew, to the utmost of its value, the worth of being prominent in the sight of the world if you seek to lead it.

Rome went to Cincinnatus in his farmstead solitude; but modern Europe would never seek a Sulla once retired to his Cuman villa. Strathmore knew this; none better; and while he smiled at the follies of mankind, turned them to his own profit, and surrounded himself with luxury and circumstance, because he recognised in them the most intelligible symbols of rule and power to the purblind sight of the masses, though he held both in disdain, and in his own tastes was almost ascetic, in his own life almost austere.

The gatherings at White Ladies were noted through the country; and Strathmore was as courtly a host as in his earlier years: his genius was one of those which, essentially facile, are never laborious. The amount of work done by him was vast, but it was done without effort; though he never wholly laid aside the political harness, none saw a gleam of it through the silken surcoat he wore in society; and whilst the chief secret of his power over men lay in the entire absence of sensitive self-consciousness, or Utopian ideology from his career, not a little attraction lay for them in the brilliant ease with which this ambitious and arduous career was covered by the same art with which the Damascus armourers covered their keenest steel with the light elegance of the chasing;—while the chasing blinded the eyes before which it flashed, the cunning smiths knew that the steel cut swifter passage home.

The warm sun fell across the sward through the boughs of

the wych-elms, and down the ruined cloisters into the oriel room where he sat at breakfast. The purple hangings were behind him, with the dead gold of their broidered chiffre; the light fell through the painted panes and the blazoned motto, "Slay! and spare not;" without, the same lengthened shadows fell across the sward, and the same ivy roots clung about the cloisters; even his own features were unaltered, the same save for some trace of added age, some look of haughtier power and of deeper melancholy, as on the day when he whom he had loved and slain had sat at his table, and the name of their temptress and destroyer been first upon his lips. Yet of that day he did not even think once out of the thousand times that found him sitting thus: wear the spiked band of penance long about your loins, and they shall so learn to bear it, that they feel it seldom, save when a sudden blow drives the iron afresh into the flesh. Could the Furies have pursued Orestes through many years, he would have grown used to the haunting troop, and would have learned to sleep, to rest, to labour, and to love in the loathed presence of the Avengers; and only at rare intervals would he have started from his slumber to shudder at the accursed forms, or flee in the dead of night from the sacred temple, because they hunted him from rest, and pursued him for the blood of Clytemnestra.

Strathmore's life was a successful one; not a contented one, because his insatiate and restless ambition always desired wider and more irresponsible dominance than in this country the highest can ever wield, and because all happiness had been stricken from it with the betrayal of the woman he had worshipped, of the lips for whose kiss he had stained his soul with guilt. But one of those lives which, full, grand, eminent, make "happiness" look tame, insipid, and needless: and in such a life it was but the solitary hours when silence and sleep were nigh, or the rare days when the eyes of Lucille met his own, which remorse could claim; for the rest Strathmore was the world's, and the world his.

There was a brilliant party gathered about him at breakfast: English statesmen, German princes, French nobility, with lovely women, who sometimes discussed the question over their Orange Pekoe before the dressing-bell rang, whether he would ever marry. Negligent of their charms, and wedded to public life, brilliant eyes softly wooed him, never to awake response: the burning passion which had once consumed his life seemed to have seared out every trace of warmer desires. After that mad, guilty, but devoted love, none could assail him; the sternest ascetic who had ever dwelt in that Dominican monastery was not colder to women than he who, beneath its roof, had been the lover of Marion Vavasour.

With a large party he went out that morning deer-stalking for the day in the forests which belted in White Ladies, where red deer were as abundant as in the wilds of Exmoor. The sun had sunk, and the windows of the grey and stately façade were all lit, as they returned and dispersed to their several chambers; while Strathmore went to his own room, fronting the State Apartments, which had been unused from the time when they had harboured the loveliness which had tempted and forsaken him. Of her he now thought, as he left his chamber and returned along the corridor; one of the long line of windows stood open to the night, and from the gardens below was up-wafted the heavy, rich scent of the roses; and the remembered perfume suddenly rising, made the memory which lay within, coiled to stillness, but never dead,

> like a dreaming snake,
> Drowsily lift itself fold by fold,
> And gnaw and gnaw hungrily, half awake.

It had been the love of his manhood, that single burning passion of an ambitious life; and—though changed in one swift hour to deadliest hate, which had pursued her with unquenched and insatiate vengeance, which would have watched her still, with unrelenting gaze, starve as a beggar at his feet, and die of a beggar's dole denied—when memory uprose, and with it burned again upon his own the lips which had betrayed him, and with it he beheld again the loveliness for which he had rent down and trampled under foot the laws of God and man, the old agony uncoiled from its rest, and pierced him with its poisoned fangs.

He had loved her, till ambition, honour, conscience, life itself, had all been given to her hands; he had loved her with delirious, ungrudging worship, that saw in her kiss his heaven, in her smile his world, in her will his deity; and that dead passion awoke, not less in hate but more, while yet across the stretch of many years it was stricken afresh with the stroke of its betrayal, and sickened afresh over all its wealth wasted, its treasure mocked, its idolatrous love poured out—in vain! in vain!—upon that lovely, hideous, beautiful wanton thing, upon a courtesan, and an assassinatress. And it was thus it awoke now, stirred to memory by the odour of the roses that stole upwards on the mist through the opened window, as he passed down the solitary corridor; and he flung the casement to, with swift hand and passionate gesture, to shut out that haunting, mocking fragrance of the flowers that Marion Vavasour had loved.

He—the cold, inflexible, and successful Statesman—shuddered and shrank from the mere scent of the summer-roses!

A low, ringing laugh, echoing gaily on the air, startled the silence of the corridor: it came from the unused State Chambers. He started as he stood by the casement, and looked up. The long passage leading thither was dully lit, for the gas burned low, and at its foot the opposite door of the State rooms stood open, and—with a light held high above her head, so that while the arched doorway and the chamber behind were deep in gloom, its luminance fell upon her and about her, brightly shed upon her young and radiant face, with the bloom of childhood on the cheeks and the smile of childhood still haunting the fair eyes—he saw Lucille.

Strathmore gazed at her, as men have gazed upon the spirits which, born of their own haunted memories, have seemed to fill the air with the forms of the dead.

What place had she beneath the roof of White Ladies, when across its threshold lay the shadow of a guilt which, known to her, would have turned her steps from it in loathing and in horror? The house of her father's murderer was no home to harbour her dawning life and shelter her innocent sleep!

"In *that* room—in that room!"

The words were muttered unconsciously in his throat, as he stood silent and motionless for the moment; to see her thus, and there, made the air round him teem with the shadows of the past, which whispered that the work, wrought by his own hand when it dealt out death and retribution, must for ever endure, the blood-stain never effaced by expiation, the dead days ever lying in wait to devour and destroy the future.

That moment passed,—the weakness was crushed down and conquered; he welcomed her with kind and courteous words, as Lucille sprang towards him, lifting her lips for his caress of greeting, her face brightened still with her happy and melodious laugh.

"Oh, Lord Cecil! I could not help being amused, you threw that window to, with such a passionate gesture; and I had never seen you anything but calm and still and tranquil! Whom were you angry with in thought?—not me! I shall be afraid of you in future, as they say all the world is——"

"Hush! hush!" her careless words smote him in that moment with keen pain. "Lucille, you would never fear me, shrink from me, dread me? I have made your life too happy——"

She looked at him surprised; he, the haughty and arrogant leader of men, sought this assurance as a boon from the child-ward who owed him all! But her mood was changed to his in an instant, her hand softly closed on his own, and she leaned caressingly towards him, till her hair, with white violets woven in it, brushed his breast, and her deep loving eyes were uplifting to his:

"*I* fear *you!* Oh, never, never! Whom can I love and

honour and trust to, like you, who have filled, and more than filled, the place of all I lost?"

He drew her gently to him, and kissed her brow, recovering the self-command which for one moment had been shaken:

"Think of me always so—always; as one who has striven to supply to you your father's loss, and to fulfil your father's trust! But how came you here, Lucille? I did not know you were at the Abbey. My mother left the day of your arrival uncertain."

"We came an hour ago. Lady Castlemere felt better, and I was so impatient to see you and White Ladies. What a stately place it is! I love its grey, solemn, time-worn grandeur. Take me all over it—now, will you—now?"

The earnestness, too deep and thoughtful for her years, with which she had spoken of her trust and love for her guardian had passed away; now she was only a child, used to the gratification of every bright caprice and momentary fancy as she looked up at him with longing in her eyes and eagerness upon her lips.

He smiled:

"Not now, Lucille; we dine at nine, and it wants only a quarter; to-morrow I will take you wherever you wish. But how do you come here—and alone! The rooms where you were are never used. They have not given you those chambers, surely?"

He spoke with impatient anxiety: he could not have had her rest *there!*

She laughed amusedly:

"I lost my way! When I was dressed, I sent Babette to ask Lady Castlemere some question for me, but she was so long gone that I grew tired, and thought I would go myself. But I could not find the room so well as I fancied; I missed it among all these passages, and found myself wandering in those chambers. Why are they never used?"

Strathmore avoided answer.

"You must not wander alone about White Ladies till you

know its intricacies, my dear. You may very easily lose yourself. I will take you to my mother now—they ought to have placed you close to her—and then we must go down to the drawing-rooms. There are plenty of people very desirous to see you."

Lucille sighed a little:

"Ah! I do not care much for strangers," she answered him, as she ran up the steps, where she had hastily set down her little silver lamp.

The spaniel which he had given her in her infancy, and with which she never parted, though it was now very old, had remained in the chamber, and she went back to fetch him. The dog did not come immediately to her call, and Strathmore, following her, stood once more in the State Apartments, where his step had never entered, and his eyes never rested, through the many years which had passed since he had first returned to White Ladies.

"What beautiful rooms! Why are they never used? Because they are only for the Royal Family, is it? Who slept here last, then?"

She spoke, holding the lamp high above her head, so that its light was shed on her, and flickered fitfully on the azure hangings, the Venetian mirrors, the gold services, the silk, and lace, and velvet, the costly cabinets near, and the dark shadow afar off, where the silvery rays could not reach, but left half the magnificence of the room lost in the darkness of the night.

At her innocent question he shuddered as at the scent of the summer-roses! His eyes glanced for one moment over the luxurious chamber, with its costly adornments and its depths of gloom, in sickening memory—then they fell upon the form of Lucille, where she stood in the halo of the light, one hand holding to her heart the little dog which had once kept its faithful vigil crouched in the bosom of the dead. The hideous past seemed to breathe through the chamber with its pestilential odour, its avenged passions, its eternal guilt—and he stretched his hand, and drew her with a sudden gesture out from that unholy place.

Yet his voice was tranquil and his smile calm as he closed the door on her, and led her forward:

"Those State rooms are damp, they have been unused so long; it is not wise for you to be in them at night, Lucille. Besides, every one will think that I have deserted my guests."

And, with the suave and graceful dignity of a courtier, he conducted her along the silent corridor, and down the broad oak staircase, in the full gleam of light, giving her urbane and courtly welcome beneath the roof of White Ladies, where her father's laugh had so often rung in clear and joyous music, and her father's hand closed in love and friendship on the hand which now held hers—the hand which, unfaltering, had dealt him death.

Lucille, introduced into the splendid circle gathered under her guardian's roof, struck and touched all there with that ethereal and rare loveliness, of which its own unconsciousness made not the least and most common charm. She was still but a beautiful child, with all a child's unstudied grace, a child's artless transparence; and the manner in which she had been reared, while it had given her that nameless ease which only belongs to high-breeding, had brushed nothing from the innocence of a youth which had loved the birds as its friends and the flowers as its teachers. Her young beauty charmed those who approached her like music, the upward gaze of her eyes, always earnest even to sadness, had for all the haunting sweetness of some remembered melody, and the joyous gladness of a life, on which no shade of sorrow had ever fallen, contrasted touchingly with the mournfulness which in moments of silence stole over her face, born of a nature musing, sensitive, and essentially poetic. The princes and the peers, the statesmen and the men of pleasure, staying at White Ladies did their best to teach her her power by subtlest flattery and most delicate court; they had seen nothing for years fairer than the way in which she listened to them in naïve surprise, and turned from them in graceful indifference; while the titled beauties, something jealous of her, yet sought her with courtly kindness, and wondered among themselves that Strathmore, the coldest, most heartless, and most ascetic man of his age, had so much of gentleness and consideration for a young girl to whom he was merely guardian: it could not be from her beauty, they thought, for was he not negligent of *theirs*, and of all!

To Lucille the sumptuous, glittering, brilliant life led at the Abbey seemed to her like a *conte des fées;* all had the spell of freshness for her, her light laugh rang under the arches of the grey cloisters, her youthful steps echoed down the vast area of the banqueting-hall, her eyes gazed at the Strathmore portraits, and—the shadow which lay across the threshold of White Ladies cast no shade upon this sunlit, dawning life, and the winds which sighed through the boughs of the monastic elms, and blew softly among the long grasses over her mother's grave, brought her no burden from the history of the lives to which her own owed birth. She was so happy!—life looked to her so beautiful in its still half-folded glories, like the illumined pictures of an uncut book, like the closed leaves of the passion-flower, which keeps its richest beauty shut in its core till the last. She was so happy! —for, for the first time, she was beneath the roof of Strathmore; she saw him daily, hourly; she was always in his presence, or watching for it; could sit and listen to him while he spoke with his guests or his fellow ministers, never weary of hearing the voice which, chill in its very harmony to the ear of others, to hers was the sweetest and most mellow music that it knew. And her heart, child-like in its purity, but far beyond childhood and beyond youth, in the vivid depth of all it felt, cherished as the life of its life, her love and reverence for him to whose guardianship her father had bequeathed her. From her earliest years she had clung with a strange affection to Strathmore; while yet so young that comprehension of his career was impossible to her, she had delightedly listened to all who would tell her of his greatness; she loved to think how much she owed to him, and how deep must have been his friendship for her father that he took this care for her. All that was powerful, generous, and grand in his character drew her to him; all that was darker was veiled from her; she thought it as stainless as it was unrivalled, and the fair, fond dreams of a luxuriant imagination had clung about him as their centre till that affection had become the religion of her life. It seemed as though the love which her father had borne to him had been transmitted to her: natures such as Strathmore's, which are indifferent to love, are not seldom those on which most love is lavished.

"What are you so absorbed in, Lucille?" asked one of the women staying there, a certain lovely leader of the fashion.

Lucille, half lying on a couch in the library, resting her head on her hand, looked up with a smile:

"I was reading 'Indiana.'"

Lady Chessville laughed, and turned to Strathmore, who had just entered the library with the Duke of Beauvoir, his son the Marquis of Bowdon, the Prince de Volms, and Valdor.

"Lord Cecil! here is Lucille absorbed in 'Indiana.' Do you permit that as her guardian?"

Strathmore smiled as he approached:

"Lucille will not be harmed by Georges Sand, Lady Chessville: Rousseau or De Kock would leave no stain *there*; the soil must be fit ere impure plants will take root. Still—you are right. Where did you find that book, my dear? It is not my edition, I think."

Lucille looked at the cover.

"No; there are not your arms on it. I found it in my room; it amused me, and so I brought it down. There is a name on the title-page, though the ink is faded. Look! 'Bertie Erroll.' Who was he?"

She held the book up to him, her hand on the faded writing, her eyes raised to his, and a sharp agony struck him again like the stab of a mortal blow, for his grief for *this* sin was great and deathless.

But his smile did not change, not a muscle of his face moved, and he took the volume without even a moment's hesitation, carelessly glancing at the title-page:

"Yes, it is one of Erroll's; he was a friend of mine. Keep the book if it amuse you, Lucille."

Lucille saw no difference from his habitual manner, which, when others were with them, was always gentle but cold. Lady Chessville connected nothing with the name, for she had been a child at the time of that tragedy in the Deer Park of the Bois, and the world had long since forgotten that darker story of its successful Minister's earlier manhood. Beauvoir, a good-hearted, kindly man, whispered to Lord Bowdon as they went out:

"He shot that very fellow Erroll through the heart years ago about a notorious woman, and now speaks of him like that! Bosom friends, too, they were! Able man, Strathmore, very able, but cold as ice and cruel as a Borgia. Don't know what remorse is!"

So bystanders judge! Valdor alone noted, to judge differently, the singular indifference, the perfect tranquillity with which Strathmore spoke Erroll's name and looked upon his writing: he had seen them precisely as calm, precisely as negligent an hour before sunset, when he went out with a murderer's resolve, brutal and inflexible, in his heart; he had so seen them when the sun had sunk, and the murderer had stooped to sever the golden lock from the trailing hair of the dead man. By one of those instincts which the mind cannot trace, but which it involuntarily follows, it struck him that Strathmore had spoken thus *for the sake of Lucille;* he would not have thought it needful to have assumed such complete indifference towards Erroll's memory merely for men who knew how Erroll met his death, and would have rather respected him more than less for some show of remembrance also. From that hour she became associated with the memory of Erroll in Valdor's thoughts; he felt convinced that the

cause of Strathmore's care for his ward arose in some way
or other from her connexion with the man whom he had
slaughtered in cold blood: and Valdor was keen, hot, eager
in the scent, for all concerning Lucille had interest for him,
this guileless beautiful child, reared in seclusion by the English
shores of the Atlantic.

Strathmore saw this interest, saw it in Valdor, as in many
others under his roof, throughout those autumnal weeks, and
it woke anger in him whenever their glances fell on her, or
their words made her eyes grow dark and wistful in half-
shrinking, half-disdainful surprise, as they whispered subtle
flatteries in her ear. Anger which was twofold: first, because
they would rapidly destroy the unworn freshness and the innocence, earnest whilst it was childlike, which were beautiful
to him in her; last, and more, because each might be one who
would wake her heart from its rest and imperil its peace.
He had sworn to make his atonement by securing her happiness at whatever cost; he had looked on hers as the life on
which hung his single power of expiation. How could he
secure it when once she should have been taught to place it
in the hands or embark it in the love of any one of those who
sought to dispel her childhood by their honeyed whispers?

Strathmore, who held that Will can work what it chooses,
and who, in the arrogance of a great intellect, conceived that
he could mould fate like potter's clay, felt passionate impotence as he realised that the work of his atonement might
be wrested from him incomplete, and dashed to pieces before
his eyes. It was here that his error had lain; his remorse was
holy in its intense contrition, its sincere agony; but he did
not seek its expiation in that humility and self-doubt which
a great guilt may well leave upon the proudest and most self-
sustained nature: he had set it before him as he had set the
ambitions of his public life, as a purpose to be effected by his
own foresight and his own will, guarded by him alone from
all chance of miscarriage, all touch of opposing will, all
danger of human accident, as his strength of steel and his
unscrupulous force bore down all that was antagonistic to him,

and pioneered his road to power. Prostrate and chastened by misery, he had vowed to fulfil the trust bequeathed him an hundred-fold beyond all which that trust enjoined; but to the fulfilment of his oath he had gone in the same spirit with which he had dealt out death and meted vengeance; the spirit which relied on the masterly skill of his own hand to mould what form it would, and still conceived that Life would bend and bow to his haughty fiat: "*I* choose this!"

"You gave me leave to hope; but what chance of hope, sir, is there for me with all *these?*" said young Caryll, bitterly, one day, as he glanced at the knot of titled and famous men gathered about Lucille in the cedar drawing-room.

Strathmore had extended his invitation to the young man, true to his promise, to give him opportunity to advance his love on her affection, for he was scrupulously just, and never broke his word in private or public matters.

Strathmore smiled—that smile under which young Caryll winced as under the cut of a knife:

"I gave you leave to hope, certainly; it is for you to give your hope a basis. I never told you *I* deemed it well founded; but you should know how to make it so. If you have so little of the necessary love-lore, I cannot help you; *ce n'est pas à moi!*"

"But—but how, when she has so many to teach her her power——?" began the youth, hesitatingly.

Strathmore raised his eyebrows:

"'*How!*' If you be such a novice in the art, it were wiser you should abandon it altogether."

He spoke with that slight laugh which was more chill than most men's sneer; but, though his words had stung his nephew as the young alone can be stung by the light contempt of a man of the world, Strathmore's disdain for him was not unmixed with a wish that his suit might prosper. If Lucille's heart were fastened on Caryll's love, and could be content in it and with it, her happiness might be more surely and safely secured than with those more brilliant in station, who now sought her; and over his nephew, who would be his debtor, and whose career would be moulded and checked by him, he would have still a sway, where, if she wedded any other, he would lose his influence for her and over her life for ever. Yet the same bitterness which had arisen when his mother had first spoken of marriage for her, rose in him now, as he looked across to where she stood in the conservatories, caressing a bright-plumaged bird, and trying to lure another from the topmost boughs of an orange-tree, too absorbed in her wayward favourites to be conscious of the glances bent upon her by the group around.

"Can they not let her alone for a few brief years, at least!" he mused, with an acrid impatience. "That bird's wing which brushes her lips is fitter caress for her than men's embraces. Marriage! Faugh!—it is profanity to speak of—to think of—for her!"

"Strathmore, if you are disengaged just now, give me five minutes," said the Duke of Beauvoir, touching him on the arm at that moment.

His Grace was a heavy, cheery, generous gentleman, to whom *Mark Lane Express* panegyrics on his prize short-horns were dearer than European encomiums on his policies, and who in the Cabinet was very utterly under the lead of his subtle and astute colleague, though the reins were so excellently managed that he was wholly unconscious of his own docile obedience.

"I want to talk to you about a merely personal matter," went on the Duke, as Strathmore led the way into the billiard-room, just then empty; "in fact, about your young ward, Mademoiselle de Vocqsal. Have you any marriage in view for her?"

"None, my dear Duke."

"Well! Bowdon has lost his head about her," went on his Grace, in his usual sans façon, good-humoured style, which flung dignity to the winds as humbug, and yet somehow or other never entirely lost it. "Never saw him so much in love in my life! You've remarked it, of course, eh? He has asked me to-day to speak to you. In point of fact, I should be very glad to see him married myself, and I have so high an esteem for Lady Castlemere, that I should have been perfectly satisfied if I had known nothing more than that the young lady he sought had been reared under her tutelage, so I told him I would mention the matter to you this morning. I presume the alliance would have your concurrence?"

"A more brilliant one it would be impossible to find for her! You do me the highest honour in soliciting her hand for Lord Bowdon," answered Strathmore, with his suave, chill courtesy, which was never startled into surprise as it was rarely warmed to cordiality. "His proposals, then, have your full sanction? May I ask what has been said on the subject to my ward?"

"Nothing!—nothing definite, at least. She is so exceedingly young—not brought out, indeed—that Bowdon and I both concurred in seeking her hand from you first. Will you mention it to her as you think best?"

"With pleasure. We may postpone, then, any further discussion of your wishes or mine until we are aware how Mademoiselle de Vocqsal receives your most flattering proposal?"

"*How?*"

His Grace looked fairly astonished—a little amazed, moreover; it was so very new a suggestion to him that his son, the future Duke of Beauvoir could possibly be rejected!

Strathmore smiled, that suave, courtly smile which always a little worried his noble colleague:

"My dear Beauvoir, I need not say that alliance with your House surpasses the most splendid aspirations which my ward could have indulged in for herself, or my mother and I as her guardians for her; at the same time, I do not prejudge Lucille's answer, since I should never seek to sway her inclination. But there is little fear, doubtless, of what that answer will be; Lord Bowdon could not woo in vain."

His Grace's pride and consternation were both soothed, and he passed on to speak further of his proposals in his son's name with that hearty *au point*, straightforwardness, which in the Cabinet made so strong a contrast to the fine finesses and inscrutable reticence of one who, from his earliest years of public life, had recognised the essential art of success to lie in knowing "how to hold truth, and—how to withhold it."

"I must be the first, then, to taint her mind with marriage offers!" thought Strathmore. "Rank more brilliant could not be given her; every woman in England will envy her her lot; he is a handsome, amiable, inoffensive—fool! Such men make the kindest husbands. There will be no fear for her happiness, if—if—she love him. And yet, that soft, delicate, innocent life! Good God! it is defilement!"

The thoughts flitted, scarce shaped, through his mind; the sudden offer of the Duke's alliance had struck him with keen, though vague pain—the same pain, but more intense, which had smitten him when his mother had first spoken of Lucille's future. Young Caryll's love for her had been some distant thing, viewed by him with some contempt, and subject to long probation; he had not realised it in connexion with her; but the Duke's words had set sharply and vividly before him the inevitable certainty that, ere long, the loveliness to which so many testified would be sought and claimed in marriage, and that, once given to another, his right over the life which he alone now protected, and directed, must pass utterly and for ever from him. She might be happy in her husband's home, and in that happiness he would have no share; looking on it, he would no longer see in the beauty of her days the symbol of his own atonement: or—she might be wretched in the union which bound her, or in the grief of a wronged womanhood, and he would be powerless to give her freedom and consolation, and must see the life he had sworn to the dead to keep unstained and unshadowed, consume hopelessly before his sight!

To the man who, high in power and arrogant in strength, had a scornful unbelief in the power of Circumstance to overthrow Resolve, the sense of the impotence of his will here was bitter as it was strange. For the moment, maddened by it, he felt tempted to exert his title as her guardian to forbid all marriage for her, all love to her; but this, again, he was forced to surrender; to secure her happiness, free choice must be left her, in that which, thwarted, often makes the misery of a life; and Strathmore's nature, merciless to others, was one to the full as inflexible to himself in any ordeal self-chosen, any sacrifice self-imposed. It smote him with pain, with aversion, almost with loathing, to be the first to speak to her of what must lead her across that boundary she had told him wistfully she feared to pass, which oftentimes parts Childhood from Womanhood by a single step. He revolted from his office; but it devolved on him as her guardian; as such he had accepted it, and he went to fulfil it.

As he descended before dinner, he saw her upon the terrace leaning over the parapet in the warm glow of the western light, which slanted across the broad flight of steps, and fell about her where she stood; strange contrast, in the bright and aërial glow of her youth, to the grey monastic walls of the Gothic façade behind her, and the dark massed branches of the cedars above her head.

He approached her, and laid his hand gently on her hair, turned simply back from her brow in its rich silken waves:

"Where are your dreams, Lucille?"

She looked up, and the warm light which ever came there at his presence beamed upon her face:

"I was thinking of all those who have lived and died here; of all the histories those grey stones could speak; of all the secrets which lie shrouded in those woods since they saw the Druidic sacrifices, and heard the chant of the white-robed Dominicans:—the dead days seem to rise from their graves, and tell me all that is buried with them!"

She spoke only in the fanciful imagination which loved to wander in the poetic mysteries of the past, but her words now, as often, struck him with that deadliest Nemesis of crime—the doom which compels the guilty to hear reproach in every innocent speech, and feel a blow on unhealed wounds, in what, without that remembered sin, had been but gay jest or soft caress.

"You are too imaginative, Lucille," he said, quickly. "Why dream of that dark past, of unholy sacrifice and insensate superstition? The past has nothing to do with *you;* live in your own fair present, my child. Your sunny seashore suits you better than the monastic gloom of White Ladies."

She lifted her bright head eagerly:

"Oh! I love White Ladies best."

"Surely? But Silver-rest is your home?"

"Yes; but this is *yours.*"

He smiled; all expression of her affection was dear to him, not because affection was ever necessary to him, but because hers was like the pardon and purification of his crime. Then the office which he came to execute, recurred to him; they were alone, no living thing near save the deer which were crossing the sward in the distance, and the peacock trailing his gorgeous train over the fallen rose-leaves on the marble pavement. But that solitude might be broken any second; he employed it while it lasted.

"Lucille! you may command another home from to-day, if you will."

Her eyes turned on him with a surprised, bewildered look, while a happy smile played about her lips:

"Another home! What do I want with one, Lord Cecil?"

"Many will offer one."

The surprised wonder in her eyes deepened, she looked at him hesitatingly, yet amused still:

"I do not understand you."

A curse rose in his throat on those who made him destroy the yet lingering childhood, and awaken thoughts which he himself would have bidden sleep for ever.

"I am not speaking in enigmas, Lucille; I tell you merely a necessary truth," he answered her gravely. "As your guardian I have the disposal of your future; of that future those who love you will each seek the charge; it is for you, not me, to decide to whom it is finally entrusted. His Grace of Beauvoir has to-day sought your hand from me for his son. What answer shall I return to Lord Bowdon?"

Her eyes had been fixed wistfully on him as he spoke, scarcely as if comprehending him; at the clearness of his last words a blush, the first he had seen there, flushed her cheeks, her lashes drooped, her lips parted, but without speech, and he fancied that she shuddered slightly.

His task revolted him, he loathed it yet more in execution than in anticipation; but Strathmore let no trace of repugnance appear, he addressed her calmly and gravely, as befitted one who filled to her, in her eyes and the world's, her father's place:

"I do not need to tell you, Lucille, that such an alliance is almost the highest in the country, and one of the most brilliant it would be possible to command. His father tells me that Bowdon loves you as much even as the fancy of youth can wish to be loved. To exaggerate the rank of the station you would fill would be impossible, and your happiness——"

"Oh hush! hush!—it seems so strange."

The words were spoken rapidly under her breath, and almost with an accent of terror, while the flush was hot on her cheek, and her head was drooped and slightly turned from him; it might be the startled shyness of girlish love, the momentary agitation of a flattered pride; he took it for these, and a pain, keen and heavy, smote him, and made his tone more cold, though as calm and even as heretofore, as he went on:

"Nay, you must hear me, Lucille. I but repeat to you what the Duke has said, and it is no light matter to be dismissed hastily either way. I am no ambassador of a lovetale; but I should err gravely in the place I hold towards you if I did not put fully before you the eminence of the rank for which your hand is sought, and the splendour of the alliance into which you may now enter——"

He paused suddenly, for she turned towards him with a

swift movement and that caressing grace with which as a little child upon the sea-shore she had leaned against him, thinking she had done wrong to touch a stranger's dog.

"Hush! you pain me. Why do you speak to me so? Are you tired of me, Lord Cecil?"

The colour still was warm in her face, but her eyes as they questioned his were pleading and reproachful, and there was a naïve plaintiveness in the words, and in the action, with which she turned to him, which touched him, even while they struck him with a sense of keen relief, of vivid pleasure: it would have cost him more than he had counted to surrender his right to gladden, to guide, and to control this young life; it would have been the surrender of Erroll's trust, and of his own atonement.

He drew her gently towards him with that tenderness which existed only for her, begotten of circumstance, while foreign to his nature.

"Why does it pain you, my love? Have you heard me aright? I but speak to you of a marriage for which my consent has been sought, and which is so exalted and unexceptionable a one, that as your guardian I should be deeply blamable if **I did not** fully set before you all it offers. I should never **urge your** inclination, but I must state truly all which may await you if you accept it. Decide nothing hastily; to-morrow you can give me your reply."

A look of aversion shadowed her face, she clung to him with that caressing reliance as natural and unrestrained now as in her childhood, and lifted her eyes in beseeching earnestness:

"Oh no! Why? What need? Tell them at once that I could not—I could not!"

A gladness which had never touched his life since Marion Vavasour destroyed it, swept over him for a moment at her words; he loved her for the sake and in the memory of the dead; and he rejoiced that he was not yet bidden to bestow her on her lover, to give her up from his own keeping:

"It shall be as you will, Lucille. I have no other aim

save your happiness. But are you sure that you know what you refuse; that you may not desire to speak of it further with my mother? You are very young, and a station so brilliant——"

Something proud, pained, wistful, perplexed, which came into her eyes, again arrested him; the delicate and spiritual nature shrank from the coarser ambitions imputed to her, the worldly bribe proffered to her:

"Why do you tell me of *that*, Lord Cecil?"

"Because it is my duty as your guardian, *not* because I think that it would sway you. I do not. Yours is a rare nature, Lucille."

His answer reassured her, and the shadow passed from off her face as the warm sunlight of the west fell on it, the smile upon her lips, so like her father's in its gladness and its sunny tenderness, that it smote Strathmore as on the night when she had wakened from dreaming sleep on the bosom of her dead mother.

"Then—then—whenever any others speak to you as the Duke has done, you will answer them without coming to me? You will say 'Lucille has no love to give strangers, and needs no guardian save the one she has!'"

He smiled, moved to mingled pain and pleasure by her words:

"I cannot promise that, my child, for I fear they would not rest content with such an answer. And—Lucille—the future must dawn for you as for all, and you will find other loves than those you now know."

She put her hand up to his lips to silence him, and her eyes grew dark and humid:

"Never! Never! If the future would differ from the present, I pray God it may not dawn. Are you weary of Lucille, Lord Cecil, that you would exile her to other care?"

"Never ask that! I wish to God my care could shield you always."

His answer sprang from the poisoned springs of a deep and hidden remorse: she heard in it but a sure defence and promise for the future, as he stood resting his hand upon her shoulder in the evening silence, while the sun sank from sight behind the elm-woods, and the shadows of twilight stole over the terrace, where the winding waters glistened through the gloom, white with their countless river-lilies, as on the night when Marion Vavasour had been there beside him, wooing from his lips the first words of that guilt-steeped love in which all the beauty of his manhood had been cast and wrecked.

Laughing in soft, child-like gaiety—for his words had made her very glad, and banished even from memory the momentary vague pain and fear which had fallen on her, she scarce knew why—Lucille stooped and wound her hands in the luxuriance of the late roses, which still blossomed in profusion over the steps and balustrade of the cedar-terrace, covering the white marble with their trailing leaves and scarlet petals, and filling the air with their odour. Her hands wandered among them with that delight in their beauty which was inborn with her artistic and imaginative nature, and drawing one of the richest clusters from the rest, she held them to him in their fragrance:

"I do not wonder that the Greeks and the poets loved the roses best, and that the Easterns gave them to the nightingales as the burden of their song and the choice of their love! How beautiful they are—the Queen of Flowers!"

The words, the action, the sight and scent of the roses, as she held them upward to him in the twilight, recalled, in sudden vivid agony, the memory of the woman who had stood there with him on that very spot, with the subtle, poetic lies upon her fragrant lips, which gave the flower that she loved value and sweetness in his sight because their kiss had rested on its leaves:—it was among the roses that he had seen her in the morning-light at Vernonceaux; it was among the roses that he had seen her in the summer-noon, when he had spared her from death only that she might live to suffer! And the flower was accursed in his sight.

Those scarlet roses, with their heavy fragrance and their clinging dews, gave him a thrill of horror as he saw them lifted to him by the innocent hands of Lucille; they were in his eyes the bloodstained symbol of the assassinatress, of the destroyer!

With an irrepressible impulse he seized them from her, and threw them far away, till they fell bruised and scattered on the turf below.

Her look of surprise recalled him to himself.

"Roses have a faint odour to me, my dear; I have not your love of them," he said, hurriedly. "Your lilies of the valley become you best, Lucille; those roses have nothing in common with *you*, the flowers of orgie, of revel, of secresy!"

She looked at him surprised still, for she had never seen his tranquil repose of manner broken until now at White Ladies, and it seemed to her very strange that he, the haughty and inflexible political leader, should be thus moved by the unwelcome fragrance of a few autumn roses!

Her eyes dwelt on him wonderingly, wistfully:

"Have I vexed you, Lord Cecil? You are not angry with me?"

He passed his hand softly over her hair, deeply moved in that moment by the tender and pleading words.

"No! God forbid! Act as your own heart dictates, Lucille, and you will ever act as I would have you. I rejoice that you do not risk your life in other hands than mine. Keep your beautiful youth while you may!"

## CHAPTER X.

### The Night Whisper of the Past.

"So you have sent poor Bowdon away, Lucille. It was very cruel, and a refusal must seem so remarkably odd to him!" laughed Lady Chessville, the night after, as she came into the young girl's dressing-room before the déshabille. The Peeress, young and omnipotent herself, was one of those women who like the beauty and grace of others.

Lucille shook her head a little disdainfully:

"It is a cruelty he will soon forget."

"It is not so easy to 'forget' always, mon enfant, but you have not learnt that; you have nothing to blot out," said the Countess. "Come, tell me, Lucille, how could Bowdon fail to please you? What was it you disliked in him? I am curious; he is accustomed to be thought perfection."

"I did not *dislike* anything; I never thought about him at all."

Lady Chessville laughed a silvery peal of hearty laughter:

"Poor Bowdon! if he could but hear that! I must really tell the Duke of the degradation to which his beloved has come. But you are very ungrateful, my beautiful child. Can none of them move you any more? I shall say your guardian has taught you his own coldness."

The colour flushed into Lucille's face, her eyes darkened and dilated, she raised her head eagerly, while the rich masses of her unbound hair shook over her shoulders to the ground:

"'Cold?' You must never use that word to my guardian. Oh! how little you know him! There is no one on earth so gracious, so gentle, so generous, so full of kindly thought and noble acts. There is the coldness of his world, of his years, of his ambitions, perhaps in his look and in his words, but there is no coldness in his heart. Look what he has been to me, merely because the father whom I lost was the friend of his youth. Would one cold at heart cherish such a memory so sacredly, and fulfil a trust of the dead so unweariedly?"

The firelight shone warmly on her upraised face, through which the soul within seemed itself to beam; her eyes looked upward proudly and lovingly, with the bright hair brushed from her flushed brow, and her lips slightly parted with the eager words; she might have been painted for Vivia Perpetua in her young and holy loveliness, willing to endure all things even unto death in defence and in reverence for her Lord.

Lady Chessville looked at her and sighed: there was that

in Lucille's face which vaguely touched to sadness all those who gazed on her.

"He was your father's friend?" she said, musingly. "I never knew that!"

"Yes; and he loved him so well!" answered Lucille, while her voice grew low and tremulous, recalling the memory of him whom Strathmore had taught her to dream of with more than a filial affection, hallowed towards the dead as it could never have been to the living. "I cannot remember him, but Lord Cecil has spoken of him to me till I think of him as dearly as though he were living now. He died in my infancy, Lord Cecil was with him at his death, and it is because they had lived as brothers that he has such goodness and tenderness for me. Do you think any man, cold at the core of his heart, could retain such a memory of one lost friend? It will show you alone that the beauty of his character to those who know it aright, equals the greatness of his career; eclipse it, it cannot do!"

"You are eloquent for your guardian, Lucille," said Lady Chessville. "What you tell me speaks very differently for Strathmore than what society says usually; we all know his intellect, his power, his statesmanship, are masterly, but we never held him anything but icily heartless with his subtle, delicate sneer, and his world-steeped egotism. I remember, I fancy, however—I don't exactly know what—but I think I once heard that many years ago he was passionately in love with some woman who deserted or betrayed him; did you ever hear anything of it, Lucille?"

"Never!" She started a little, and a certain look of disquiet and pain shadowed the eyes which were gazing happily and dreamingly at the flashing fire-rays.

"Ah! I dare say not," said the Countess with a little yawn of ennui. "It was a romantic, terrible story, I imagine; it was so long before my time that I never heard any particulars, but very likely it may be the reason of his utter indifference to women. I cannot possibly picture Lord Cecil Strathmore loving anything but power, or heeding anything save himself!

But you will rebuke me if I say so, ma belle; and since he is so kind to you, I shall do my best to believe that there *is* a heart under that polished surface of courtly and ministerial ice."

Lucille did not seem scarcely to hear her; her eyes were fixed with their gaze of vague disquiet on the ruddy glisten of the fire-flames.

"Betrayed him—deserted him," she muttered, musingly. "Oh, surely no woman could——"

Lady Chessville looked up quickly and scanned her face, from which the warm colour had faded; and she passed her hand caressingly over Lucille's brow as she rose.

"Good night, my lovely child. Do not sit up and think over that bygone story I was silly enough to name to you; you may be very sure that Strathmore has never suffered, and (I would stake much) has never loved, even in his early years, except, indeed, perhaps, as people—*petri du monde* as he is—do love, which is very worthlessly. I will not have you waste so much of your thoughts and tenderness on your guardian, Lucille—that cold, negligent, ambitious man, whose only passion is power!"

Lucille drew slightly away from her hand, and a faint smile came on her lips.

"You only know Lord Cecil as the world knows him, Lady Chessville; he merits from me a thousand-fold more than all the gratitude and reverence I can give him."

The Countess looked at her again in silence for a moment, then stooped to give her a light kiss, and floated from the chamber. Lucille sat where she had left her, not changing her attitude, but, with her head bent forward and her hands lying lightly on her bosom, gazed into the hot and glowing embers of the burning wood, with a vague and unknown sadness oppressing her, she knew not why.

Strathmore had told her aright that one day suffices to destroy for ever the barrier which parts childhood from womanhood; and Lucille had that day lost much of the golden radiance of childhood, which is happy in its unconsciousness and content in its present. But what had dispelled it, was not so much the love which had been proffered to her, which, though it had startled her for the moment, had had so little hold on her thoughts, that it had been shaken off from them, leaving nothing of its significance, and having taught nothing of its knowledge; it was rather this shadowy love of a long dead past, of which she had heard to-night, which woke in her own heart an unfamiliar pain, and made her wistfully muse on its meaning and its story.

For the first time in all her innocent and guarded life she felt an intangible disquiet and uneasiness, and, rising, she went, as was her nightly custom, to Lady Castlemere's chamber before going to rest—her own apartments had been altered by Strathmore's order, and now adjoined his mother's in the west wing of the abbey. She was received with the affection which had encircled her only too tenderly from her infancy, and which the peeress in her aged years did truly feel to this bright and loving child, who had been given to her care by so dark a tragedy, orphaned by her son's own hand, and made desolate by his crime. Haughty still to most others, his mother was invariably gentle to Lucille; and her hand fondly stroked now the floating silken masses of loosened hair, as she lay at her feet in the warmth of the fire-glow resting her head against her knee; Lucille loved warmth and light like any tropic bird.

They were in strange contrast, the age and the youth—the grave and venerable patrician, bowed by the weight of many years, while something of the fire of her superb womanhood still gleamed from her proud sunken eyes; and the young girl in all the dawning glory of her unspent life, with the grace of childhood in every pliant limb, and the unworn brightness of childhood in the bloom of her cheek and the golden light of her hair.

"You are silent to-night, Lucille?" she said, gently, at last, when some minutes had passed by. "Where are your thoughts?"

The colour stole into her face, and she did not lift her head from where it rested.

"I was thinking—I was thinking, Madame—of what Lady Chessville said just now."

"And what was that?"

"Madame," was the familiar title Lucille had given her when too young to pronounce her name, and Lady Castlemere had encouraged her to continue it, since it supported the foreign extraction from which all were led to attribute her birth.

"You can tell me, Madame, did—did Lord Cecil, many years ago, ever love any woman who betrayed him?"

The hand which lay on her waving tresses moved with an involuntary start. Had any been hinting to Lucille the outline of that tragedy so long, so scrupulously, so anxiously concealed from her!—had any been unfolding the first pages of that dark history, which, opened to her, would reveal to her that the hand which she loved, and which cherished her, was the hand which had slain her father, as the pitiful among men would not have slain a brute!

But with the blood of the Strathmores in her veins, his mother had the inscrutable serenity under trial of her Norman race; and she looked down into the girl's wistful eyes with calm surprise.

"Why do you ask, Lucille? It is a strange question."

"But tell me, is it true? Did he ever love any one who was faithless to him?"

Her voice was very earnest, even to tremulousness, and in her upraised eyes there was a plaintive anxiety; and her listener saw that entire denial would rather increase than lessen the little Lucille could as yet know of the truth.

"Long ago, my love, Strathmore loved unwisely and unhappily. But it is a matter so entirely of the past, that it is folly to recall it; and you must never allude to it to your guardian. What was it, Lady Chessville could tell you; she was a mere child in his early manhood."

"She told me very little. She said she knew nothing; but

she had heard of the story, and she thought it was the reason why he was now so cold. Why should she call him cold; he is not?"

"Not cold in your sense, my dear, but in hers. He feels deeply—here and there—as he feels for you, and for the memory of your father; but Lady Chessville means that he has long ago left to younger men the follies of love, and is entirely given to political life. In her sense she is right."

Lucille's head drooped again; and as the firelight flickered on her face, it wore its unwonted look of new disquiet, of brooding and unanalysed pain.

"Oh! how could any woman betray him?" she said, half aloud, with an accent in her voice it had never borne before. "How could any one forsake him and make him suffer—throw away such a treasure as his love?"

Lady Castlemere caught the intonation of the words, and stooped to look upon her face; a thought crossed her which filled her with a ghastly and horrible terror. Better, better, she felt, that Lucille should learn the truth of that fatal history, shrouded from her birth—learn it in all its hideous nakedness, its merciless and deliberate crime, and learn to shrink from the hand she loved and honoured, as the hand stained with her father's blood, than that the fear which crossed his mother's thoughts as she looked on her should ever ripen into truth!

"Lucille!" she said, almost hurriedly, "do not let your thoughts wander into buried years of which you can tell nothing, and which can be nothing to you, my child. It is sorrow wasted, to grieve for so long dead a thing as your guardian's past. All men love, some wisely, some erringly, but love he himself has long abandoned and put aside; it had a charm for him in his earlier years, but it can never now be anything to him, not even a regret; therefore waste no regret for him. In the ambitious life of a statesman, such weaknesses are quickly forgotten; associate them with Lord Cecil no more than you would have thought to do with your father, whose place he fills."

Her words were purposely chosen; and Lucille listened silently, her head bent, her eyes gazing at the falling embers, the warm colour in her face wavering. The vague pain still weighed upon her, and each syllable fell chilly on her, like the touch of a cold blast; the last yet more than any.

"Lucille! look at me," said his mother, anxiously.

The terror which had floated through her mind strengthened with that silence, and the shadows which flickered over the face she watched. Lucille raised her head with a half-broken sigh, and her fair eyes looked upwards to her gaze, guiltless, fearless, trustful, even while their natural sadness was deepened: the fear which had seized on her watcher was slaked for the time; if it had grounds, as she prayed it might never have, she saw that Lucille, at the least, as yet knew nothing of her own secret. She bent and kissed her.

"Go to your bed now, my darling; it is late, and you are used to early hours at Silver-rest. And, Lucille, the question you have asked of me you will not ask of others?—it would displease your guardian."

A faint, proud smile, tender and mournful, came on Lucille's lips as she arose:

"Oh! Madame, you are sure his name is too sacred to *me* to talk of it idly with any! I would never have asked of Lord Cecil's past of any one save yourself."

And his mother knew, as the girl's good-night caress lingered on her brow, that Lucille spoke the truth; that unless any remorseless hand tore down the veil which hid the past, and forced upon her sight the secret which it shrouded, her lofty and delicate nature would never imperil its own peace by restless search or curious interrogation. Yet the new and different fear which had arisen in her that night for the first time could not be banished; and, as she sat in solitude, she shuddered at the memory with which a long and varied life supplied her—the memory of how often, baffling men's justice and men's expiation, the harvest of the past, sown by the guilty, is reaped by the guiltless, and the curse of sin lies in wait to prey on the innocent.

In her own chamber, Lucille did not at once obey the words which had bade her seek rest. She dismissed her attendant earlier than usual, and stood alone gazing into the embers of the hearth, while the little spaniel which had loved her father nestled to her bosom, and her eyes grew dark and humid in deep and dreaming thought. This causeless pain was on her still; she could not have told why.

A long-drawn breath, broken as a sigh, unconsciously parted her lips as she turned at last from watching the woodsparks fall in showers on the crimson ashes, laid the little dog down upon his cushions, and, moving to the nearest window, drew the curtains aside, and looked out at the night. It was almost a habit with her: from infancy she had loved to watch the stars shining over the face of the ocean, which had been to her a living poem, a never-ending joy, a divine mystery, a beloved friend; here the distant sea was hidden by stretches of wood and hill, but its familiar murmurs reached her ear upon the stillness, and the stars were many in the cloudless skies. She stood looking out into the brilliant night, over the vast forests and the monastic ruins of White Ladies—those silent yet eloquent relics of a long-dead past—as the moonlight shone through shivered arch and ivy-covered aisle, on crumbling cloisters and decaying altar-stones, memorials of a religion and a race whose place now knew them no more. Below her windows ran the cedar-terrace, white and broad in the moonlight, with the roses growing over its balustrade, and covering its pavement; and the fantastic coils and branches of their foliage caught her eyes, and brought the memory of Strathmore's action, and of Strathmore's words:

"He called them 'the flowers of orgie, the flowers of secresy;' perhaps he associates them with *her*," she thought. "Oh! how can they say he never suffered!—how can they know! His love must have been so strong, and his suffering as great! Who could she be, that guilty woman, who could give him misery and betrayal——"

And the dangerous thoughts, which wandered dimly and

blindly towards a dark and unknown past, filled her heart with their pain and her eyes with their tears—tears rare and unfamiliar, which gathered there, but did not fall.

Then she turned away from the silvered light lying on the sward, and leaving in deeper shadow the masses of the woodland; it looked chill and mournful to her—and, kneeling down beside her bed, while the glow of the warm wood-fire gleamed on her loosened hair and on her young bowed head, Lucille prayed her nightly prayer to God, for him whom she knew only as her father's friend.

## CHAPTER XI.
### Under the Aisle of the Palms.

OF the many who at White Ladies flattered the beauty and sought to win the smile of Strathmore's ward, the only one to whom Lucille gave heed, was Valdor.

She was indifferent to all; they neither banished her childhood, nor taught her her power; and the graceful flatteries which might have done so, she heard half amused, half surprised, while they fell from her thoughts as the rain falls from rose-leaves, leaving no stain behind. To Valdor alone she showed favour; not because his pursuit of her was made with all the skill and fascination which lengthened experience in woman's favour had lent him, but because she found in him what she thought a sincere friendship towards Strathmore, which she found in no other. The young girl perceived, what she did not reason on, that Strathmore was rather followed and respected as one of the chiefs of a great party, than surrounded by men's warmer sympathies; and that, while he led and influenced them, he lived isolated from, because independent and negligent of, their personal cordiality. This *she* never traced to its due cause, which lay in his own neglect and contempt of the esteem and support which most men seek—his own cold and all-sufficing self-reliance, which withdrew him from the pale of human sympathies. *She* blamed for it a world which she thought did not read aright a character that, in her sight, was little less than god-like. And the single reason which made her listen to and like Valdor was, because he spoke to her as Strathmore's friend.

He did not wholly mistake the cause which gave him this preference; he knew women too well, and read this soilless and transparent heart at a glance; but the very sense, which he felt from the onset, that he who had been the courted of patrician coquettes might perchance fail here, lent his love but fresh charm and new excitement. He saw that the way to Lucille's confidence and regard was to speak of Strathmore to her as she held him; and this way he took with the subtle tact of the world. Strathmore himself watched his intercourse with her with vigilance, almost with apprehension, which at times foreshadowed to him what, in the face of the past, he refused to acknowledge—that circumstances may net in the power and outweigh the might of the finest foresight, the keenest strength; a creed he scornfully left to weaklier and humbler men. It was not without fear that he saw approach her one who had read the murderer's intent within him ere the shot had sped home and the life had fled.

But all knew that history, though the world had long since let it drop into oblivion, buried by that sure palliator of all error—success. Moreover, he relied upon two things; first, that none would ever whisper to her evil of one who stood in her sight and theirs as her legal guardian; and again, which was yet more sure, that the secret of her birth had been so carefully suppressed, its every slightest trace effaced, its every faintest link broken and buried, that nothing could ever suggest it to the wildest dreamer or the subtlest speculator. Careful provision and fortunate accident combined to make it impossible that the will of Erroll, which was to his destroyer more sacred than any law, could ever be disobeyed—the will which had written, "Never let her know that it was by your hand I fell."

"Lady Chessville tells me, mademoiselle, that your father was Strathmore's friend. Perhaps I knew him also," said Valdor, one day, as they rode homeward through the deer-forest with the river making music as it wound under the leaves, and foamed over granite boulders.

Lucille turned to him with glad surprise: "Do you think so?"

"I think most probably. I knew many, indeed most, of Strathmore's friends. I must ask him, for I would give much to recall in the past one who stood so nearly to *you*."

He spoke gently, for Valdor saw that her nature was one to be wooed by tenderness, but revolted by flattery; his eyes were eloquent, his voice meaning, but Lucille's gaze met his with the innocent look of a child, grateful for his interest in her father, but unconscious of his homage to herself.

"He was my guardian's dearest friend," she answered him. "You may believe how much so, when you see how, for my father's sake alone, he gives such care to me."

"Indeed! I can well believe it, for I know that he can feel very deeply, act very generously, though the world looks on him as cold and austere."

"Ah! but what can the world know of him? It sees him in office, it discerns his intellect, it listens to his eloquence, it admires his statecraft, but what can it know of his nature? Such men as he do not court the world, they lead it; they show the chill iron glove to the masses they rule, it is only the few to whom it is given to feel the warm, firm touch of the generous hand, which is mailed for the many."

The sun shone down through the leaves upon her face bright with reverent eloquence, while her eyes darkened, her colour deepened, her voice grew low and tender; she was very lovely in that sudden glow of proud rejoicing, mingled with the poetic veneration which she gave to one whose darker traits were all veiled from her, whose lawless passions she knew of no more than she knew of the evil and the bitterness of human life, from which he had guarded her.

Valdor for the first time forgot his tact and his resolve in the irritation of a jealous impatience.

"We who know him, mademoiselle," he answered, quickly, "are accustomed, on the contrary, to say that Strathmore has an iron hand under a silken glove. I have seen it grip very brutally, though (to be just to him) I have known it give very generously. Why feel so much gratitude to him as your guardian? It is an office most men would but too gladly discharge to such a ward; and—you do not know that he remains, now your early years are passed, so wholly and purely disinterested!"

"Disinterested!" She echoed his last word in wonder, in rebuke, in as much resentment as could be roused in a nature which had all the gentle softness of her father's; and, in truth, she did not even faintly understand him.

"Yes, you have yet to learn your own loveliness, your own power!" said Valdor, with impetuous bitterness; "and Strathmore, though he is an ascetic now, may not be dead to all the passions which once ruled him quite as utterly as ambition does at the present."

The moment his words were spoken he repented them; he knew how rash and ill-advised they were, by the effect they wrought. Her eyes gazed at him like the eyes of a startled bird, darkened and dilating; the colour burned in her face with a deep and painful flush; she breathed fast and unevenly. His words flashed on her as lightning flashes before the sight, bringing a vague, voiceless terror, and throwing its sudden gleam on depths and danger never feared or known before. With an unconscious, irresistible impulse, half born of the innocent shyness of childhood, half of newly-startled consciousness, Lucille shrank from his side, and rode after those who were in front, as swiftly and breathlessly as the fawn flees from the stag-hounds.

"Lucille! what has frightened you?" asked Strathmore, in surprise, as he glanced at her face where the warm light fell on it through the crimson and amber leaves of the autumn foliage.

"Nothing."

And in truth she could not have told what it was which filled her with a sudden breathless terror, nor what it was which mingled with that terror an unknown, nameless sweetness, which seemed to tremble through all her life. Valdor vainly strove to approach her; he was bitterly resentful with his own folly in having let such words escape him in the moment of jealousy, for he did not believe them himself. Mainly swayed by impulse and caprice, of a transparent and impetuous character, little altered at the core by its surface of indolence and indifferentism, he was consumed with angry self-remorse that he had allowed such words to escape him, treacherous to his host, and indelicate to her. He saw that they had startled, alarmed, shocked her with a force he had never foreseen; whether they had revolted her by the supposition of such a passion in one who filled to her her father's place, or whether they had awakened her to that which she had never dreamed before, was a doubt which unceasingly tortured him, crossed now and again by a hope that this half child-like, half woman-like terror might be born of some feeling for himself. The very action with which she had fled from him was not unlike the first dawn of love in such a nature as Lucille's, spiritual as Una's, poetic as Undine's, which seemed—

Too pure even for the purest human ties.

He was impatient till he made his peace with her; impatient till by look or word from her he could put his last faint and new-born hope to test. Brilliant, handsome, and still young, the French noble was pardonably sure of his fascination over women; here, for the first time, he misdoubted his power, perhaps because, for the first time, he genuinely and honourably—*loved*.

He saw a change in her when they met again a few hours later; slight, not to be defined, yet something which was unmistakable. The colour was deeper and more uncertain on her cheek, the lashes drooped over her eyes, which had lost the clearness and cloudlessness of their regard, and on her face there was a new look, half light, half shadow; the transparent waters of her thoughts had been stirred and troubled, never again to know their perfect peace.

Valdor knew its cause, and his pulses beat quicker as he thought that it might be himself for whom stirred that still half-conscious love. Strathmore saw it also; when he addressed or approached her, her eyes no longer met his own in glad smiles or pleading earnestness; he saw that something had been said or done to her to scare away the unthinking peace of childhood, as a single touch suffices to scare from its rest the brooding bird.

He turned to young Caryll as he passed him in the drawing-rooms in the evening:

"Have you broken your word?"

The youth started and looked bewildered; the angry colour flushed his face:

"No, Sir. I have the same blood in my veins that you have!"

The answer was spirited, and to its truth the young man's candid, unflinching glance bore witness. Strathmore bowed his head with that warm, frank smile now so rare upon his lips:

"True! The question wronged you, and I beg your pardon sincerely for having insulted you with it."

Lionel Caryll had disliked and feared him before, had dreaded his word, and shunned his presence; at the courtly amende rendered, because it was his due, as gracefully to a young dependent kinsman as it would have been to the highest among his peers, the youth saw for the first time all that was generous and best in his nature, and ceased to marvel that Lucille found much to venerate, and much which fascinated her, in a character which until now had seemed to him to possess many grand traits, but not one human sympathy.

"Mlle. Lucille, you shun us," whispered Valdor softly, late that night, as he was at last alone with her in one of the conservatories, whither, missing her from the circle, he had tracked, and found her; the light from above falling on her, about her broad-leaved palms, brilliant creepers, and eastern citron-trees, while the waters of the fountain by which she stood fell musically in the silence.

She started.

"I did not shun you. I only came to fetch my spaniel."

"The dog is very dear to you, is he not?"

"Yes! He was my father's; the only thing I have of his."

Valdor looked at her in her silence where she leaned against the marble basin: that fugitive likeness which perpetually evaded him wavered before him now, and, like some strong light which brings what is shadowy into palpable shape, the memory of one whom he had often seen in the very place where she now stood, arose before him, invoked by the groundless fancy with which he had associated her. In the remembrance of Erroll, he saw whose it was that her face recalled to him, and the wild dreaming folly of a thought he had contemned grew into a sudden vivid belief, rootless, unproved, untenable, but clear as the day in his sight. Was *this* Strathmore's secret?

"The spaniel is very happy to have such a claim to your affection," he said gently, and almost hesitatingly, for she arrested the words of flattery and love upon his lips. To whisper of passion to this beautiful child seemed impossible.

She did not answer—perhaps she did not hear him; but she bent her head till her lips touched the shining silky curls of the dog. As he saw the caress given to the animal, by the young lips which he longed to teach to tremble and grow warm under a lover's kiss, the new hope that he cherished stirred and strengthened in him. He bent tenderly towards her:

"Lucille, you so gentle to a dog, will be merciful to me! I deeply regret the words which I was so rude as to offend you with to-day; will you forgive them?"

She did not raise her head, but he saw the colour rise, deepen, and burn on her cheek, and her heart beat with quick, uncertain throbs; they gave him more than hope, almost certainty itself, and he stooped lower still, fearful of scaring this shy and dawning love from him by a too swift grasp.

"I would not for an empire breathe one word which should ever wound you, and I spoke in haste and error. You will forgive me, will you not?"

Resentment could not exist in her nature; she turned to him and held out her hand, with pardoning and winning grace:

"Oh, monsieur, yes! I forgive——"

As his lips touched her hand in gratitude more eloquent than speech could offer, the broad drooping leaves of the tropical foliage fringing the path through the conservatories moved; and Strathmore, who had that moment entered from the rooms beyond, stood looking on them. He saw the blush on Lucille's face, as it still lingered there—he saw the kiss which Valdor left upon her hand, and he knew then who had wrought that shadow of disquiet on her face, who had banished childhood and awakened love.

Valdor released her, and turned to Strathmore with the easy carelessness of a man of the world.

"My lord! I tell Mademoiselle Lucille that you and I have had so many friends in common, that I feel sure I must have known her father. Did I do so?"

"I told you once, no doubt you did."

"But not well enough to recall him? Dieu! that comes of leading a crowded life! Wait! I think I knew a De Vocqsal once, one of the Viennese Bureaucracy; was it he?"

"No! not the same race. I remember whom you mean, but he is a governor in Galicia at the present time. There are none of Lucille's family living."

He spoke so naturally that Valdor was for the moment deceived; there could be no mystery here, it must be a chimera of his own imagining—a bubble without substance!

At that moment the groom of the chambers approached him with a special despatch, marked "Immediate." And with an apology he quitted the conservatory, and left them.

Strathmore was alone with her, and the silence between them was for once unbroken, save by the falling of the fountains; and for the first time he saw that she stood embarrassed before him, that her eyes shunned his, and that she bent away from his gaze over the border of the marble basin. It smote him with a fierce and cruel pain. This was the first sign of the alienation which would ensue between them when her heart wandered to her lover—to her husband.

But, whatever he was to all others, with her he allowed no personal feelings to move him from that gentleness which he rendered her, for in his eyes she was sacred, and to secure her peace he would have sacrificed himself at any cost. He bent towards her, and his eyes, cold and unrevealing, the eyes "fathomless and darkly-wise" of the Legend, softened with an unspeakable sadness:

"Lucille! have you a secret from *me?*"

The reproach quivered to her heart, and her face grew pale, even to the lips. She started and trembled as she leant over the water, playing with the lilies on its surface, and the pain of alienation smote him deeper and more cruelly—he was answered.

He had not deemed it possible that this young life so late laid bare to him in its every thought, wish, and instinct, could learn so soon to harbour a concealment from him. But his voice did not lose its gentleness, nor his eyes their fondness, as he bent still downward to her:

"Lucille! will you not trust me with it? No one can already have taught you doubt of how entirely I am sure to sympathise with your every wish, and give you happiness, if human means can make it?"

She lifted her head quickly, and in her eyes were all their old love and reverence.

"Doubt *you?* Oh no! I could as soon doubt the goodness and the mercy of God———"

He passed his hand over her brow caressingly.

"Then tell me what has changed you since this morning? What is this new barrier, my child, which has arisen between us?"

The colour burned afresh in her cheeks, her eyes glanced at him shy, hauntingly, half ashamed, yet filled with a new light, then drooped beneath his own.

He stood silent beside her for a moment, mastering that bitter pain which gnawed within him: a stern word or a harsh thought he would not have given to her to purchase his own life. He waited till he could speak calmly and gently.

"Lucille, tell me—as your guardian I have a title to ask—did you refuse the Marquis of Bowdon's hand, because your own preference turned to some other?"

The flush deepened over her brow and bosom, and she twisted the lily-leaves unconsciously together, as she stooped over the fountain away from his gaze: again her silence answered him.

"Lucille, can you not trust me in so little? Tell me whom it is—that you love?"

He had no answer, save the flush which burned and wavered in her face, the tremble of the drooped eyelids, the quiver in the silent lips, as she bent down over the water—these were eloquent enough. Leaning over the fountain, she too saw her face reflected in the water, saw all that it told, and all the change which had come there, and with a sudden movement, almost of alarm, she turned and would have left him—his hand arrested her.

"Lucille, I will not force your confidence, but I must sue for it. I did not think that a few hours of a new and dearer fancy could have so soon estranged you from me."

His voice was gentle still, but the restrained pain and rebuke in his words vibrated through it; her swift desertion from him stung him painfully. Held by his hand, she stood motionless for a moment, her head drooped, her face flushed with its hot, betraying blush; then she broke from him, and throwing herself down beside the fountain, with her head bowed, she sobbed bitterly—tears half sweet, half bitter, born from what spring she barely knew, risen from the heart which was half unconscious, half fearful of all which was waking in it. Her tears were terrible to him!—they were the mockery of all the care and prescience with which he had sought to work out his atonement by the guardianship of this single existence from every touch of pain or misery! And mortal griefs seemed to have no part or share with Lucille's life.

These broken, voiceless sobs thrilled like fire through his soul, callous to pain, and dead to mercy with all others; he raised her fondly from where she knelt, and drew her to him till her bright head was bowed upon his breast.

"Lucille, my child, what has been done to you? Have any dared to grieve—to pain—to tamper with you?"

She turned her eyes on him one moment, beseeching and fearful through their tears:

"No, no! I do not know why—what——"

The words were barely above her breath, hurried and tremulous; her face was very pale now, her glance shunned his:—at that instant the leaves were swept aside by some entrance from the rooms beyond, and starting from him, Lucille fled through the screen of Oriental foliage, and left him ere he could arrest her.

Valdor had entered.

Strathmore stood silent by the fountain, under the fan-like leaves of the palms and banyans, his face as white and fathomless as the marble on which his hand leaned, and he did not greet the approach of his friend and guest by word or sign, as the other hurried to him with an open letter in his hand.

"Read that, Strathmore, and you will see, however rude it be, that I am compelled to leave your hospitality to-night."

Strathmore glanced at the paper silently, and returned it: he was intimate with all the hopes, plans, and intrigues of Valdor's party. He neither favoured nor condemned them, but it was a portion of his policy to be more thoroughly and early acquainted than any other with the movements of all foreign schisms or projects, and Valdor, passionate, transparent, and open as the day, with all the chivalry and indiscretion which have so fatally characterised all extreme Royalists of every age, confided in and to him without reserve.

"I much regret a summons which will deprive me of the pleasure of your society," he said, with cold courtesy. "But since you must leave us immediately, there is a subject on which I desire to speak with you at once."

Valdor looked up, his animated and eloquent eyes losing all their languor:

"You do not desire it more than I. No doubt you mean concerning my love for your young ward!—perhaps you imagine that I may have been without serious thought or intent——"

"I imagine nothing—I never imagine!" said Strathmore, impatiently. "I have the honour to await your explanation."

"Pardieu! it lies in one word—*love!*" answered the French noble, the indolence and indifference of custom breaking away before the warmth of his passion. "Strathmore, I know well enough you will command offers of marriage for her far more brilliant than mine; many will offer her riches, affluence, station, all that I have lost in a thankless cause and for a lethargic prince; but rank better than mine there is not in Europe, and love truer and warmer she will never win than she has roused in me——"

"Had you not better pour out all this eloquence in her own ear? I fear I interrupted your tender scene a few moments ago?" interrupted Strathmore, in his soft and languid voice, the slight sneer falling like ice-water on the impassioned and eager tones of the chivalrous Legitimist.

Valdor pardoned the sneer for the permission it conveyed:

"Can I do so? Finding you alone I feared she might have retired for the night; it is so late. God only knows how bitter it is to me to leave her at all—above all without a farewell—but what can I do? My honour is involved."

Strathmore did not answer, but rang for the groom of the chambers:

"Order horses to be put to, horses to post twenty miles; but inquire first if Mlle. de Vocqsal be in the drawing-rooms."

The servant returned in a few minutes:

"Mlle. de Vocqsal has gone to her own apartments for the night, my lord."

Strathmore signed to him to retire:

"It is impossible you see," he said briefly, as they were left alone; and with these few words he crushed out, as a matter of not the slightest moment, the glad, vivid hope he had inspired, whose disappointment made Valdor's cheek pale as he turned away with a swift movement and paced the conservatory with fast, uneven steps. Suddenly he halted before Strathmore, who had not moved from his position, standing under the palm-trees, with his hand on the marble basin.

"I must trust myself to your mercy and intercession then. Will you be my ambassador with her?"

"Have you grounds for supposing she returns your love?"

Valdor hesitated a moment:

"Grounds? No. I dare not say that I have, though she has seemed at times to prefer me to others, and to-night——"

"What of to-night?" The question was sharp and imperious.

"To-night I could have sworn that her heart had wakened, and wakened for me; her blush, her shyness—tell me, you saw her the moment I had left her—do you believe that I deceive myself or not?"

"I believe that you do not. I believe that Lucille loves you."

The answer was cold, but it was rigid to truth. There was this that was grand in Strathmore's nature—he never *spared himself;* and those words had judged him justly which had drawn him "a dangerous man always, but a false man or a mean man—never."

Valdor's face lightened with a frank, glad, passionate joy:

"Thank God! And when I return you will give her to me?"

"I will never oppose what concerns her happiness."

"And I may ask you to be my intercessor now?" went on Valdor, swiftly, in the quick eagerness of a nature which knew hot joy and scorned a timorous hesitance as cowardice, as he stood before Strathmore in the midnight silence under the aisle of the palms. "I am compelled to leave her in what will seem to her a manner so cold and strange, that it may well look incompatible with any love worthy the name: may I trust to you to make it clear to her why I go, and why I could not wait even for the assurance and the farewell tomorrow could have given? Will you leave no doubt, no cloud, no mystery, on my departure which might wound her or chill her towards me, as one who has not loved her as she has a right to be beloved? Will you feel for me in the absence, to which every law of honour binds me, in the moment of all others when honour is most hard to follow?—will you remember that I am driven from her in the very hour when I have learnt to love as I never learnt before? and while I am far away, defenceless and powerless against all those who will strive to rob me, will you guard for me what you yourself believe that I have won?"

Strathmore listened, the lids drooped over his eyes, his face impassive as the marble against which he leaned, whilst Valdor, forgetting all that he knew, and all that rumour said of the heartlessness and callousness of the man to whom he pleaded, poured out his rapid words, while his voice grew mellow and his eyes dimmed with the earnestness of what he felt.

"Will you, Strathmore?" he repeated again. "I do not ask it for my own sake alone, but—if she *should* love me— one doubt is a woman's curse, and that soft, delicate, lofty nature will never love but once."

Strathmore stood silent, still, his face in shadow under the drooped palm-leaves, his eyes looking down into the water where the lotus-lilies she had toyed with floated lazily; none could have told what might be passing in him; his thought was deep, but none could have said it was painful. After some moments, he lifted his head, and his voice was clear and serene:

"Before giving you my promise, you must give me yours to one thing—your love for Lucille is genuine?"

"It is, so help me God!"

"Sufficiently so to concede what I should exact in the event of your becoming her husband (I speak to you now, of course, not as your friend, but as one who fills her father's office), namely, that you would relinquish and give me your word never to rejoin political risks and intrigues? I could not consent to place her peace in the hands of one who would unavoidably jeopardy it by hazarding his own safety—for a Patriot is but a Conspirator if he fail. You would do this?"

Valdor hesitated a moment; his political creed was portion of his very blood and life, and the ardent Henry Cinquiste revolted from condemning himself to the inaction from which he could not rouse his party; but the stronger ardour of a new-born passion prevailed at last; he bent his head:

"I would, I swear to you. And now, Strathmore, may I seek your word, that you will guard my hope from being destroyed during my absence, and will say to her of my love all I would myself have said to-night!"

"Yes, I will do so."

His voice was tranquil and passionless; it had no inflexion

of reluctance, but equally none of willingness or friendship; it was simply the assent of a man who undertakes a duty, but it also bore with it the unmistakable assurance of an honour which will unfailingly execute its word once pledged. And that assurance Valdor recognised; he stretched out his hand, a grateful light gleaming in his eyes, with unwonted emotion:

"Thank you from my soul! You have relieved me of all fear, for I know, Strathmore, that though those who trust to your mercy may be in danger, those who trust to your honour are safe. In a brief while I shall return to claim Lucille at your hands."

He spoke in the thoughtless candour, the transparent warmth, of his own heart; the shadow which fell across his listener's face from the swaying palm-trees above hid from him the light which, for a second, leapt to Strathmore's eyes, like the sudden flash of steel in the gloom. But Strathmore gave him his hand, and bade him good speed—and without falsity. He would be no traitor; he would keep true faith with this man, since it was this man whom Lucille loved.

As Valdor left the conservatories, he saw a spray of lilies of the valley fallen from Lucille's dress, natural flowers preserved by some peculiar art; he recognised them, and, stooping, took them up; for this new love of the French noble had something of the knightly reverence of old. He put the flowers in his breast, and went out into the night; his heart was heavy with the pain of enforced absence, but it was warm with hope and with the firm belief of love returned, belief he would never have so cherished but for the testimony of Strathmore—a testimony he felt instinctively was sincere because unwilling; and he thought of her tenderly, longingly, trustfully, while he looked back at the grey, stately, melancholy pile of White Ladies.

He whom he had quitted, pledged to fulfil the office trusted to his honour, stood for awhile motionless beside the lotus-fountain, his hand clenched hard on its marble rim.

An evil of which he had never dreamed uncurled about him up from the poisoned ashes of dead years; a contest which he had never foreseen nor feared was before him through which to wrestle;—and he was no coward, no traitor. He could not shrink from that which lay before him, he could not sacrifice the life he had sworn at all cost to preserve joyous, and knowing not pain, only to secure to himself a selfish and barren desire—the brute desire of the man who, banned from a treasure, destroys it, rather than let it drift, blessing and blessed, into the lives of others.

For awhile he stood motionless there, with his hand pressed on the marble where the young girl's brow had lain; then, with swift uneven steps at first, later on with a harder, firmer tread, as though treading down the accursed shapes which rose about him to torture and to tempt, he walked to and fro the pathway bordered and shaded with the palms. This man—whom his associates deemed callous to all pain, as the bronze to which they likened him, and who in his arrogance had held that life was a thing to be moulded at will, defiant of deity or man, of death or circumstance—suffered a fearful doom, such an one as purer souls or gentler natures never know.

Once, as he paced there in the midnight solitude, he looked up at the drooping and curled leaves of the palms above, and a bitter smile came on his lips.

"The emblems that fools choose of Peace, they are fitting in MY house! Peace! peace!—there is none! Oh, God, is there peace in the grave?—or does science, that knows we rot, lie as well as nescience that babbles of our resurrection? Is there peace there—dull, dreamless peace—or in death must we even *remember!*"

And in the heart-sick mockery there was a misery greater than lies in grief.

## CHAPTER XII.

#### Can Oblivion be Bought?

STRATHMORE had an accepted duty to perform, and from what he had once set before himself he never shrank nor paused. With as little mercy as he drove the steel into the souls of others, he drove it into his own when occasion arose; self-love and self-reliance were dominant in him, but self-pity he disdained, as the weakness of the coward. It was for Lucille's sake that he had given the pledge extracted from him the night before; it was for Lucille's sake that he prepared to fulfil it rigidly and to the uttermost letter, not grudgingly, nor with constraint moreover, but with a complete and unfaltering justice to the man who had trusted him.

And on the morrow he was braced to his ordeal. He was victorious, and ready to carry through what he had appointed to himself; what he had once elected to do he was strong to do, whether it were to inflict or to endure.

It was noon, and the windows of his private library stood open to a shady and secluded part of the gardens, with the Western sea beyond the deer forests.

He sat alone, writing the history entrusted to him; delicacy to her, not distrust to himself, prompting him to relate it thus, for Strathmore, "weaker in many things, stronger in a few," having once selected that which he had to do, was of the stuff to thrust his arm into the flame unblenching, and hold it there till it had consumed without a sign of pain.

So he wrote—wrote the truth in every iota of what had passed between him and the man who loved her. A calm letter, leaving no doubt unjust to the absent, withholding no expression which could assure her she was beloved by him, speaking of him as he deserved, as one not faultless without doubt, but as a generous and chivalrous gentleman, finally leaving her free to be happy in his love if she would, with such kind and thoughtful words of personal tenderness for her own peace as became his position towards her—such as her father, had he lived, might have penned to her on the turning-point of her young life. The writing had the firm and delicate clearness of his habitual hand; the words were gentle to her, and just in the uttermost to the absent; the style was courtly, lucid, terse; there was not a trace that its composition had cost him anything, or that any feeling moved him save solicitude for her welfare and her future. Yet, when it was done, the dew stood upon his forehead as on the brow of a man who has passed through some great peril, and his head sank down till it rested on the writing-table—he felt as though the curse of his past were rising around him with its sensual murderous vapour, and stifling his life like poisonous fumes.

"It is just—it is just," he muttered, "that I should surrender her to the one who was with me when I slew him! Retribution—is there retribution? Only for cravens and fools! Do I grow a coward as well as a traitor?"

He flung the letter from him, and rose and went to the open casement, where the fresh west wind of the morning was blowing among the thick ivy which clung to the mullions. He wanted to shake from him what had newly assailed him. Strathmore was of the world, and one amongst its rulers; his deity was power, the essence of his life dominance, and that which weakened or undermined his strength he would have cut out by the roots and torn from him, no matter at what cost. Anguish might fasten on his solitary hours, remorse might seize the brief watches of the night, but it was unknown by men. As the Iron Cardinal wore the shirt of penance under the velvets and furs of his pontifical robes, and had the coarse pallet laid unseen under his sumptuous bed, so Strathmore kept his sin unforgotten, to torment him as it would, but never let it be seen of the world, or strike his ambition from his public life, and from his future hold. Like Ximenes he scourged himself, but he ruled others.

As he stood there he saw Lucille. She was feeding one of the pet fawns with rose-leaves, only a few yards from him; and in the fall of the lashes over the eyes, the smile upon the lips, the whole attitude with which her head drooped, and she held the leaves to the little animal, there was something of weariness and dejection. Possibly, he thought, she had heard of Valdor's departure, though as yet, thus early in the day, it had not become generally known among the numerous guests at White Ladies.

Turning, she saw him, and the rose-leaves fell from her hand; she came to him with the gladness and grace of her habitual greeting, fleet as the fawn which followed her, ringing its silver bells; but the flush, which he had seen for the first time by the lotus-fountain, came on her face, her steps lingered more slowly as she drew nearer to him, and she did not lift her face for the caress which she was used to receive as a child receives her father's. The new love had already stolen her from him; the shadow of estrangement had already fallen between them.

"Have you anything you wish to say to me, Lucille?" he asked, gently, as he advanced to meet her with the graceful courtesy habitual to him to all women, but which to her alone was not unreal. He asked the question with some anxiety, some hope; he would fain have kept, at least, her free and fearless confidence, it was difficult to him to believe that she had so soon learned to treasure thoughts too dear for him to share.

She lifted her eyes with something of wonder mingled with their shyness.

"No—nothing."

He dropped her hand, and was silent a moment, while she stood beside him stroking the lifted head of the fawn.

"Do not think that I wish to force your confidence, my dear," he went on, gently still, "but I should be glad of a few minutes alone with you. Will you come into the library now?"

He held open the glass door for her to pass through; but she shrank back, something of the startled fear with which she had fled from him the night just passed came on her face again.

"You wish me?—now?"

The reluctance stung him to the soul.

"Certainly not, if you be unwilling. It is no matter."

Strathmore re-entered the library saying no more; he let no living creature disobey him, but to her he would not use coercion, not even command, and he left her, lest she—who knew not the blow she dealt—should wring from him one stern or bitter word. From such she was as sacred to him as are the dead to the living: he would no more have raised his voice harshly to her than we would raise our hand to strike some hallowed and beloved face that lies within its coffin.

As he took up his letter, and sealed and addressed it, standing with his back to the windows, he did not hear her follow him, he did not see her at his side, till he felt her lips touch his hand, and started at the caress to meet her eyes raised wistful and pleading to his own.

"Lord Cecil, did I displease you? Are you angry with me?"

"I could not know anger to you, Lucille."

"But you looked coldly at me—your words are not like your own. Are you sure I have not vexed you?"

He stooped to her; and the clear, inflexible voice, which never softened for mercy, nor faltered for pain, nor altered in welcome or invective, in courtesy or in mockery, but was ever tranquil and icy alike to friend or foe, quivered slightly as he did so:

"Lucille, once for all believe me; you can only pain me if I see you pained; you will most truly obey me, most truly rejoice me, by showing me that your heart has not an ungratified wish, nor your life a single sorrow. There is a letter lying there I wish you to read: do not hasten to answer it, to-morrow will be ample time for that—to-morrow at this hour."

His lips touched her cheek in his usual farewell, and he quitted the library.

She sank into his chair, and her head drooped, as the sunlight, slanting in through the ivy leaves, fell on her brow, while her lips were slightly parted in dreaming thought; not wholly the childlike thought, poetic but unshadowed, with which she had gazed over the seas at Silver-rest, more restless, more vague, more troubled at itself.

"How good he is!—so great, so powerful, so famous, yet so untiring for me," she whispered, below her breath. "Pain him? Oh, how could any ever pain him, or disobey his lightest word? That guilty woman, who forsook him in the past, how could she ever betray such a heart as his? Perhaps her memory is bitter to him still; perhaps he has never loved another as he loved her!"

And the burden of those long-buried years, of that veiled past, she did not know, already cast its first faint shadow over Lucille, where she sat with her head bowed, and her eyes unconsciously tracing the path across the skies, of an autumn flight of swallows, winging their way to cross the golden land where her father's grave was laid, and the pine-covered mountains of her mother's Hungarian home, on towards Syrian air and Cashmere citron-groves.

Some moments had passed when she remembered the letter he had bade her read; she took it up without interest till she recognised his writing, then she opened it in eagerness, all that her guardian did or said was sacred to her. She would have disbelieved the witness of the universe if it had bid her see a stain upon the character whose very indifference to others only served to make her feel the more his constant gentleness to herself.

She opened his letter with eagerness; but as she read, the colour left her cheeks, a look of wondering pain came into her eyes, and at its close her face lost all its warmth and light; she pushed back the hair from her brow with a movement of startled disquiet, and her lips trembled. She sat silent, gazing down on the clear writing and dispassionate words; she was very young, and the love proffered to and pressed on her had little other effect upon her than that of wonder and something of repulsion, she had no need of it, no wish for it, and it had almost a terror for her. Phrases in this letter, moreover—those very phrases which most expressed solicitude for her welfare, and did most justice to Valdor's claims and story—smote her with a deeper pain. She felt for the solitary time in her bright, brief life, wounded, stricken, left alone.

"Is he weary of me, that it would give him pleasure to exile me to another life?"

It was this thought which made the mist gather between her eyes, and the wheeling flight of the swallows in the sun; this thought which brought over her face a look which it had never worn in her sunny life—a look of that pain from which Strathmore, for the sake of the dead, had set his will to guard her, as though he held the making and the marring, the warp and the woof, of that tangled web of Fate which is woven by hazard in the shadow of a dark uncertainty, and is not to be coloured or riven by the art or the strength of man.

"Lucille! what is it that has grieved you?"

She started, and looked up in the sunlight. Before her stood young Caryll, whom she had sent for rose-leaves for the fawn; the boy's face was troubled at the shadow upon hers, and his frank eyes shone with the love he was forbade to speak, and in which she, used to tenderness from her youngest years from all, and specially from him, never dreamt of danger. "All things loved her," as she had once said in her early infancy; and of another love than this affection which had always surrounded her, of the passion which her beauty awakened, or of the misery which it might cause, Lucille was utterly unconscious. Her life and her education had been such as to leave her, far longer than most, the guilelessness and purity of her childhood. It would be long ere the world could teach such a mind, grosser taint or darker knowledge; it would shake off the evil lessons as a bird's wing shakes the night dews.

"What has grieved you, Lucille?" the young man repeated, as he knelt before her.

"Nothing; at least—I do not know," she answered, slowly, while she pushed the hair from her temples with a certain heat and weariness.

"Something has," he persisted. "Perhaps my uncle ——"

Her face was flushed with light in an instant, and her eyes turned on him with rebuke:

"Nello! for shame—hush! When was Lord Cecil ever otherwise than generous and gentle and kind for *me?*"

The youth set his teeth hard; with the keen insight of jealous love, he feared none of his brilliant rivals who circled about her, free to whisper what they would, while his own lips were sealed to silence, as he feared this graceful and loyal devotion to the man whose years were double his, who stood in her father's place, and whose cold, world-worn, inflexible character looked to Lionel Caryll one which no feeling had ever touched, nor weakness ever smitten.

"Oh, Lucille, Lucille!" he said, with bitterness, for it was a cruel ordeal to chain down his words to go no further than his honour had pledged, "have a few weeks changed you so, that you have forgotten all the years from your infancy, and will not even share what grieves you with one whom you used at least to trust and love as a brother?"

She looked down on him surprised and regretful; the change was not that she gave less, but that he longed for more, and she wondered, self-reproachingly, how she had wounded him.

"Dear Nello, you *are* my brother, and I am not altered —not altered in one shadow! I could never change to those I love."

"And I am among them?"

His voice trembled, his heart beat loud; it was difficult not to pray with all his soul and strength for *one* love greater than all the rest, but it was much to keep his hold on the silver cord of her child-memories. Her hand strayed among the waves of his hair, while the eyes that were clear with the single-hearted loyalty of youth gazed up into her own, and the swift sunlit smile that was her heritage from her father lighted her face; it seemed to her so absurd that he could doubt she loved him, her playmate, her favourite, her brother!

"Nello! it is you who are changed! You never asked

those foolish, useless questions at Silver-rest! You know I love you dearly, very dearly. None will ever love you better than Lucille."

She spoke with the consoling, caressing affection of a loving child to one whom she fears, while she wonders how she may have wounded, and the young man's frank, tell-tale face gleamed with the light of hope and youth; the love of his years, if reverential and poetic, has much of the element of worship, and is quickly gladdened by a little, unlike the fierce, imperious, egotistic passion which, if it have not all, has nothing. He thanked her with joyous, tender words, which he found hard to rein in to the limits of his promise, and led her out into the sunlight.

"I see nothing of you, Lucille, here," he pleaded. "Give me this morning alone, as though we were at Silver-rest."

She hesitated a moment, listening; it was to the roll of carriages taking Strathmore and several of the men to a meeting twenty miles away, which, as Lord-Lieutenant of the county, he had promised to head. Then she went with Caryll where he liked, her guardian's letter lying on her heart, and lying—she knew not why—with a dull pain there.

The park was very beautiful in the autumn noon, with surge and beach, cloud and sunshine, golden woods and winding waters, all molten together in the amber light, and they wandered where chance led them. To her, to whom the brown chesnuts in her path, the sweep of a flight of deer, the glance of the ocean through an avenue of forest-trees were poems, all life, all nature were full of beauty; and he had no world but in her face, and knew no music but her voice.

They came at last to the small, grey, mediæval church of White Ladies, ancient as the Abbey, with dim storied windows, and Gothic walls all wreathed and darkened with ivy scarce less old. It stood shut in with foliage, and singularly still and peaceful, with the sheen of the sea gleaming below through its trees, and the lulling of the waves making solemn melancholy requiem over the buried dead.

"Hush! it is so beautiful!" she whispered to him, as if the

sound of his voice jarred on her in breaking the silence, while her face reflected the tender and holy memories of the place, as it reflected all such things but too deeply. "Listen! the sea itself murmurs softly and low, as though it were afraid to wake them. It is not death *here*, in the stillness, in the sunlight, under those shady leaves—it is only sleep!"

He was silent, gazing on her as her eyes filled with a reverent tenderness and a softened light, as they looked far and wistfully, beyond the beauty round her, into those sublime and mournful mysteries of life and death, in which the poetic spiritual mind had wandered away where his could not follow.

"I love the German name, God's Acre," she said, softly, after long silence. "It seems to say that while the world is only busy with the living, and so soon forgets its best when they are gone, He loves, and has garnered, the lost."

"Do not speak of those things, Lucille; death seems too brutal a thing to remember with *you*."

The youth felt, as all felt in her presence, something more tender than awe, more vague than fear, as looking upon a flower whose brilliance is too delicate and fragile to bloom long on earth, a sunshine too shadowless and too pure to be long lent of heaven. She smiled a little dreamily, and her hands wandered among the long waving grasses and coils of ivy, putting them tenderly aside from the nearest grave, whose single grey stone they had overgrown in their luxuriance; and, as she did so, she traced the moss-veiled letters of the inscription, which was but one word only—

### Lucille.

She gave a low, startled cry:

"Oh, Nello! look—it is my name."

Young Caryll bent over her, startled also more than so slight a coincidence warranted; it gave him an emotion of pain to see the name he loved graven on a tomb, and in the sequestered village churchyard, where none but the peasantry had been buried century after century, save where the lofty mausoleums of the great race of White Ladies rose, it seemed one strange and foreign to find there.

"Yours! Whose can it be? There is no date," he said, as he swept the grasses farther off the low headstone.

"No! Perhaps she died young, and they laid her here with only the name by which they had loved her;—and it told all to them, though nothing to us. Ah! death is cruel, desolate, sorrowful! The sun is warm, the sea is calm, the birds are singing, and *she* lies there—alone!"

Her voice was hushed, and her eyes were filled with a sad and tender light, as she wound the foliage reverently about the tomb, leaving clear the name that was her own, the name which touched her strangely, found on this unknown and lonely grave, which she knew not as the grave of her mother. Her temperament was vividly susceptible and deeply tinged with the reflective sadness which usually marks imaginative natures, and Lucille, to whom, personally, sorrow was but a name, felt for all things that suffered, for all who were lonely and in pain, with a divine and yearning pity. Life in her hands was a beautiful wonder-flower, just unclosing without a soil on its white virginal leaves, and the richest gold in its calix still hidden like the amber stamen of the half-opened lily. It seemed so cruel to her that there should be any for whom that beautiful flower was bruised and broken, and left colourless and crushed, and without fragrance, to be flung at the last into the darkened solitude of a closed grave!

And she sat silent, her hand still wandering over the foliage that covered the carved letters of her own name, while at her feet the wide blue sea lay shining in the light, and the honest, tender eyes of Lionel Caryll gazed upward to the face which he had loved from childhood. But her thoughts were not with him as she looked far away through the shady leaves of the church elms over the sunny waters: they were with the unknown life which lay buried and lonely beneath the moss, and with the words of the letter, which rested on her heart with a vague and heavy pain.

Strathmore returned late. He came and addressed a few courtly, gentle words to her, according to his custom, but he did not even with a look seek to learn the effect which Valdor's love had had upon her as he approached her.

"This day has been like an Indian summer! How have you spent it, my dear?"

He noted that her cheeks flushed and her eyes drooped at his presence.

"In the park with Nello. The air was so lovely! And ——Oh, Lord Cecil!"—her face was raised now, and her eyes full of wistful inquiry—"there is a grave here, in White Ladies, with my name, 'Lucille,' on the stone—only that! Whose was it? Do you know?"

"Your name? Had it any date?"

"No; nothing but the one word."

He smiled a little; and even his mother, who knew the history of that grave, could not see any look on his face save some slight amusement with the marvel of youth at the ordinary trifles it meets.

"Were you abroad, Lucille, you would see your name on many graves, though it is an uncommon one here. Several French refugees came to White Ladies, I know, in '89; possibly it belonged to one of them. The stone bore no date, you say? Now, your wandering fancy can dream a mournful story of exile and of severance, and weave an idyl from that single word!"

Those around them laughed; she smiled; the explanation she never doubted, yet the remembrance of that lonely grave lying beneath the waving grasses and the ivy coils, with its incessant requiem chanted by the melancholy seas, saddened her still; and Nello Caryll, as he listened, felt vaguely and causelessly, that in some way or other that nameless tomb under the shadow of the old monastic church was one of the links which bound Strathmore to the young girl, Lucille.

The day had been like an Indian summer, but its warmth and serenity had been treacherous. It had become very chilly as the evening drew near; the "wild white horses" of the sea dashed in, flinging high their snowy foam; dark, ominous clouds drifted before the wind as the sun went down; and the fisher-people farther down the coast looked up and saw the sure heralds of the coming storm, as the grey gulls and curlews flew with a shrill scream over the angry waters.

In the same hour while the tempest was rising to break over the ocean and the beach, the forests and the hills, of White Ladies, a steamer was ploughing its swift way across the Channel, running fast before the gale to reach the French coast ere the night and the storm were down; and Valdor leant against the side of the vessel with the little delicate lilies of the valley close against his heart. He was on a perilous mission; his name had become suspected, all but proscribed, by the existing government, a trifle made known of his present errand, and he might be "detained," or worse: and yet his thoughts were bright and trustful ones, for the chivalrous nature of the Legitimist Noble knew nothing of the craven hesitance of fear, and—he loved and he thought himself loved.

"A rough night coming on, but we shall be in port in half an hour," said a voice beside him.

Valdor started from his reverie with a courteous "*Plaît-il, monsieur;*" and as he raised his head saw a tall, bronzed, soldierly man, whose face seemed to him familiar. The recognition was mutual, though indefinite, on both sides.

"Pardon me, but we surely have met before, though I cannot recall your name," said the Englishman. "I am Colonel Marchmont, Queen's Bays——"

"Whom I think I had the honour of knowing very well in Paris years ago; is it not so?" said Valdor, as he gave his own name, and acknowledged the acquaintance. "Surely the last time I had the pleasure of seeing you we acted together in an affair of honour?"

"Ah! ages ago," said Marchmont. "To be sure, I remember now; a shocking affair, when that incarnate brute,

Strathmore, killed poor Erroll. I beg your pardon for calling him so; no doubt he is a friend of yours still."

"A very valued one."

"Then I offer you many apologies, but the words slipped out," said the soldier, puffing Havannah smoke from under his long grey moustaches. "I have killed off plenty of men myself in the field, but there was something I didn't like in that affair; it was cold and deadly; one saw he 'meant murder' by his eye. They'd lived like brothers, and he shot him like a dog, and felt as little remorse afterwards! I dare say Strathmore's forgot the whole matter, hasn't he?"

"I have never heard him allude to it, nor any one else, for many years."

"No doubt. The world soon forgets, especially what its great men like to have forgotten. He is a wonderfully successful statesman; his politics are not mine, but there is no denying his power."

"He is the most able man of your country; he was always 'plus fin que tous les autres' in diplomacy," answered Valdor, as his hand wandered in the breast of his coat, where the fragrant lilies were hidden; "but you wrong him if you imagine him brutal. Cold he is, and when he is aroused, perhaps dangerous, still he has generous, and, indeed, great qualities. But you were intimate friends with Erroll, perhaps?"

"Poor fellow, yes! We were in the same corps."

"Do you know if he had any relatives?" Valdor's hand was on the lily-sprays, and a vague instinct connected in his thoughts the memory of Lucille with the memory of the dead man.

"None, I think, except old Sir Arthur, and some cousin or other, who had the baronetcy."

"There was no one to mourn him, then?"

"Nobody, except—all who knew him! He left me a letter for Strathmore, and one for a woman in England, if I remember right; that was all."

"A woman! Who was she?"

His hand was on the flowers, and he felt a sudden, keen, breathless impatience, as though it were closing on the thread of the mystery which he had always felt encircled the life he loved, and connected her with him whom the world saw as her guardian.

"Haven't an idea," answered the Englishman. "Some lady-love or other, I suppose."

"Do you remember her name, monsieur?"

"No, it is so many years ago. I fancy it was something foreign; but I recollect he addressed his letter to her at White Ladies. I remember that, because it was Strathmore's place, and poor Bertie was often down there."

"Would you know the name if you heard it?"

"I might."

"Was it De Vocqsal?"

Marchmont thought a moment.

"Eh? I don't know. I think it was. Yes, I am almost sure. Why?"

"Only because I had a fancy of my own about a story of his past, and I was curious to know if I were right. How the wind is rising; but there are the Boulogne lights. Are you going to Paris?"

"Yes, but only en route for a little farther; to India, for the next ten years, perhaps, if those mountain robbers go on worrying us," answered the soldier, too careless and too indifferent to the matter to wonder why Valdor had any interest in the past history of his long dead friend. Soon afterwards he was called to the cabin, where his wife, but lately wedded, had taken refuge, and Valdor was left alone, leaning on the rail of the ship, while his eyes watched the phosphor light flashing on the crested waves, and his hand held the lilies of the valley as though holding the pledge of a fair future in those delicate, withered sprays.

His pulses beat quicker—he had learned Strathmore's secret! That which every forethought had environed, every care veiled, every prudence and expedient concealed beyond reach of sight; that which had been buried for ever in the graves of the dead, in a sepulchre whose seal no human hand was to break, lest the poisoned miasma should escape to touch with its taint the young and innocent, had come into his power. Dark, uncertain, shadowy as the past still was, he knew enough to know what was the link which fettered Strathmore to the fragile tenure of a dawning life, in so strange an union; what was the knotted cord of expiation worn beneath the chain armour, and the broidered velvet, of public ambition, and of worldly fame, by the man whom the world deemed remorse never smote. He had unearthed Strathmore's secret, and he forgot how pitiless to those who braved him, how unscrupulous where his passions were roused, or his will was opposed, how intolerant alike of those who stood in his path, or trenched on his power, was one whom nature had made inflexible, whom a woman had made cruel, and whom the world had made merciless. He only felt:

"*I* will never tell her; his remorse is sacred, his secret shall be safe with me."

And the French Noble thought with a generous pity, a noble faith, of the man whose atonement he had learnt, as in the shadow of the night he lifted the frail fragrant lilies of the valley to his lips, and kissed them reverently, like some hallowed relic, as he leaned over the dark angry waters while the vessel bore her way to France.

## CHAPTER XIII.

### "Morituri te Salutant!"

IT was near midnight; the fires were warm and the lights bright in the cedar drawing-room at White Ladies, flashing on the silver and azure panellings, the countless trifles of art and luxury, the clusters of exotics, and the delicate hues of the women's jewels and dresses. Some were playing chess or écarté, some softly flirting, some talking of sport and some of slander, while the clear contralto of Lady Chessville echoed from the music-room beyond, where she and her idolaters were singing the music of "Figaro," which they would perform on the morrow in the private theatre.

Within, it was brilliant, still, peaceful, with no sound higher than the murmur of voices attuned to one soft, languid key, which never varied in pain or in pleasure, in repartee, flattery, or spleen. Without, the winds were rising shrill and high among the old monastic woods, and the lightning was swirling about the fretted pinnacles of the Abbey, and in the lull of the music the hollow, angry roar of the seas, answering the challenge of the storm, pealed through the silence. It was a rough night on the coast.

"Bad night out," said the Earl of Fernneley, with a suppressed yawn, as a blaze of lightning flashed through the length of the drawing-rooms, outdazzling the wax-lights.

"Plenty of casualties," suggested Sir Philip D'Orvâl.

"All the better for wreckers, they thank Heaven for foul weather!" said a pretty woman, castling her adversary's queen, and nestling herself in her causeuse to await his next move.

"Wreckers! You touch our esprit de corps, Lady Adela. We are all Ministerialists here," said Johnnie Vaux, a whip and a wit.

A languid but general laugh gave him the answer that flattered him most, as a minute gun was fired, faintly heard in the pauses of the thunder, but not stopping the cards, the chess, or the flirtations.

"Many lives lost off your coast in the year, Strathmore?" asked the Prince de Völms.

"Scores, I believe," answered Strathmore, with negligent indifference, as he pursued his écarté with D'Orvâl.

"Pray don't talk about it, then; it is terrible!" cried a Spanish beauty, with a shiver of her fan, drawing her perfumed lace about her.

Strathmore laughed his slight, gentle laugh:

"*Je n'en vois pas la terreur, madame!* Men must die, it doesn't much matter *how*. If casualties, epidemics, and wars didn't take off our surplus population at intervals, we should soon be overrun. Nothing is more superfluous than those romantic laments for most convenient laws of nature! I mark the king, D'Orval."

Another signal of distress broke on the ear, muffled by the moaning winds, as he turned to pursue his game. With the proficiency of old, he brought the same skill and the same rules to cards as to the Cabinet, and won in both.

He had been perfectly sincere in what he had just said. His political economy taught him its truth. He had a profound indifference for mankind; loss of life did not concern him; with a cold, but correct, philosophy, he held that a thousand people killed by an accident, a battle, or an endemic, mattered no more in the aggregate, and was, therefore, as indifferent to men of sense, as the butchery of a thousand sheep in the shambles.

As he looked up to deal the last game he glanced across the room, and saw the gaze of Lucille fixed on him. Her eyes watched him under their long lashes with something of wonder, of reproach, of sorrow, mingled with their earnest and reverent tenderness; to *her* he never spoke such words, to her this side of his character was never shown, and at its pitilessness her heart which loved every living thing down to the lowliest flower, and grieved for the broken wing of a bird, felt a shuddering incredulity and pain: death would have been sweeter, and more mercy to her, than to have found an error or a stain in him. And that gaze, as he met it, was so like that which had dwelt on him in compassionate pardon, in mute reproach, while the sun sank down upon his wrath, that the life his hand had taken smote his conscience with the sudden memory of irrevocable crime.

He played the game out — played, and won with unchanged science and skill, or he had not been Strathmore;— then, crossing the drawing-rooms, he approached her.

"You look sad, Lucille. Are you afraid of the storm?"

She sat a little apart, no one was near at the moment, and she lifted her eyes to his as his hand lay on her shoulder:

"Afraid? Oh no! I was thinking of the people out at sea,

and of their misery. You only said that in jest; you would save them, I know, if you could? It is so terrible to sit in light and gaiety and comfort while the ships are perishing?—it seems like guilt to be careless and rejoicing while others suffer, and death is close at hand? There is something so fearful in life taken!"

His hand dropped from her shoulder—the hand which had "taken life"—and, stricken by those words, he went out away from the light, the murmur, the music; out into the solitude of the dark and stormy night.

No rain was falling, and the night was still, save when the winds, sweeping up through the forests, shrieked and moaned upon the air, and the noise of the waves arose with a hollow roar, like desert beasts seeking their prey. The ringed lightning, whirling down the sky, lit up the black masses of woodland and the ruins of the cloisters where the graves of the dead Dominicans lay; and at intervals, above the tumult of the wind and sea, the signal of distress broke faintly, and then died away.

He stood on the terrace, looking seaward, his head uncovered, his eyes meeting the blaze that was laden with death or blindness, braving the fury of the storm as he had braved the curse of God and Man. Its wild work rioted unnoticed, unfelt, around him; one of those dark hours was upon him of which the world never knew, when the pride of an arrogant and egotistic philosophy was rent asunder, and the throes of an undying remorse possessed the soul which knew itself but the more deeply damned because the loftiness of intellect by which it was companioned left it no plea of the dullard's brute ignorance, or the murderer's coarse apathy, in its crime. He had wrought his guilt wittingly, deliberately, and, though trodden down from memory by an iron heel, and forgotten through long stretches of time in the pursuit of power, in these hours—rare, solitary, horrible as those hours in which the men of earlier ages, passion-riven, deemed themselves fiend-possessed—it rose from the coiled and slumbering past, and twisted round him as the serpents round the Laöcoon.

Rare, but the more terrible for their rarity, these hours came upon him. He lived again through the commission of his crime; he heard the sullen splashing of the pestilential waters; he saw on his right hand the luminous glory of the sun; he watched the last-drawn breath shiver through the dying limbs, while the white and quivering lips gasped their last words of pardon: "I forgive—I forgive!—he did not know——" Pardon even in the throes of death! And the love that he had borne him, the love of youth's rejoicing brotherhood, uprose before him in all its glad communion, and the very earth beneath, the very air about him, seemed to call for vengeance for that guiltless life hurled into a brutal grave!

Arrogant to the living, before the memory of his sin he bowed, prostrate, stricken, accursed in his own sight. For his work was *irrevocable:* and in its despair, its fruitless yearning, its hopeless impotence, remorse looked mockery, expiation blasphemy.

What is done, is done for all eternity.

He stood looking seaward, while the thunder echoed from hill to hill, and the roar of the deep rose hoarse and sullen to its call, and as the wild winds lashed and moaned about him, his eyes looked up, and met the lightning unquailing. The great lost soul of this man, which knew a supreme remorse, but was never smitten with a craven's fear, found the echo of its own agony in the throes of earth and heaven, and from his lips broke a bitter cry, lost in the beating of the storm:

"Oh God! release me from my guilt!"

In the silence, as the tempest lulled and the winds sank to rise again in deadlier wrath, there echoed from the ocean raging below, the piteous signal, and the prayer for human aid, of men in their last extremity, perishing nigh at hand. He heard it, standing there, looking down into the darkness with his face towards the sea; and as from the night around him there arose that faint and weary moan of mortal misery, his conscience whispered, "Let the hand which took life save it. So may its sin be redeemed!"

Then as men obey an imperative command, he bowed his head and went through the tumult of the storm down towards the sea.

In the dark-arched portal of the door leading from the western wing, gazing at him with the loyalty of her innocent love, while the wind drowned and wafted from her ear the cry to God of her father's destroyer, stood Lucille. Unseen and inspired by that instinct which lends courage to the weak and strength to the frail, she had followed him through passage and corridor to the silent and deserted western wing of the Abbey. The bright and delicate figure was strangely framed in the grey stone of the pointed archway; her eyes looked wistfully out into the weird darkness of the night; her hair gleamed golden in the flame which played about it; fragile, imaginative, impressible, fearful in much, the storm had no terror for her, its grandeur had been the music which had filled her heart with its own solemnity in earliest childhood, and to which she had loved to listen as to the sublime rhythm of a Miltonic poem. Moreover into danger or death she would have followed Strathmore without pause or fear.

When he bowed his head and went down towards the sea through the winds and the gloom, she left the archway of the door, and silently and softly pursued his steps over the mossy ground, strewn with rent boughs, and fallen fir-cones, along the steep and winding path which led to the beach. The gusts loosened her hair and tossed it floating on the air, the thunder of the skies and waters echoed from hill to hill, the lightnings made their mad war about her feet. Still she went on—she whom the storm could destroy as it destroyed the fairy-bells of the forest lily—went on without fear, for she followed him.

A wild night!

A night to drown death shrieks like the cry of a curlew, and play with men's lives as with wisps of straw. A night with the black seas yawning in fathomless graves, and the hissing of the surge, filling every moment that the thunder lulled. No rain fell; the air was hot and arid; the dense clouds looked to stoop and touch the wave where it rose, a mighty wall of water, mountain high. A darkness impenetrable brooded over land and sea, when the lightning ceased for some brief second, and when it blazed afresh the heavens were filled with its flame that lit up the white stretch of beach, the Titan rocks that glittered, steel-like, in its light, the vast Druidic forests of the Abbey stretching westward, and the boiling, seething, roaring abyss, where the sea devoured its dead in the horror of night, to smile calm and sunny in the morning dawn, when its work would be done, and its prey rot below, with the sand in their eyes and the salt weeds in their hair, and the nameless things of the deep creeping over their limbs—over the childish brow that had been flushed warm with sleep a few hours before, over the long floating tresses that had been played with by a mother's hand, over the lips which had been sought in the bridal softness of a good-night caress. For the sea is fellow-reaper with death, and, like his comrade, will not spare, for youth, or love, or pity, for childhood's cry, or mother's prayer, or gallant strength of manhood.

It was a wild night. The wind rose in sudden blasts swift and fierce as a simoon, sweeping down from the wooded heights of the ancient monastery over the darkness of the sea, and driving against each other the great masses of the clouds like armies hurled together. The deafening roar of waters met the thunder of the skies as they rolled back peal on peal; and in the occasional glare the ship was seen, black and spectral, with sails rent away, and masts broken like willow boughs; flung from side to side as a lame bird is flung in cruel sport, now lifted on the crest of giant waves, now sunk from sight in the chasm of the closing waters, reeling, rocking, driven at the mercy of the winds, alone in the trackless waste. The minute-gun was silenced now, or drowned in the tumult of the storm; but ever and anon from the tempest-tossed vessel there rose the shrill, piercing wail of perishing souls, the cry in which Strathmore had heard a voice as the voice of God, bidding him who had destroyed life save it.

The beach stretching beneath the wooded cliffs of White Ladies was almost deserted. There was no fishing village near for several miles along the coast, and there were no fisher-folk, no coast-guard men, no boats, save the pleasure-boats kept for the Abbey, pretty toys, shaped like Turkish caïques, that would have been beaten to pieces in the storm like painted butterflies. A few men had gathered on the shore—gamekeepers, lodgekeepers, woodsmen, labourers, cotters—looking helplessly on, full willing to succour those in peril, but incapable of lending any aid; they had a great coil of stout rope with them, but they gazed vacantly and sadly at it; they had no means to use it for any chance of rescue unless the storm lulled, and some dared swim out to sea. They fell back, and uncovered their heads as Strathmore's step was heard on the surf-splashed sand, and the lightning shone upon his face; he did not seem to see them, but stood looking outward to the ocean where the ship was reeling through the trough of the waves. In the uproar of the night, in the fury of the storm, in the violence of the winds that swept the sea apart in yawning gulfs, and piled it high in beetling barriers of foam, and flung it over the quivering vessel as though it were some living thing they strove to stifle and entomb, help from the hand of man seemed hopeless; nothing but a life-boat could have lived through such a sea.

He stood looking in silence outward, his head uncovered to the winds, his eyes meeting the electric glare unflinching, behind him the granite pine-crowned slope of the cliff, at his side the group of men, silent, too, and watching him with something of wonder, for they had never seen their lord take heed of the waste or cost of life upon the coast; with much of anxiety and hope, as the light flashed flickeringly about them, for they knew how bold a swimmer he was, and had heard through what storms he had brought his yacht in distant tropic seas in years gone by. Unseen by him, for she knew he would forbid her braving the risks of the night if he saw that she had followed him—stood Lucille. Her arms were close wound about a tall pine to lend her resistance against the gusts that swirled through the forests, and bent the old witch-elms like silver larches; her long hair was unloosed, and filled with sear brown leaves blown in it by the wind; her eyes were gazing on him through the blinding flashes, her face white to the lips, but in awe with which fear for herself had no share, awe that was filled with the pity, the terror, the sublimity, the grandeur of the storm. The ocean, in her imaginative creed, was the mighty servant of God, moved by his voice and ruled by his will; eternal power spoke to her in the rushing of the storm, as eternal mercy smiled on her in the sunlight of the seas. She had no fear; and she stood with her arms wound about the knotted pine, and her hair floating backward from her brow, as in the pictures of old masters the young angel stands, serene and filled with an infinite compassion and love, while the earth is tempest-rocked beneath his feet.

On the beach Strathmore looked outward over the boiling waters, and alone far out to sea the lost ship laboured.

The heavens were riven by a sheet of flame, the vessel was distinct against the glare, so nigh, that from the shore the crowd swarming on the deck and clinging to the ropes were seen in the spectral light. Then one huge wave dashed over her and laid her down on her leeward side; there was a crash, a crushing splitting noise, that echoed to the land; darkness fell over the face of the waters; the moaning wail of perishing lives pierced above the tempest roar—the ship had struck.

When the blaze shone out again, the wreck lay with its hull out of water, stranded on a sunken rock, a black and shapeless mass, a bow-shot only from the shore; more than a third of its freight of human life had been swept off by the sea that had engulfed it, and the remnant left clung to the shattered timbers, their faces turned towards land, their shrill shrieks ringing through the night. Strathmore's eyes glanced over the short stretch of the channel which lay betwixt the shipwreck and the beach, and measured it unerringly—as unerringly he gauged the danger, almost the impossibility, of any swimmer living through those seas. Nevertheless he turned to the men beside him:

"Fetch me a coil of rope."

"I've got rope here, my lord," said his head-keeper, as they hauled the great coil nearer.

"We can't do not nothing, your lordship," said another man, one of his tenant farmers. "God knows I'd risk a bit to save those poor drowning wretches; but even a boat, if we had one, my lord, wouldn't live through that ere storm."

"Most likely not," answered Strathmore, indifferently, stooping to try the strength of the cable with his hands, while the men grouped about him with white scared faces and eager wistful eyes, that strained now towards the wreck where it lay in the heaving waters, now towards his movements, with the dull mechanical anxiety and marvel with which those, whom peril and emergency stupefy, look on at him whom they only nerve and arm. He was flinging off his evening dress, lashing a lantern to his shoulders, and knotting tight about his waist one end of the rope. He knew that hazard ran a thousand to one that the boldest and surest swimmer could ever breast the mad fury of the seething waves and return alive; death waited for him in a hundred forms. He had no pity, no yearning for those dying in the darkness of the night; and his philosophic creed had held in its calm logic that death, as the universal law, reaps its sure average every year, and that the mode of its advent is of little import. Life was precious to him, for his power, his intellect, his ripened triumphs, his gathered honours, his influence over men and nations; it was as wide waste to risk his existence for that of a ship's crew—common sailors, wailing woman, useless children—as to risk a man's for that of a dog. It was not for them that he came to wrestle with the storm, to rescue them or perish; it was for the memory of the dead; it was for the wretched law of expiation, which he had set to himself with the iron sternness of Mosaic law; it was for the remorse which in its dark hours forced him to any travail, to any sacrifice, to any ordeal, which could wash the blood-stain from his hand. Thus he had done great things unknown to men, things of a noble charity, wrought on one inexorable principle of atonement, in silence and unseen of the world, even as in monastic days the soul strove to cleanse and justify itself by pitiless penance in cloister and in battle, among the plague-stricken and the infidel, in the death-ranks of the Crusade, and the reeking pestilence of the Lazar-wards.

He knotted the cord close about his waist, and glanced once more across the boiling seas; he was a skilled and daring swimmer, and held all danger in the sure measurement, yet the cool disdain, of a sagacious courage.

"For heaven's sake! my lord, you won't try those seas!" said the men, involuntarily crowding nearer, their deference to his rank, and their first awed wonder at his cool rapid movements, breaking down before the imminence of the peril that he was about to encounter, single-handed and unaided.

"Strathmore, for the love of God, what are you about!" shouted one of his guests, who, with Caryll and another, sprang down from the cliffs above, having left the drawing-rooms soon after him to visit the shore, not naming where they came lest they should alarm the women; the thickness of the pine-boughs and the wood parted their path from where Lucille stood, and they saw her no more than he did on the beach, as they plunged headlong through the blaze of the storm down the slippery precipitate path, strewn with broken branches and with loosened boulders.

"Nothing wonderful," he answered simply; "only what any of my yacht's crew would do in a second."

"But no man can live in those seas!"

"Oh, I don't know. I have swam the Bosphorus in rougher weather still."

Young Caryll laid his hand on his arm.

"Lord Cecil! let *me* go! I swim like a water-dog, and your life is too great to be flung away on a risk."

The youth's face was very pale, and his eyes shone with excitement; he was of a generous, impressible nature, and it touched him strangely to see one whom he had known but as a haughty ambitious and caustic man of the world, ready to face death for (as he deemed) the mere sake of those who suffered, ready to peril life to succour perishing strangers.

"My life is required of me; yours is not."

The brief, calm words bore no meaning to the boy's ear, save that they refused to yield up place to him, but his hand tightened still on Strathmore's, and his voice, hurried and low, was drowned to any other ear than his in the din of the storm.

"Let me go first at least, sir! *She* would never forgive me if I stood by to see you perish."

Strathmore started, and Nello could not tell whether the quiver which passed over his face was one of pain or was but the shiver of the flickering flash. He put him aside with a brief command:

"I forbid you to peril your life!—and while you talk the wreck is sinking."

Then, shaking himself free from the other men, he plunged without pause into the dark, seething breakers;—the wild, broken cry of a young voice rang out upon the night, as the waves closed over him, but in the crash of the tempest, and the tension of high-strung excitement, none heard, or none regarded it.

In the glare from the rent skies, those clinging to the wreck saw him fling himself down into the boiling chasm of the seas to save them, and gave him one ringing cheer that pierced above the thunder and drowned the dying, stifled shriek of those who were washed at that instant into the darkness yawning round. He knew that death was nigh; he knew that the keenest skill, the boldest daring, could do but little against that mad mass of loosened waters; he knew that in a second's space the chance was, as a million to one, that he would be flung back upon the rugged granite of the rocks, torn, mangled, bleeding, lifeless, or be beaten down under the weight of the waves, never to rise again. Yet he gave himself to the fury of the seas without hesitance, and let their surging billows yawn for him and close above his head, while over the wide waste of ocean the great darkness again fell, and those who gazed, awe-stricken and with tight-drawn breath, knew not whether the issue would be life or death. The lightning shone out afresh, and he rose, flung to and fro upon the heaving foam, grappling hard with death and danger, and refusing to be conquered: then, from the broken, shapeless wreck a great cheer rose again, and rang over the seas, sublime as a Te Deum, grand as the Io Triumphe of the victor's pæan;—it was the "Morituri te Salutant!" of the dying to him who died for them.

Thrice he was hurled backwards to the shore; thrice, bruised, buffeted, borne down by the weight of the waters heavily as by an iron mace, he swam out again, striking the waves with steady, unceasing strokes. The salt foam was in his teeth, and in his eyes, the seas threw him hither and thither, and flung him down into their depths. They cast him, now, outward to the waste of the ocean, now, backward towards the jagged beach rocks, where, once dashed upon the granite, he would lie a shapeless corpse; now high upon the crested billows in the lurid glistening light, while the great bulk heaved and rocked beneath him; now, down into the chasm of the yawning seas, while the breakers swept over his head, and in the darkness he heard the sullen roar sounding in his ear and beating in his brain, and felt the surging of the waves seeking whom they should devour.

Neither from wreck nor shore could his path be traced, —now and again when the lightning lit the skies they saw his arms stretched out upon the black expanse, where he wrestled with the winds that blew in his teeth and drove the waves upon him, and swayed him to and fro as the current sways a straw. Once through the shroud of darkness that covered the deep, on which the wail of the drowning lives

alone was heard, the light lashed to him shone out for one
fleet instant, to be lost in the impenetrable gloom. When it
sunk from sight they could not tell whether he yet lived
amidst the fury of the seas, or whether he were dashed upon
the sunken reefs to rise no more, until a rigid, sightless,
broken corpse should float upward in the dawn of the morrow's sun.

A great awe fell on those who watched and waited for the
issue of this contest of one human life with the tumult of
ocean and storm; their lips were white, their breath was held,
their brows were wet with dew. They feared, they trembled,
they suffered for him as he never did for himself; for in the
jaws of the grave Strathmore was calm, and with danger the
dauntless and defiant courage in his blood rose resolute. He
beat his path through the salt blinding water, recovering
again and again every yard from which the wind drove or the
sea dashed him back. None wrestling through the tumult of
the night, to reach what they loved best from the fast-sinking
wreck, would have fought a more enduring conflict with the
death which menaced him on every side, than he who, with
no human love, no human pity for one of those for whom he
gave himself, cast himself into the devouring seas, for sake
of a sterner and nobler duty, for sake of the atonement
which should save life by the same arm which had once taken
life, and wash out the stain of blood-guiltiness by the ransom
of lost souls.

The night was holy, the storm was sanctified to him.
With each time that he arose from the salt, fathomless abyss,
he was nearer to the expiation for which he laboured. With
every stroke by which he forced back the murderous waters,
he was victor over the remorse which in its dark hours made
him accursed in his own sight. With all the bruised, exhausted pain of that wild work, as the ocean flung him downward, and the winds hurled him against the rocks, and the
salt surf dashed in his aching eyes, he felt but as in ancient
days, those guilt-laden and athirst for freedom from the
memory and the burden of their guilt, felt the points of the

iron in their flesh, or the torturing baptism of fire, as an atonement welcome and hallowed, a purification before God.

For in these hours the dark, grand, wild barbaric nature latent in him broke out and ruled; and shattered down the creeds of the Statesman, the Courtier, and the World.

At last he neared the rock, beating his way through the uproar and the gloom, while above him the great waves were like the towering crest of an Alpine slope. For a moment the lightning died out, and in the thick darkness he lay, waiting till in its glare he should be able to reach the side of the stranded and shattered hull. The blaze flashed out afresh, illumining sea and sky, the measureless waste, and the dark woodlands of the shore; and—at the instant when the dying saw their deliverer, and in the stead of death hope came to them—the curled, reared waters rolled, and swept up with a hoarse roar, like a lion's when he is an hungered and baffled of his prey, and broke upon the wreck. When they again severed and left it free, the crowding lives had been swept with them, and garnered to the grave; a remnant alone was left: he was too late. The elements themselves mocked and denied him his expiation!

Where he looked upward to the shapeless, sinking mass, the cry of the drowning, devoured ere he could reach them, rang on his ear; and from his own lips a moan broke in the silence and solitude of the vast waste.

"My God! my hand is too accursed to *save!*"

As though in answer, from the riven clouds the soft radiance of the moon shone out for one brief space, bathing land and sea with its pale light after the lurid glare of the storm. A few were left upon the wreck—four or five women and children and youths; these, in their mortal misery, turned their eyes upon their saviour, and with that mute and terrible prayer besought his succour. No wild shouts greeted him as he swam to the wreck, and made his footing on its slippery woodwork; those who would so have welcomed him, had a second before been swept away to death; yet, as he reached the sinking ship, one, yards distant, wrestling for life in the trough of the sea, saw him, and gave him a single ringing cheer, the Moriturus te Saluto of the dying to the victor;— then the voice ceased which in the throes of death had been lifted to hail him who had come too late, and in the black whirling water the sailor sank, with that greeting on his lips to the stranger in whom courage found its comrade.

The moon was shrouded now in darkening clouds, that were driven swift as the hurricane across the skies; but the almost ceaseless play of the lightning made it clear as day. He saw the white faces of dead men rise up about him, and the dark floating hair of women's corpses was blown over his hands as he swam towards the reef, through the seas, which were strewn with the flotsam and jetsam of the shattered ship, and mounted with steady grasp the shelving, slippery mass, which was all that was left of the stately vessel that when the sun had gone down had been steering calmly before the wind, with white sails set, through a fair and balmy evening, over a laughing azure sea. When the few who were gathered together, trembling and praying, waiting for instant death, and scourged by the brutal stripes of the salt billows as they broke, saw him ascend and stand amidst them, giving his life for theirs, they fell upon their knees and lifted their blanched faces, and blessed him and prayed to him with tears of agony: their saviour looked to them not man, but deity.

And as they wept and clung about him, and worshipped him as their deliverer from death, he neither saw nor heard them; but in that moment when he stood upon the deck, with the tumult of the storm between him and the land which he might never reach again—between him and the life which was filled with wealth, and power, and honour, and the ripe fruitage of a great ambition—Strathmore remembered but one, the Dead who in the long-buried years had fallen by his hand: and from his lips a prayer broke, more bitter and more yearning than any which those who wept about his feet prayed for their deliverance from the grave:

"Oh God! Let *this* atone!"

He bade those trembling and quivering in the terror of the night be still and of good cheer, and with the aid of the youths—lads who had been passengers in the ship, and could not swim—he unwound the rope from about his waist, and fastened it tightly to a ring-bolt; the other end had been held by those on shore, and, made taut, it stretched a narrow bridge through the pathless waters, a frail yet precious aid through the great abyss that yawned between the drowning, and the land where lay deliverance and safety. It was a hideous passage—through the curved walls of the giant waves, through the black salt chasm filled with the hollow roar of voracious billows, through drenching, merciless blows of solid waters, with but that one vibrating cord as plank between them and their destruction!

Yet the love of life is a master-passion, and makes the feeble strong, the coward daring, the weakness of womanhood cope with the force of giants. It was their sole chance: one by one, in the glare from the heavens or by the flickering lantern-light, he directed them to descend, and pass along the rope where it stretched through the foam and the gloom. There were wild disorder, delirious panic, the fever of hope conflicting with the horror of despair, the abject anguish of helpless women. But the same tranquillity and resolve which bore down the opposing factions of states and ministries made their might rule here; he who is calm and resolute in peril is a king among his fellows. One by one he made them descend, holding back the reckless, encouraging the fearful, warning, guiding, commanding each, bidding each be of strong heart and of sure courage through the perilous and dire passage. Seven lives were launched by him on that frail bridge which he had perilled his own life to give them, where it hung vibrating above the boiling surf, and passing through the gorge of the waves. One alone was swept down into the abyss, and perished; six were rescued, and one by one he saw them reach the shore, and received by those waiting there, in the ruddy gleam of the beacon-fire hastily piled on the sands from the broken pine-boughs and the resinous firs. He had saved them. Six lives wrestled for with death, and brought from out the grave;—might not these expiate *one* taken?

Standing on the wreck, which he refused to leave while any were still unrescued, he looked across the sea as the wild shouts which welcomed those whom he had succoured, and saluted the grandeur of his act, rang loud through a pause in the uproar of the storm; and on his face a light shone which had never been there in the days of his youth, and in his eyes came a sublime serenity; the peace, the gratitude, the rest with God and man, of the soul which, after lengthened years of travail and remorse, is at the last released from the brand and burden of its crime, and purified by expiation.

The holiest hour of Strathmore's life was this in which he stood alone in the wide desert of the ocean.

## CHAPTER XIV.
### Lost in the Hour of Redemption.

TWO yet remained, young boys but little out of infancy, for whose delicate hands and fragile limbs the passage by the rope was hopeless. Their mother had been swept from them when at the first crash upon the reef the vessel had parted amidships, and half her human freight had perished: the children, by the wild caprice of the seas, had been spared, and sat locked in each other's arms, the elder comforting the younger, strangely stilled and in the awe of a voiceless terror. Strathmore looked down on them, then stooped and touched the elder, a little fellow of some seven years, whose fair locks were drenched in the brine and surge.

"Leave your brother and trust yourself to me. I can only save you one at a time."

The child gazed up at him with sad and dreaming eyes; the horror of the awful night had left him passive, his eyes were tearless, and his face very white. He loosened his arms from the little four-year-old, and motioned Strathmore to take him instead. They were French children, for the ship was a Havre vessel bound for America.

"Take Victor first, not me; my mother loved him best."

The plaintive heroic answer was drowned in the hurricane, but Strathmore heard it, and lifted up the younger, as the boy bade him.

"I will save you both. Have no fear. You are a brave child."

He took the other in the grasp of his left arm, who was all but unconscious from cold, from terror, and from the blows of the heavy billows, and plunged down once more into the waters. As he quitted the wreck, he saw one whom he had not noted—a woman lying prostrate, insensible, perhaps dead. It was too late to go back; when he returned for the boy he could rescue her if she lived; and he gave himself once more to the madness of the ocean, this time with the dead weight of the young child hanging wearily upon him.

From the shore they saw him leave the deck thus laden, then they lost sight of him in the deep trough of the heaving seas; in the darkness they knew not whether his life had been laid down in ransom for those whom he had saved, or whether he wrestled with the seas again to be again their victor. The blackness of night brooded over land and water, while the sullen roar of the thunder rolled through the air, and the equinoctial fury of the winds lashed the storm to its height—they knew not whether he lived or perished.

Then, where the gleam of the fire on the beach was cast red and lurid upon the breakers, as they rolled upward, crested with white hissing surf, they saw him rise, bearing the burden of another life.

Swift as thought, Lionel Caryll flung himself into the sea, and swam to meet him. Strathmore threw the young boy to him, and, without pause, turned and went backward to redeem the word he had given to the child left there by his own will to perish, that his brother might be saved. Once more back through that terrible travail of life with an impending death; once more through the passage of the trackless seas, through the darkness of the tumultuous night, through the massive waves, with the brine in his eyes and his teeth, with the bodies of the dead floating around him, with the winds hurling him hither and thither, and striking him blindly with great masses of curled water. Once more; —while now, his breath came in laboured gasps of pain, and every sinew throbbed with the unnatural strain, every muscle quivered, every bone ached;—while his throat was parched, his eyes starting, his temples aching; while he had to combat with a yet direr and more insidious foe than the ocean, in the exhaustion which was slowly gathering over all his limbs, and stealing out the life and power from his frame.

Yet strength of the will conquered weakness of the body; he reached the rock afresh, and the wistful eyes of the boy, gazing into the night, saw his deliverer return faithful to his word, though it was but pledged to a lonely child. Strathmore ascended the stranded wreck, and paused to rest, and gather force to reach the shore in this last passage, whose peril was more imminent than all. A brief breathing-space sufficed to give him back some strength; his muscles were of steel, his powers of endurance great, and his ascetic life had left his frame firm knit as in his earliest manhood. As he paused, and looked down to where in the darkness the waves were dashing the wood and iron of the devoured ship together, and whirling the dead bodies of the drowned men in wreathing phosphorescent light, he heard a sullen menace roll and groan through the shattered hull on which he rested —it was the sure and ominous sound which preceded the parting of the few broken timbers which still held together. They were no longer safe for a single second: one moment more and the sea would break away, destroying all life which should remain near the abyss which yawned for then. It was quite dark; the uncertain glimmer of the lantern he had left upon the deck was cast about his feet, but it shed no light on the wide waste around, where the cry of the waves was like the cry of desert lions, and the bodies of the dead were washed against the reef, lit only here and there by the weird phosphor-glitter on the surf. There was no time for pause, for thought; he stooped and touched the woman lying at his feet; she was unconscious from terror or from a swoon, but he laid his hand to her lips, and felt them warm; in her bosom, and her heart was beating. She lived; he could not leave her there to certain death.

He bade the child mount on his shoulders, and cling close so as to leave his arms free and his limbs unshackled; the boy, quiet and intelligent beyond his years, comprehended and obeyed him; then Strathmore raised the woman's form, and grasping her firmly in his left hand, felt his way with his right along the rope down the side of the wreck, which every moment might yawn, and crash, and disappear, and so committed himself yet again to the fury of the seas, thus heavily laden with the burden of two lives. The thick darkness was around him; he could see neither the waste that stretched before, nor the vaulted skies which brooded above him. He sank as he first swam out from the side of the ship; the great waves washed over him, and he held himself as lost, with the child's hands clinging round him, and the weight of the woman hanging on his arm. The waters closed over his head and over the boy's fair curls, and he felt the salt billows surging in his ears and stifling his breath: he heard the rushing of the surge, he knew that he was sinking to his grave. Better, he thought, for him to perish so—better to die thus in the supreme martyrdom of a grand labour, in the great ransom of a holy expiation. His death might absolve his life; he might then yield up his soul in peace with God and man; having sinned much, yet much atoned!

But death was not for him in that hour.

The long hair of the woman swept across his lips; he shuddered and sickened at its touch, he knew not why, as he had never done at the sharp agony on the jagged rocks, or the blinding blows of the massed water. By his involuntary movement his foot touched the projecting timber of the sunken wreck; instinctively he struck with all his force against the beam, so that the impetus given might send them upward to the surface; he rose, and they breathed again, floating in the impenetrable darkness on the face of the ocean. Life was yet his and theirs whom he had saved, and he lay on the waters, parting them with the strength of his single arm, while afar off through the dense gloom gleamed the leaping flames of the beacon fire. His hand grasped the woman's form, which he bore up against the force of the hurled billows, and her hair swept again against his lips, and her breath was on his cheek, while she faintly awoke to consciousness from her trance, as they moved through the icy air. Thus they passed together through the darkness of the night, through the tumult of the storm, through the valley of the shadow of death.

Thus they passed together amidst the devouring waters, with the innocent face of the young child nigh them, and the cold limbs of the lost dead washed against them.

As the last ransom of his soul from guilt, as the last travail in his ordeal of redemption, he was bidden to save this woman's life.

Above, in the brooding skies, the dense clouds driven by the hurricane were hurled on one another; the shock vibrated through the air, and pealed over earth and sea. There was a hideous light which lit in it land, and heaven, and ocean—and in its gleam he saw her face, the lips close to his own, the eyes filled with a fearful agony, the trailing length of the amber hair lying loose upon the waves.

And they knew one another, they whom guilt had bound together, while they looked down into each other's eyes, where they lay on the boiling, hissing, bitter waters with the livid light upon their faces, as, in the vision of the Poet, the doomed behold and recognise each other sinking in the liquid fires of the Lake Avernus.

She gazed on him with a dumb and terrible appeal, for his will alone upheld her from the yawning abyss, and back upon her ear through the midst of many years rang words once uttered to her in the hour of her extremity:

"If you were drowning before my eyes, and my hand stretched out could save you, you should perish in its need."

Beneath her, around her, leaping up to seize her as hounds leap on their prey, the waves surged and roared; between her and destruction there stood but the mercy of him to whom mercy was unknown; death was upon her unless he gave his life to save her—he whom she had made a murderer!

A worse temptation than any that ever had assailed his life, assailed him now, in the hour of his atonement: had he still strength to rise above it?

Afar off, on the hanging rock, under the monastic woodlands, with her arms wound about the great stem of the pine, her fair hair floating in the wind, her eyes gazing down into the raging seas, unblinded by the storm, and opened wide with straining, yearning pain, stood Lucille; and her young face, white and pure, and filled with a sublime light, was as the face of an angel, and on her lips was one voiceless unceasing prayer to God for him, in whom she saw but the deliverer from death, the saviour of the lost. Had he looked *there* he might still have conquered, still have endured; and saved himself from the fresh guilt which uprose and curled about him from out the slimy bitter waters like some loathsome shape from the depths of the sea. But the ringed lightning circled him, eddying round in its ghastly glare, a whirlpool of flame—fire burning on the icy gulf—and by its light he and the woman who had betrayed him gazed alone on one another as their faces rose above the seething mass.

They met again.

In his eyes there came the dark, merciless gleam of the passions which were not dead but sleeping, the ruthless thirst of the vengeance which no time could satiate, no draught could slake: she was his temptress still. The noble serenity, the thankful rest of one who has laboured for absolution, and won his way to meet atonement, passed from his face—perhaps for ever. Where the lurid flame gleamed on it as he rose above the foam, it grew white and rigid with deadly menace.

And his hand unloosed its hold, and left her alone upon the fathomless seas.

"Die—as you condemned him to die!"

The words hissed to her through the tumult of the storm, and her eyes gazed up to his with a mute, appealing terror, yet with a hatred bitter and brutal as his own, where she was left to perish, the water reaching to her livid lips, her brow turned upward in the scathing light. Then, in the circle of the azure flame that played upon the chaos, Marion Vavasour sank, downward, downward, till the loose trail of her floating hair was beaten beneath the billows.

A moment, and he knew what he had done. An agony of horror fell upon him, he plunged down again into the depths—again and yet again,—he swept the waters with his arm; he searched for her in vain search; he grasped the gliding waves, the salt and slippery foam:—that was all!

Darkness fell over the ocean, and darkness as of the night covered his own soul, which for one hour of travail and of martyrdom had soared upward to God's light, and had failed in the supreme instant of victory, in the crowning ordeal of temptation. She had been his temptress again, and again he had fallen; again through her he knew himself accursed! And on his face a great misery gathered, for the weight of his guilt lay afresh upon his life, and the work of his expiation was tainted and shattered, and in vain;—his ransom had been lost even as it was redeemed.

No human sight had looked upon that awful meeting on the waste of the ocean; its history was hidden in the shroud of the storm, in the wildness of the hurricane, in the beating of the seas; the darkness brooded over land and water, darkness impenetrable, filled with the rushings of the winds and the roar of the ice-chill breakers. When the light broke forth again from the riven skies, they saw him towering above the boiling waters, and holding the young child aloft; erect, and with measured movement he came through the surf breaking breast high upon the shore, the glare upon his face, the cold surge parted by his arm. Then, as the shout of those who welcomed their deliverer vibrated through the midnight, Strathmore reached the land—and, without word, without sign, reeled and fell as one dead.

A cry, wailing through the night, rang on the silence as he fell.

There was a swift, noiseless sweep, as of a sea-bird's wing, past those who gathered round him; in the beacon's light they saw what seemed to them a face, rather of heaven than of earth. Lucille sank down beside him, where he lay on the wet beach.

"He is not dead? He will be saved?—he will be saved?"

Her voice, in its anguish of appeal, thrilled above the tumult of the storm, above the hoarse roaring of the breakers; it pierced through the mists of the exhaustion which clouded and dulled his reason; a shudder ran through his frame where he lay stretched, felled in his spent strength, like a stately pine that the tempest had broken and laid low.

"Saved? No. *Lost!*"

His mind awoke to its guilt ere his senses revived to the world; but the low delirious words died muttered and unheard upon his lips. Life was dark and meaningless to him; he remembered nothing save that dim horror of unexpiated guilt; the noise of the rushing seas was in his brain, the throes of a great suffering throbbed and quivered through his strained limbs, an iron weight seemed to lie on him, crushing the breath from out his chest, as the lead and beams were piled on the condemned in ancient days; he was sinking down, down, into a fathomless abyss, while the amber hair of his temptress twisted and writhed and netted round him, and would not let him loose!

His eyes unclosed, and opened blindly and in pain to the wild fury of the night, to the whirling of the lightning blaze, till he saw the child-face above him, with its fair angel light. What had she to do there, in the night, in the storm, with the black seething waters, with the giddy flame? In a faint, unconscious gesture, he stretched out his arms:

"Lucille!"

Their eyes met;—and with a low, delirious laugh of joy she sank senseless down on the dank sands, her head bowed unconsciously on his breast, her bright hair trailing in the surge, the virginal flowers that crowned it tangled with black beach-weeds.

And in that moment, as he met her eyes in the dizzy glare that swept over earth and sky and ocean, a light more terrible than the death-fire that played upon the sea flashed through the blind mists before his brain.

He knew that Lucille loved him.

## CHAPTER XV.
### "And Retribution arose."

THE dawn broke, the pine-boughs were bathed in the light, the snowy surf was tossed upon the beach, the waves swept up with stately measure, and broke in melodious murmur on the shore, and the curlews flew through the fresh air. Earth, and sky, and ocean kept no record of their work, and over the sunken reef where the ship had found her grave, the wild blue waters, rearing in the sun-gleam, broke in joyous idle mirth, crested with snow-white foam.

Beneath the waves, far down in the salt depths, were floating lifeless limbs and trailing hair, tangled with the noxious weeds and briny grasses of the sea-bed; on the shore dead forms were stretched and dead faces were turned upward to the light, presently to be lain, nameless and unmourned in the shadow of the old monastic church, in the shelter of the still Druidic woods; and—as the sun rose, and shed its warmth upon the waters—one life trembled between earth and eternity. It was that of Lucille.

Through the horror of the night, through the peril of the storm, an unnatural strength had upheld her while his life was ventured; when he was saved, the tension broke like a bow over-strained. The nature which had found its power in love, and had kept its vigil in the air laden with death, was like the sacred light which burns in a porcelain lamp; the brighter, the fuller, the purer the light from within, the frailer the human-wrought porcelain which prisons it, the surer to break and be shattered to dust, that that light may escape heavenward, to be lost amidst its own likeness, which it has not found on earth.

With her cheeks deeply flushed, with her hair still wet by the heavy sea-spray, with her eyes closed in a stupor that was never sleep, or opened wide in vague wild fear, she lay unconscious of all which passed around her. She deemed herself still on the sea-shore, clinging to the fast-rooted pine, and beholding the war of life with death, waged in the dark seething waste below. Her low, swift voice, full of the softest music, was never silent; incessantly and incoherently, with a sad, sweet, wild pathos, it spoke—now, of the black mountainous waters, that were burying him beneath them; now, of the terrace-roses which he had told her were the flowers of sin, the flowers of revel—why had he said that?—what was it that he meant?—now, of the solitary, nameless grave lying under the ivy coils and woodland grasses by the old monastic church, which she had seen in the morning light; why was it Lucille's grave?—was *she* to lie there when she died?—and now—ever and again—of the wild storm-night, of the dying cries ringing above the tumult of wind and water, of the dead floating in the white lightning glare of the seas which stood betwixt him and her, of the fathomless ocean-depths where he had sunk for ever, of the death whence he would never return.

It was strangely piteous that delirium which spoke of him unvaryingly as dead, and betrayed in its unconsciousness a love which was the core of her life.

Pacing the terrace beneath her windows, which stood open, Strathmore heard it; and had his foes beheld him in that hour, they would have known, then, where to strike, and reach the life which, in all else, was chill and invulnerable as the cold polished steel.

Those who did see him when the day came, thought that the haggard, broken look which his face wore was the weariness of shattered strength; that the dark and hollow circles beneath his eyes, the air of spent force and worn-out pain, which had displaced the repose of his face and the proud, negligent dignity of his bearing, were but the result of the past night, were but the physical prostration attendant on his physical injuries. They did not know them *as* they were; they did not know that bodily suffering, and the exhaustion of powers overstrained, were unfelt by him. What made him sick unto death was the dark knowledge of the guilt shrouded in the blackness of night, buried in the sepulchre of the seas; what bruised and broke the haughty egotism of his strength, was the impotent, baffled sense of despair, before the expiation which was undone before his sight, and beyond the power of his hand to stay.

He had striven to a great atonement, and he had given his life to its travail; and as he reached it, it had perished from his grasp, and left the guiltless to suffer for his sin!

He knew that Lucille loved him.

Standing there, where he had made his way into the cool fresh air, he heard in every accent of the voice, which thrilling with pain and rising in plaintive appeal echoed to him through the opened casements above, the love which he had never dreamed or feared until that hour when his eyes had met hers, and he had known it as no words could ever have told it to him. And his first sense then had been one of fierce, sweet, sudden joy. No other could steal her from him! The next, remembrance returned, and a revolted self-accusing agony swept away all touch, all chance, all thought of that forbidden gladness which it only needed memory to destroy for ever.

He knew himself a murderer; his hand could not seek hers with a husband's touch, knowing that on it lay the stain of blood-guiltiness; knowing himself for what he was, he could not take a soilless life to lie within his bosom. Shrouded from her sight, between them arose the eternal barrier of his crime, severing for ever the guilty from the innocent. Though through long years of joy she were never to learn the secret of the heart on which she were bidden to rest her own, never to hear in the still watches of the night one unconscious word which should unfold her the covered crime which haunted sleep, the union would yet be unholy—a dark, forbidden sin against her sacred innocence.

For the blood-stain was fresh upon his hand; and where he stood in the silent dawn, looking outward to the sea, he shuddered. In the light of the breaking day he saw but the black chasm of the yawning waters, and the livid face turned upward, and sinking slowly in the guilty night downward and downward till it was lost for ever.

He abhorred himself, as he thought of the atonement so hardly laboured for, so nearly won by the strength which had passed through its martyrdom, to be vanquished by its own passions at the last ere it had grasped the victor's crown. For although the one sin lay buried in the past, and the other had been shrouded for ever from all human sight and ken, in his conscience he was none the less branded as the destroyer of Life; in his own knowledge divided none the less from all innocent and hallowed things, from all pure and holy youth.

And Lucille loved him!

He, who for the sake of the dead would have given his life for hers, was powerless before the retribution which arose from out the office of his solitary expiation. She must lose all the beauty and the glory of her youth in the shame of a hopeless and an unaccepted love; and he must never let loose one word of consolation, one caress of tenderness! He was powerless; she must suffer, and he must behold the life he had sworn to guard from all breath or consciousness of human grief and worldly evil, smitten and accursed through him!

He had never by the faintest thought foreseen this issue of the care, and the fidelity with which he had followed and fulfilled the trust bequeathed to him by Erroll; he had never feared or dreamed that she could ever feel for him any emotion deeper than the filial and childlike tenderness she bore him as her guardian. Of the good that he had done, the fruit was evil! And far back through the stretch of many and forgotten years the words of Redempta the Bohemian came to him:

"The past has been wrought by your own hand, but the future will escape you . . . . . . The sin to the guilty has been avenged, but the sin to the innocent will never be washed away!"

The future escaped him. And a great despair was on him: he fought against fate, he strove as with God's vengeance for a slaughtered life!

From above, in the silence of the waking day, he heard ever the plaintive wail calling upon his name with the delirious words of an unconscious love. He could not hear them and not seek her; he felt that he must silence them at all or any cost. Were she to die for him, to die through him!

He entered the house and approached her chamber; on the threshold his mother met him, but he motioned her aside.

"Let me see her! I stand in her father's place."

In the hour of extremity the world is forgotten; she let him pass, and he stood in the stillness of the early day, in the chamber filled with the ceaseless moan of the voice that called upon his name.

Where Lucille lay, the light from the sunlit east fell on her, deepening the golden hue of the hair, damp and clogged with the clinging sea-water, the fevered, scarlet flush upon the cheeks, the wistful, haunting pain in the dreamy eyes; and as the full light on the heather-bell, where it lifts its delicate head, on the bloom of the flower, or the hue of the sea-shell, shows their beauty, only also to show their fragility more, so in the brightness of morning he saw, as he had never seen before, how frail was the life on which the work of his expiation was garnered. All of atonement that could be made by him to the dead hung on this brief existence.

He stood in the shadow of the chamber and gazed on her; in that hour he loved her, purely, deeply, willing to give his peace for hers, as he had never loved;—the one sacred and unsullied thing in a life world-corroded and sin-stained.

Where she lay her face was turned towards him, her hair swept backward from her brow; her eyes looked upward with a sad, wild pain, and she raised herself, with a piteous gesture of appeal, as the vague, unconscious words came swift and plaintive from her lips, murmuring the strange burden of a weird, mournful, Scandinavian legend, woven in her thoughts by the unbidden wanderings of fever:

> "Roses my secret keep,
> While those around me sleep!

What does that mean? The roses may hear, but they cannot whisper again? He would not have me gather them; he called them the flowers of sin. Why, why? Others must have sinned to him; *he* never sinned. He is so great, so noble. He cares for me for my father's sake; only for that! If he loved me he would not have bidden me go to strangers? He knew Lucille had no love but for him. Perhaps he was angered because I gathered the roses?"

The words died away wearily, while in her gaze came a troubled, wondering look. And he on whose ear that innocent voice rang, stood, with an iron calm on his face and the darkness of guilt on his soul; smitten by those words as by the voice of an accusing judge.

Then a wild terror leapt into her eyes; she lifted herself, with her hands outstretched, and a wailing cry:

"He is dead! He is dead! The seas have covered him; he cannot rise! Look, look!—it is so dark,—there is no light; the waters are on him; they have buried him! Let me go, let me go—oh my God!—and die with him!"

Her voice rose in passionate anguish, her hands were stretched out to the empty air, her eyes were filled with the misery with which they had followed and sought him through the horrors of the storm; she lived through all the torture of that awful night, in which she had seen his life ventured and given to the mercy of the storm.

He heard the piteous appeal of the love which in that hour he would have suffered a hundred deaths rather than have known, given to himself; and he saw that if any could save her he could alone. He moved from the shadow where he stood, and drew near her bed. He took her hands within his own, and his voice was calm, with that tranquillity with which Strathmore could rein in and veil his deepest passions, his most bitter agony.

"Lucille, look at me; I am with you! My life is safe, and what harm can touch you whilst *I* am near?"

His words pierced through the mists in which her brain was wandering; he held her hands within his, and his eyes looked down with a serene and loving light into her own, which met them with bewildered pain. And slowly and soothingly the calm fixed gaze magnetised hers, and tranquillised her like the stealing peace of the lotus-fumes, which give rest to the weary limbs, and lulling dreams. The love which had endangered now restored her life; she knew his voice, his touch, his gaze, as she had known no other's; the terror passed from her face, a smile, faint but sweet as the glad light of the dawn, shone on it; and, as her head drooped and sunk in exhaustion, her eyes looked upward to him with the love so unconsciously betrayed.

The sun rose higher over the laughing seas, the white mists of the hills rolled back before the brightness of the day; still she lay there, her head resting on his arm, her hand lying in his, her hair sweeping his breast, and while a touch could waken her he would not move. His strained sinews ached and throbbed, as those of men taken off the rack, his limbs were bruised and torn by the conflict of the waves, sickening pain and blindness were still on him from the unnatural tax his strength had borne. But he did not stir, nor seek to release himself from the constraint of the attitude in which he leant over and supported her, till her restless, wakeful, still half-delirious slumber had deepened in the hushed calm of the silent chamber into the surer sleep of safety, with which the fevered flush faded from her cheeks, her breathing grew low and tranquil, her face lost its look of pain, and the life of Lucille was spared. Then he gently loosened his hands from hers, unwound the hair which had coiled about his arms, moved her from him without breaking her rest, and going out from her presence passed to the solitude of his own chamber.

Unseen, his mother followed him. He did not move, nor turn his eyes to her; he stood silent and motionless, while the dark, heavy folds of the portière swung behind her; he knew her words ere they were spoken in his ear.

"It is *you* whom Lucille loves!"

"I know it."

"You *know* it, Strathmore?"

"I knew it last night."

His mother's hand tightened where its light tenacious hold lay on his shoulder, and her voice, haughty and mellow still in her declining years, sank lower yet:

"And you——"

He put her hand from him, and moved to the deeper shadow of the mullioned window. She was answered.

A shudder ran through her frame, and her lip quivered, her voice sank lower still, as in the awe of an unutterable horror.

"Oh, my God! It must never be!"

"No. It must never be."

His voice was calm; but there was that in its tranquillity which appalled her with a great terror; she was his mother, and she loved him. It was not for *her* voice to lift itself and say, "Behold! the guilt was yours, it is but just that its chastisement should overtake you, and be also yours! It is but meet and due!"

She was his mother, in his remorse she had succoured him, in his retribution she yearned to him.

"My son! my son!" she cried, wearily. "You suffer——"

"I!"

The word rang out in passionate loathing and condemnation of himself; Strathmore had in him the nature of those who, in the days of Basil and Chrysostom, in the austerity of remorse, gave up to pitiless torture their bodies for their sins.

"I! What matter how *I* suffer; it will be but just. It is she—she—the guiltless!"

His voice fell, the dark veins swelled upon his temples; he moved from her again, and sank down with his head bowed upon his arms. She had broken the deadly calm which in men of his blood and race she knew and dreaded most; but where she stood by him, she—the aged and imperial woman, who, in all her years, had known no fear—trembled, and was afraid, for she had never until this hour beheld the bonds of his passions loosened, or the cold pride of his strength beaten down.

"Heaven help her!" she said, brokenly. "She will suffer—she must suffer. But it could never be, Strathmore! It were too horrible! You—you——"

"A murderer! Say out the word."

His voice rang loud and hoarse, with his hatred of his own life, of his own soul; and she did not know that the darkness, as of night, which was upon his face, was that of fresh guilt; that in the morning light he saw but the whirl of the giddy waters, and the white face upturned in the phosphor glare, and the amber hair floating out on the black waste, and beaten down beneath the foam.

"You have striven to atone—you have done all you could," she murmured. "Effort is man's, Cecil; but the result is with God."

"Atone! Ay! I have laboured to atone, but the end of the atonement is accursed. I can destroy—that is devil's work!—but I cannot expiate. My peace, my life, my soul, I would give them all for expiation! and I cannot reach it. Cain bore his brand for ever; so do I."

The words were wild and hollow in their pain, their bitter

futile yearning; the one cry wrung from the shattered strength of a great lost soul.

And his mother shuddered as she heard, and covered her face, trembling even as Eve before the guilt which wrecked the mighty sin-stained life which she had given, and which had once been nurtured guiltless in her bosom.

For a long space there was silence between them, and he seemed not to note nor remember her presence where he stood looking outward to the early day, with the darkness on his face, which had come there when his hand had unloosed and left the dying to her grave, and the light of sacrifice offered, of redemption won, had died for ever from his eyes.

His mother lifted her head and looked at him, and in her haughty eyes, which had rarely known such weakness, blinding tears gathered—tears for the force and the weakness, the grandeur and the guilt, the sanctity of remorse and the brutality of hate, so strangely blent and woven in his nature, whose will had power to conquer all save the passions which wrought their own curse. She drew nearer to him, while her voice was dropped so low that its whisper scarcely stirred the air:

"Strathmore—one word—you will not seek to expiate the past by what would be but added sin? Love between you and his child could never, must never, be?"

"Love!"

He shuddered as he spoke, and the haggard weariness upon his face deepened, while his eyes were bloodshot and filled with pain. The word was horrible in his ear; the name of that mad, sweet, delirious sorcery, which he had known once, never to know again; which even now, in hours of memory, he longed for, as men yearn for their dead youth; which had been the well-spring of his crime, the poison on his lips, the tempter in his soul, the beautiful vile lie which had betrayed him and driven him to his crime.

"Love!—from *her!* My God! if she knew me as I am! .... She would abhor me—she would hold my very touch damnation. Wed her to her father's destroyer! Ay! it would be but added sin. *My* life cannot—and yet—who would have cherished her as I . . . . ?"

The last words his mother did not hear, they were stifled almost ere they were spoken; and with a gesture he signed to her to leave him, and let him be. His nature was too kindred with her own, she knew too well the intolerant and silent souls of the men of her race and blood, to disobey his will, or rob him of the sole solace which is left to suffering—solitude. She stooped her proud head, and her lips rested on his brow, and trembled there in the tenderness which in his childhood and his youth she had never given him, and which throughout her life had been very rare in the high-souled imperious woman.

"My son! God comfort you; I cannot!"

Then with that broken, murmured prayer, his mother left him; and Strathmore was alone. Alone to see ever before his eyes the white upturned face, met, after the lengthened stretch of many years, in the darkness and tumult of the night, his temptress and destroyer still! Alone to know the labour of his expiation stricken from his hands, the atonement he would have yielded up all sacrifice to attain, broken from out his grasp; the life he would have given his own to save, wrecked and condemned through him!

## CHAPTER XVI.
### The Choice that was Left.

BEFORE long, sleep, unbroken and restful, became the sure saviour of youth. Lucille was left fragile, fevered, with a certain startled fear in the dreamy depths of her eyes, a certain weariness in their drooped lids, but restored from the exhaustion and the pain which turn by turn had succeeded to the exposure of the night which she had braved.

The days passed slowly by, heavy, gloomy, early autumn days, with white mists on the yellow woodlands, and stormy sunsets in the dark western skies above the sea. The guests

had all left, and the hours wore lingeringly away at White
Ladies, while the spent strength and physical injuries, consequent on his recent peril, with whose story the country
rang, gave sufficient reason for Strathmore's brief retirement and rest there.

"'Heroism,' 'Sacrifice,' 'Nobility!' God help me! If they
knew me as I am!" he muttered, where he stood in his
private library, his eyes falling on the newspaper which lay
open before him, where were painted in vivid detail the terrors of the shipwreck, in which alone and unaided one who
was of value to the nation, had given himself to the madness of the waters and rescued six lives at peril of his own.
The act was grand and simple, and thrilled through to the
heart of the people. They gave him but that which was his
due; yet Strathmore turned from it abhorring himself; for
this man judged himself more rigidly and cruelly than others
would have judged him, and in that innate truth which remained to him through so much that was evil, recoiled from
homage which worshipped that in him, which *he* held solely
as atonement for his crime, and atonement wrecked and
forfeited at the last beneath temptation.

"They kneel to a false god!" he said, bitterly, as he flung
the paper from him; yet, perchance, he might be judged
more mercifully than he judged himself, and the travail of
self-sacrifice was not wholly worthless, though imperfect and
guilt-stained at its close?

He rose, and walked up and down the chamber; he had
an office to perform, and he feared the durance of his strength,
for—he loved her. Not with that sweet, wild passion which
had broken asunder all laws of duty and man, and been world,
conscience, eternity, to itself—*that* comes but once in a lifetime—but more holily, more tenderly; and with the intensity
which those natures alone know, which are, like his, cold to
all the world save one. And—God help him!—he longed to
be enabled to believe his love hopeless and unreturned, with
more agonised passion than ever a man prayed to have his
love echoed in the heart he sought. Loneliness, pain, misery;

ay, even the fate which should bid him give her with his own hand to her husband's embrace, he knew he would have strength to bear in silence, without self-betrayal; these, in all their suffering, would have been mercy to that love which would curse her through himself, while on his soul lay the memory which forbade him to shelter, and shield, and mingle with his own the young life which was guiltless!

For one long hour his steps unceasingly paced the room in solitude, then they turned towards hers. It was the first day that she had risen—the first hour that they had met—and he feared that ordeal as he had never feared the death with which he had stood face to face.

Her couch stood near one of the windows, and she lay resting her head on her hand, and looking outward to where the deer swept beneath the golden foliage; there was a fitful hectic on her cheek, a weary drooping of the eyelids, a certain look of pain and fever on her which smote him with sharp agony. *His* was that touch which he had hidden be accursed, by which her childhood and her peace had for ever been scared from their rest! Yet he must live as though blind to it, speak as though he had no knowledge of, no tenderness for it, as though he were steeled and dead to the innocent fondness of the sole living thing for which he cared!

Lucille knew nothing of the delirious words by which she had betrayed herself. She had been vaguely conscious of his hands holding hers, of his eyes gazing on her, till the sense of his presence soothed her pain and fear, and lulled her into happy rest. She had been sensible of no more; and it was with no fuller consciousness of her own heart than that which instinctively awoke with the first touch of love in a lofty, delicate, and but too sensitive nature, that she saw him now. It could have no alarm, it could have little strangeness for her, this affection which was still that of her childhood, only deepened and taught to know that no other could ever reign beside it; to love Strathmore seemed as much the religion of her life as to love God. Her head turned swiftly as he entered, a glorious light beamed upon her face. With a low cry that thrilled his heart with anguish, she rose and sprang towards him, all forgotten save that peril from which he had returned to her, the heroism with which he had offered up his life for others through the hideous dangers of the storm.

They were alone; Strathmore stood silent, motionless, his face white, the veins standing out darkly upon his temples; *he* could suffer, he had passed through enough to be well used to that, but the trial that awaited him was one far deadlier, it was to see *her* endure the fruits of his own guilt!—to know that with one whisper, one gesture that should bid her come to his heart and rest there, he could make her happy, yet to have that single word, that single sign, forbade him, and made horrible even in his own sight by the foul crime of his own past!

Power, riches, station, fame, the world's homage, and the dignities of men, he would have given them all to have stood *guiltless* before that one unsullied life.

With that glory on her face which pierced him to the quick, she drew his hands in hers, and laid her soft lips on them in reverent worship, and looked up in his face with broken words of love and honour, and tears beyond all eloquence, beyond all gladness; he was a thousand times more beloved and reverenced, come from the conflict where storm and death had been braved, with martyr sacrifice, for the pure sake, as she believed, of one grand, simple, human duty. And he stood beside her, chained back by the bonds of crime from all communion with the only thing he loved, while on his hand her sinless lips gave their kiss of sweet religious veneration, as to the hand which had *saved* the sanctity of life!

All utterance of her affection had been so natural with her to him from her childhood, that her heart could not wholly awake to the knowledge that this was that love which others begged from her; a desert child whom no breath of the world had ever touched, and to whom no lips of man had ever whispered, could not have been more divinely unconscious of all profanities of passion than Lucille. Yet—at the look that was in his eyes as they met hers then — the words of homage paused on her lips, a light shyer, sweeter, than had been ever there, came upon all her face, with a flush sudden, and warm, and fitful, bright as the blush of the wild rose; she loosed his hands, and her head sank. It was so lovely that tremulous, half-conscious dawn of love! One who should have had no love for her in answer, looking on her then, would have known but one instinct and one response, to raise her in his arms, to gather her to his heart, and bid her rest there; to soothe with fond caress the loveliness startled into new beauty with the new pulse that stirred it. And *he*—who would have given his life for hers—stood beside her, silent, responseless, forbidden from her by every law of conscience.

Silence fell between them.

In that brief hour Strathmore suffered deadlier chastisement than pursues guilt in the scaffold and the grave; he suffered as those suffer who behold what they love and cherish slain through them. Yet still—that moment of silence given him—he addressed her with his accustomed gentleness; he rebuked her tenderly for the peril she had braved for his sake; he let her note no change in him. Only—his voice unconsciously grew cold in the strain which kept it calm, and he never sought or gave that familiar caress which at meeting or at parting Lucille had used to receive from him, as she would have received her father's kiss.

That was for ever ended: the peaceful guardianship of the life bequeathed to him could never again be as it had been; her love seemed to sunder her farther from him than her loss to another could have ever done; his very hand was not fitting to touch hers *now*, stained with the fresh guilt of an added crime.

He moved suddenly from her side. He had a duty, bound by honour, to perform to an absent man, and Strathmore had no thought to be false to that—not even to spare her. He had a trained strength to endure, and his code of truth was lofty and severe. His face was somewhat turned from her, but his words were calm as he spoke:

"Lucille—you read the letter I left with you some days since?"

"Yes!"

Her voice was very low; a heavy misery began to weigh upon her young fair life, still vague, still nameless, the same which in delirium had found its plaintive shape in the words; "he does not love me, or he would not bid me go to others!"

His eyes were still turned from her; his voice was still tranquil and sustained. Such honour to the one absent, who had trusted him as he could still keep, he kept most faithfully.

"Lucille, I owe it to you and to him, both, that you should know I wrote no word there that was more than barren justice to Valdor and to—to the love he bears you. In a few days I shall be in Paris for political matters: he will come to me for his reply. He believed that your heart was his—I believed so also——"

"*You!*"

The one word stayed those upon his lips; the accent quivered to his soul in its wondering, piteous reproach. He could not plead another's cause whilst he knew that every fibre of her life clung to himself; he could not bid her go wed where she had no love, and live in the abhorred pollution of a joyless union.

He was silent many moments; when he spoke, his voice was hoarse and forced:

"It was not so?"

Her eyes looked upward with the gaze that had been in them when they had met his own in the light of the storm, then her head drooped upon her hands, while a flush of pain and of shame stole to her face.

"Oh no, no!—never!"

He heard the words, barely above her breath though they were, and he knew what was uttered in them; that loyalty to himself born of gratitude, of reverence, of every hallowed and endearing memory, which closed her heart to all others.

He had no need to question now what had parted them, when, in that which was her love for him, he had believed he saw her love for the one who wooed her. He knew but too well.

"It was I who misled him, then," he said, slowly, letting no sign appear of the effort his words cost, save that which made them sound cold in all their gentleness. "I told him but what I honestly believed, God knows, and to you I have done him no more than honourable justice. He loves you well—it might be better if——"

The phrase died unfinished; his lips could not end it; her face turned to him one moment with an unspoken reproach more plaintive than all words, and her eyes mutely questioned him why was the fostering tenderness of his guardianship abandoned and forgot, that he should send her to another's home and bid her be an exile to another's love? Before that look his forced tranquillity, his strained composure, broke down. Master of his own suffering still, for sake of her, the misery of his life, which saw his solitary power of expiation shattered from his hands, broke out in one involuntary utterance as he bent to her:

"Oh, Lucille—Lucille! why is your childhood over! I could guard you *then!*——"

He had said, without words, that they could never be again as they had been, and all the loneliness of abandonment weighed on her with the loss of that guardianship which had never let her know one touch of pain, one wish ungiven, or one desire unforestalled. She felt as he felt, though she knew not why, as he knew, that the bond which had bound them was severed, and could not be replaced by any other. Of a nearer tie to him she had never thought; her love was too pure, too high, too wholly born in an ethereal and reverent nature, to take grosser form and definite shape; she only knew she had no love for any save for him, and that the tenderness which he had lavished on her was for ever chilled and lost, and that he had bade her trust herself to other care and go to other hearts. He was the world to her—and henceforth she was as nothing to him.

He saw the peace he had sworn to save at any cost desolate and broken through him; he knew that he had but to lift her to his heart, and bid her lose her guardian's in her husband's love, to make his own for ever the life which had no law but his will, no joy but from his hand, and to see beneath his roof, within his home, before his sight by day, and hushed on his heart by night, the beauty of those young years, in which was garnered his sole atonement to the dead. And the work of his dead passions divorced them; the knowledge of his own sin bade him stand aloof, barred out from the life that suffered for him and suffered through him.

That his crime might be veiled from her, he must let her deem him insensible to the beautiful faith and love she bore him!—he must leave her alone in her desolation, powerless to solace or to save the life bound in him and wrecked for him!

He was strong to endure himself, but he had no strength to behold her suffer, as men have borne the torture without a moan, tearing their own sinews and rending their own limbs, but have been vanquished when they were chained to witness the same ordeal wrenching the delicate form of the woman whom they adored.

For one moment more he knew he could command himself; he stooped and laid his hand gently on her bowed head.

"You are still weak, my child. Rest now; I will see you later on."

Then he left her. A little longer, and his control would have been wrenched down, his strength would have failed him; she would have seen betrayed the darkness of a buried crime, the despair of a sleepless remorse, on the face of him whom she thought great and sinless, and held second only in her worship to that God in whom she believed not more holily and utterly than she believed in him.

Hours afterwards, as he crossed before the open door of the great library, he saw Lionel Caryll; the young man leaned against the embrasure of one of the oriel casements, his forehead bowed upon his arm, his whole attitude full of a deep restrained dejection, his face very pale as the light streamed through the coloured panes upon his bright tawny hair.

On a sudden impulse—one of those vague, unstudied, and blind impulses which never before had had place in his temper or his life, an impulse of desperation rather than of thought or of belief in its own inspiration—Strathmore entered and approached him; the youth started and looked up, the warm blood flushing his face.

"I absolve you from your promise. You may urge your love to-day—this hour—when you will."

They were brief words, and uttered coldly, but to the young lover they spoke of heaven: yet even as the first startled gratitude flushed over his face in its wondering happiness, he was chilled and awed by the look upon Strathmore's. He could not translate it, but in some vague sense he felt that the proud, silent man beside him suffered.

Strathmore stood where his own face was unseen by the youth.

"You are honest, loyal, and without guile. You love purely; her life will be safe with you. If you can win her of her own will, without pressure, do so. Keep her years happy, innocent, sheltered, you whom she loves as a brother, and you shall ask nothing from me that I will refuse. Go; and speak as your heart bids you."

He turned abruptly away, with a sign silencing all reply; for one moment he heard the rush of breathless words with which the young man strove to thank him, and saw the flushed, tremulous ecstasy of joy which beamed on his face as it only beams upon the face of youth; with the next he had left the library, and the door of his own study had closed on his solitude.

Hours more might have gone by, or only minutes, he knew not which, when the door unclosed, and before him stood the boy, whom he had sent from him a brief space before, in all the wild, sweet hope, the rich undoubting happiness of youth. Words were not needed to tell his story; one glance, and Strathmore knew the issue of his errand, and the sudden rush of a hot, swift joy which swept through his veins felt to him like guilt. In all sincerity he would have given up his life to any torture to know that hers was safe where his own could never attaint it with regret, or shadow, or the dark curse of his own past.

He rose and laid his hand, with an unwonted gentleness of pity, on his nephew's:

"Poor boy! I only sent you to more pain!"

Lionel Caryll shrank from his touch, and his face was turned away, while his voice shook:

"I only dealt *her* more! She loves me as a brother! I was mad to think it could be otherwise. I have but wounded, startled, grieved her—her for whom I would——"

His words died, his head sank, and in the desolation of his grief he forgot all pride, and strength, and shrinking shame of his young manhood, and, throwing himself down, sobbed like a child.

Strathmore stood and looked on him: he had no scorn for *those* tears—they were for her—but he had a weary envy of them! and a smile of unutterable sadness came on his lips. What was this boy's first guiltless grief, beside that with which Life brims over for those who suffer and give to the world no sign?

His hand fell once more on the young man's, and his voice, deep and softened, had a solemnity and a compassion in it which had never before been in its tone:

"Lionel! your grief is bitter to bear, yet be grateful that you *can* grieve—there is suffering which cannot! Live so that you never know it; keep your life as it is now, without remorse, and it will be peace beside *that* hell, however you suffer!"

The youth lifted his head, startled and awed; then it sank again, and his stifled sobs were heard upon the stillness, vainly striven with for love of manhood, while Strathmore paced to and fro the chamber, with his head bowed, forgetful of Caryll's presence. Some moments passed; then the young man arose slowly and wearily, and the change was piteous which had come upon his frank, bright, careless face; all the sunlight was dashed from it, and a pale, drawn misery left there in its stead. He stood before Strathmore, and something proud and noble came on him as he spoke—vainly seeking to make his voice steady and calm:

"Sir, I dreamed a fool's dream, and it has been broken by—God shield her!—the gentlest heart that ever pitied pain. *I* can be nothing to Lucille; less, now that I have lost my title of 'brother,' than I have ever been. *I* have no power to make her life, as you bade me, 'happy, innocent, sheltered.' That power lies in your hands, for—it is you whom she loves."

Where they stood together he saw Strathmore shudder, and his cheek grow whiter; watching him keenly, the youth saw that it was not with wonder, but with a revulsion almost of terror that he heard him—the look which he had seen once before break down the pride and reserve of the man whom he feared, in the summer night at Silver-rest. And even in the blind pain of his sharp sorrow, Nello noted and marvelled at that look; whence could be its spring?

"You think this?—and why?"

The tone was haughty, but there was forced tranquillity in it; Strathmore ceased to stand before him, and passed again down the length of the library.

"I feared it long; I know it now," the boy answered him. "She may not dream it herself—I cannot tell—but *I* read it in the very words with which she put back my love, in the very pain with which she shrank when I told her you had sent me, free to plead with her as I would for——for——"

The joy which could never be his!

His voice failed him; and Strathmore paced with swift and restless step the silent chamber, his head was sunk upon his breast, and in his heart was a bitter cry:

"*I* deal her pain! Oh, God, which sin must I choose!— the sin that spares her, or the sin that smites her?"

"Lord Cecil! have you so much tenderness for her, and yet have no love?" cried the young man, brokenly, for Lionel Caryll's devotion was untouched with the selfishness of that passion which would slay what it cannot attain.

"No love!—*I!*"

The words were stifled—Caryll did not hear them, and pursued his generous, unselfish prayer:

"My lord! my lord! You must know that she loves you? Will you, who are so tender a guardian to her, close your heart to a fonder tie? She cannot love in vain! Men call you —you have seemed so to me—stern and heartless; but a cold nature had never been gentle to her as you are, a merciless one had never perilled life for suffering souls as you imperilled yours. Will you not have pity upon her? Can you give her in her youth to misery, to hopelessness, to the anguish which must be hers when she has learnt her own secret—for Lucille will never love *twice!*"

"Boy, boy!—hush! You do not know what you tempt."

Strathmore had sunk into a chair, his head was bowed, his face covered by his hands.

The young man stood before him, awed, marvelling, deeply touched at the power his word had to break the icy calm and the haughty pride of the nature which for one moment he saw rent asunder.

"Forgive me," he faltered, while his unselfish devotion to Lucille conquered every thought of self, and impelled him to plead for her as he would have pleaded for himself, preferring her peace at loss of his. "But—but—oh, Lord Cecil! —I spoke for *her*. It cannot be that you have no love for her? Can you refuse her a nearer place in your heart, in your home? *I* have learned the bitterness and the desolation of a hopeless love. I would give my life that *she* should never know them; they would be her death-blow!"

"Peace! for Heaven's sake!"

His voice was hoarse with a terrible anguish, and barely above his breath; his head was still bowed, his face still covered. Each word which the boy spoke in his guileless and unselfish prayer quivered like a knife in his soul. Awe-stricken, and arrested with a terror to which he could have given no name, Lionel Caryll stood mute; the great tears slowly coursing down his cheeks, his bright and gracious youth sorely shattered and stricken; yet even in all the bitterness of his own despair, vaguely conscious that he was in the presence of some grief beside which his own was dwarfed. For a moment there was a dead silence; then *in* that moment, the proud man gathered back his strength, the statesman resumed the armour of ice which he wore with friend and foe. Strathmore rose; he dreaded lest he had betrayed his secret; but his face, though haggard and dark with the traces of a deadly conflict, was calm.

"There are reasons, in my past, why the thought of marriage is painful, almost impossible," he said, slowly, and with forced effort. "And—and why should you urge this upon me? You have confessed you love her?"

The young man raised his heavy eyes:

"It is *because* I love her that I would know her peace secured, though its security left me only the more desolate."

The answer was proud and touching in its sad simplicity; it went to the heart of him who heard it; Strathmore leaned his hand heavily upon his shoulder.

"Lionel Caryll, you are nobler than *I* ever was!"

The youth's lips quivered, and he moved with a quick shudder; he had pleaded against every selfish dictate of passion for Lucille's sake, but he shrank from the touch of the hand she loved.

"My lord, you will forgive me if I leave your roof to-night. I could not stay now that—that——"

His voice failed him, and he turned his head with a quick

gesture, that Strathmore might not see the tears which choked his utterance; but Strathmore's hand was not shaken from its hold, and his words were gentle—strangely gentle for him:

"As you will. But, ere you go, remember, for your tenderness to her, you shall still ask of me what you choose, and there shall be nothing that I will refuse. Think of me as your best friend; your future shall be my care."

The young man gave him one swift heart-broken look; "the future!" to him it looked beggared for all time. Then his hand closed on the one held to him in a convulsive pressure, the dull echo of the closing door vibrated through the silence, and Strathmore was once more alone.

In solitude, beside which his nephew's fresh guiltless grief, even in all its poignancy, was mercy. He must of his own hand deal to her the deadliest blow that could smite her life; or he must seek her as a husband, hiding for ever the death-stain upon the heart on which she would be cherished!

The words that the youth had uttered, the lovely light which he had beheld on her face as he drew near—these were his tempters, his torturers. He could have bidden his own life suffer and be silent to his grave;—but hers! Too well he knew the truth, that never would that nature "love *twice;*" that never for another would dawn and smile that beautiful gladness which, through him, must be changed to a curse. He knew it—he knew it. As he had destroyed her mother's life in the morning of its youth, in the sweetness of its joy, so he must now destroy hers.

They stretched before him; that terrible, lonely loveless course of years through which she, the soft and fragile child steeped in sunlight and sheltered in tenderness, would be condemned to pass. Could he send her to them? Could he leave her to believe that she was barred from out his pity? Could he bid her be taught, that he, who had sheltered her with more than a father's care, was cold, and brutal, and dead to the holy love he had fostered? Yet—breathe in her ear the whispers of love, seek her lips with a bridal caress, gather

her to a husband's heart in her soft dreaming sleep!—he could not, he who knew himself the slayer of more than one human life.

## CHAPTER XVII
### In the Cabin by the Sea.

THE gloom deepened in Strathmore's solitary chamber; the joyless autumn twilight stole over wood and moorland; the shadows grew more sombre: still he sat there, his head sunk, his strength broken. Of what avail were pride, will, power, iron force, and haughty dominance *here?* They could not shield the innocent from the curse that fell upon her from his crime; they could not compel the expiation which he had vowed the dead; they could not assoil his life and render it purified and free to seek the sinless.

Hours had passed; he had not raised his head, nor moved, when suddenly—he knew not what it was—there stole over him with a chill sickening shudder a sense as of a presence *felt* but unseen, which froze his blood and made him start, and lift his head and look outward to the twilight. And his eyes fastened there with a blank, distended gaze; a great horror came upon his face;—in the sickly autumn mist, in the black shroud of the leaves without, he saw the features which he had seen, ghastly and livid in the phosphor glare, swept downwards to death beneath the waters.

Had the sea given up its dead?

His veins were ice; on his brow the dew gathered thick and cold; terror like a hand of steel gripped his heart, stilling its beating life; while up from the darkness, through the white cerecloths of mists, rose the form of his Temptress, until he saw her face with its grey blanched hue of haunting pain, and its amber hair driven by the autumn winds, and the eyes with their remorseless, cruel, thirsting hate, claiming him still *her own*—her own by right of their companion guilt; her own by title of their evil past.

He gazed out into the falling night, his limbs powerless,

his voice paralysed, his lips cloven, while the spectral shape grew whiter and whiter, clearer and clearer, in the stormy air, and he saw her as he had done when his hand had unclosed and left her to perish, bidding her die the death that she had given.

They looked on one another thus, under the shadow of White Ladies;—one moment, one fleeting second, that to both seemed lifelong—then the phantom faded, lost in the dull gloom, while the sough of the leaves swept alone through the silence: and he trembled in every limb, and quivered as after a blow that had felled him to the earth. The ice grip loosened from his heart, the awe of an unearthly horror unfroze its hold; and he thanked God aloud, as one released from doom, and led back to life by a gentle and compassionate hand.

For he knew that the sea had given up not the dead but the living; and that he was freed from the guilt which had risen from the depths of the ocean, and tempted him. Not wholly freed, for crime lies in *intent*, and is not washed away, because a merciful fate baffles its committal and its consummation. Yet, freed in much; and humbled in far more.

The face that he had seen in the yellow weirdly gloom was before him still; still he felt as though it stole nigh, and breathed around him—the presence of the temptress, the traitress, the assassinatress. Fierce and deadly, evil hatred, burning passions, had leapt swift as flame into life, when in the tumult of the storm he had been face to face for the first time, since he had bidden her go reap the whirlwind she had sown, with the woman who had been his destroyer, and who had been driven out to misery and shame by the flail of his vengeance. But now, in the sudden release from crime, in the chastened awe of stricken pride, freed from a fresh sin through the wild and wayward mercy of the waves, these were not on him. These for once were drowned and stilled. Truly had she said to him, in the years gone by, "If *I* sinned, were *you* guiltless?" And, strangely, as all things are strange in human life, with the sight of the woman who had betrayed him, there came upon him again the agony of that sweet, idolatrous love, the impotent regret for all that lay buried in his youth, never to be known again—never to have resurrection or successor. It was dead—dead for ever; and the great tears forced slowly from his eyes, and his head sunk lower and lower on his arms. If that love had been guiltless, if that beautiful lie had been worthy the worship, in what living warmth and light would have been bathed the life of the man whose god was Power, and whose tyrant was Remorse!

Through long hours he lay there with his head on his arms, as in the sleep of a profound exhaustion; it was the sleep of the soul, though not of the body, worn out with crime, with conflict, and lulled to rest through sheer weariness of misery. Then, after a while, he rose, and his steps ceaselessly paced his chamber, as though he trod down the memories that thronged around him, the passions that uncoiled from the past and claimed him for their own, the warring duties, the severed thoughts of the dead, and of the living, that tore him asunder as the wild horses tore the quivering limbs of the condemned. Across him for one moment glanced a thought that seemed to scorch him like the physical touch of fire, making him shrink ere it was grasped. The fresh sin, hidden from the sight of men and buried in the secresy of the seas, was not upon him to bar him from the touch, the tenderness, the presence of the youth that was pure and without soil;—for the dead years gone, had not atonement been striven for which might avail to wash out *that*, without the martyrdom and sacrifice of the life that was both innocent, and unconscious of that brutal past?

Lucille loved him: what if—— He shuddered from the thought and flung it from him, as though in its very sweetness it were added crime; cast it away with the same revulsion, almost horror, with which he had first heard its suggestion in the summer evening from his nephew. He wed her! Now, when, for the first time, the thought of its possibility came over him, it looked tenfold more forbidden and unholy than it had ever done when he had refused to glance at it for an instant, when he had had no knowledge that her love was his, no imagination that it would ever become so. With newly committed crime upon his soul, he had known that never could their lives ever have bond between them; now that he stood freed from this, he had seemed for one instant nearer to her, for one moment he had thought that he might guard in his own bosom that fairy youth, that sacred innocence, that beautiful dawn of purest love, fulfilling, till death should take him, the trust which Erroll gave; for one instant his heart had gone out with a pang of passionate yearning, a thirst of unutterable longing, to lock her close into his life, where none could ever assail her, and to make her his alone for ever, beyond the touch of evil or the accident of fate. But with its very thought, came the memory of all that severed them, making in the knowledge of his own sin divorce more wide than law could frame, divorce against which there was in his own conscience, no appeal.

*He* wed her!

He shuddered at the darkness and sin his life had known. Could he, more utterly condemned in his own sight than any felon that ever stained the earth, approach her with a husband's love? he, who held from her in lifelong secresy the tragedy of her father's death, bid her lie on his heart in the soft stillness of the night, and give him the dearest name that men can claim from sinless lips like hers? The more because now his own desire pleaded for it, his own peace sickened for it, his own love longed for it, did the mere hope, the mere thought strike him as with the horror of crime, as with the shock of blasphemy. *He* become her lover, her husband! It would be impious to the sanctity of the dead; impious to the innocence of the living!

He went out into the still late night, alone, when no eyes were on him, and the earth lay hushed and darkened as a grave. His steps wore their track in the damp grasses as he walked unceasingly on and on, to and fro, under the gloom of the woods, within the sound of the moaning seas. All the misery of his life seemed to fall short of this: she loved him: his own heart recognised it, other lips had said it; she loved him; and he had no choice left, save to give her up to a solitary and unpitied desolation, or—to do what his soul revolted, and shrank from, a thousand times the more because the answering love in him craved for it, and self-pity pleaded for it with a passionate pain that he stifled as some vile infamy towards the dead and her. Where question had arisen of sacrifice of himself to her, he had known no temptation, no hesitation, no struggle; he would have given his life for her, and would have doomed himself without a thought of pity to an eternity of woe to have saved her a single pang. But here—sparing her, he spared himself; or, thrusting back the temptation that coiled about him, and accepting the just chastisement of his past, he must sacrifice with him all her life, and through himself, destroy what he had sworn to cherish!

A young poet once wrote:

"If sorrow could be won by gifts to barter prey for prey,
There is an arm would wither, so thine revived might be,
A lip which would be still and mute to make thy music free,
An eye which would forget to wake to bid thy morning shine,
A heart whose very strings would break, to take one pang of thine."

Strathmore, no poet, and to whom the gentleness of self-sacrifice was by nature alien, felt not less than this in all its absolute self-negation, in all its passionate tenderness and fidelity to the only one that he had ever purely loved, to the only trust bequeathed him by his friend. And now he could alone spare her, by binding with his own the life that every memory of the past, and every law of conscience forbade from him, and banned from his very touch! Which choice could he make?

To the man whose path even through guilt had been firm and incisive, as though cut with steel through wax, who had never hesitated, who had never doubted as to his own course, or to his own resolve, an agony of indecision was the worst torture life could hold. Whatever he had suffered, he had never before endured this; his will, however erring, had been resolute and prompt to act, as the will of a tyrant; and this helplessness of doubt, this conflict of opposing duties, this struggle in which he could see no light save from one path that he dared not follow, was greater anguish to a nature like Strathmore's, than any clear shape of action could ever have been, even though it had taken him to a martyrdom.

Do what he would, it seemed to him that he must each way sin to her and to her father; whether he left her and let her fair youth consume in the bitterness and shame of an unanswered love, or whether he crushed the past down out of sight and memory, and took her in his heart and in his home —his wife; whichever he chose he thought that guilt must lie upon his choice. With the one he must break for ever his loyalty to the trust he held, and lose for ever his only expiation to the dead; with the other he must woo her to a union that seemed to him an outrage against her innocence, a forbidden unholy treachery that would betray her in her unconsciousness into the arms of her father's destroyer. Do what he would darkness and crime seemed to rest on it; and all he had done turned into evil. All gentler things, all nobler effort, in him had been vain; and out of his fealty to the dead man's trust came the doom that wrecked it. His tenderness for her had been pure and unsullied, the holiest thing his heart had ever known; yet even the fruit of that was evil. Unwitting what he did, he had taught her a love that he would have died rather than waken! With every caress, every gentle word, every unremitting care, given her for her father's sake, he had in cruel unconsciousness sown the seeds of a misery he had never dreamed as possible. Was there none in the wide world for her to love but the criminal whom a brutal past divided from her?

And yet—and yet—who would ever cherish as he would cherish her!

All through the autumn night, till the dawn broke greyly

over the dusky seas, he walked alone with steps that wore a weary track through dank grasses and on heavy sands; and the day broke and found him no nearer to his choice, no better able to meet and vanquish the fate that had suddenly risen up from the ashes of his dead sin, and mocked his dreams of redemption by seizing the pure life he guarded, and flinging it out to misery with his own.

\* \* \* \* \* \*

In the little hamlet that nestled above the sea on the borders of the great forests of White Ladies, and in the dip of one of the wild western valleys, stood a shealing, scarce wind and water proof, with the blasts of the early autumn moaning through its time-browned thatch, and the pomp of the autumn foliage sheltering its rotten timbers in a wealth of reddening gold. Those who made their home there were very poor, a woman old and feeble and her grandson who was yet but a child; still in their poverty they would break half their last crust for one poorer still, and such as their roof was would share it.

When the sun had risen after the night-storm, and high upon the beach were washed black drift-wood and broken wealth, and nameless sightless corpses that the fish had spared, they had found one woman tossed by the mad mercy of the waves in safety on the beach, and living still by one faint scarce-felt pulse of life. They had raised her, and brought and lain her gently on the heap of hay that served them as a bed, and, though she was poorer yet than they, since the seas had only left her this flickering remnant of uncertain life, and robbed her of all else, they did their best for her, and served her as they could, with that most touching charity of all—the charity of want to wretchedness.

Here, on the pallet of dry grasses she lay;—the woman who once had slept in the palaces of kings.

Broken, bruised, stricken, having lost almost all likeness of herself, delirious, though she kept even in fever the secrets of her past, with something still of lingering matchless beauty that would not perish;—beauty even yet in the voice that murmured wild words, in the hair flung in wild disorder, heavy with brine and tangled with black weeds, in the hand which closed on the dry hay with unconscious pain, in the eyes which never could utterly lose their lustre. She was still living, she who would have thought death a thousand-fold gentler than life, yet who had shrunk from it when it was near, with the cowardice of a criminal, and the physical terror of womanhood. Living—in such last depths of woe, that she owed the cold water held to her lips, and the wretched bed on which her aching limbs were stretched, to the charity of the lowest and the poorest hirelings of the man who once had been her slave.

He had bidden her live to suffer—and retribution had driven and scourged her into obedience to the uttermost letter of that brutal Mosaic Law.

The woman and the boy who tended her, one in extreme age, the other a young child, did their best for her, but they feared her and shrunk from her, they could not have told why. About her there still remained something of inalienable grace, of patrician haughty majesty, and on her in vague yet awful shape, that they rather felt than saw, guilt had left its seal, and shameful years their trail. Long ago, the cruelty and crime within her had flashed out even in her young soft dazzling beauty; now they reigned alone, and gave her a terror to the simple peasants who gathered round her. Yet they did their best; and when the night before, being unwatched, she had risen, and wandering in the mechanical action of delirium, had dragged her weak, bruised limbs through brake and woodland, and wide grassland and dense thickets, till she had crossed the park of White Ladies, and gazed vacantly through the windows of the Abbey in the dull mists of falling night, they had followed her and found her lying senseless and exhausted among the dank yellow ferns, and had brought her back in redoubled pity to such shelter as they could give.

There she lay now in the risen day, insensible still, and moaning wearily, with strange pathetic murmurs now and again upon her lips, and eyes wide open to the light with a blind gaze that looked out upon the earth where she had now no place, and on the sunlight which now to her could never be but mockery and pain. The broken rafters yawned above her, while through them poured the chilly autumn winds; the air was heavy with the lowering smoke of a low peat fire burning on the hearth; the pile of sear grasses and straw was beneath the form once beautiful as a dream of Phidias; squalor, misery, darkness, were around her, and in that wretched cabin by the sea lay the woman who once had bowed monarchs to her smile, and swayed a sceptre wider than sovereigns own, Suffer as she would, her suffering could never yet be so great as her sin had been.

Without, the noon was at its height, and the glancing waters stretched serene and bright; within, even the day could lend no fairness to the den where human lives lived in penury that made the kennelled hounds of White Ladies seem lapped in luxury. The old peasant rocked herself before the labouring smoke of the damp fire; a broken pitcher of cold water stood beside the pallet where she had let a stranger lie; the place was black, and close, and noisome.

Suddenly, and softly, the door opened, the freshness of the mellow autumn day flooded the cabin floor, on the threshold stood, like a child-angel that gleams out in all its golden glory from the dark backgrounds of old altar pictures, the bright youth of Lucille.

To those whom the wreck had flung homeless and beggared on the shores of White Ladies, she seemed like such a spirit, bringing balm, and healing, and hope, coming to their bereaved and desolate lives with her fair young face and her loving, exhaustless charity, which from her earliest years had known no happiness so great as to give succour to suffering, and had found compassion for the vilest, "driving away all things of sin and guilt" by its own divine unconsciousness of their shame and danger.

Lucille's life was love;— for all who suffered with that suffering whose shadows she had never felt, for all who sinned with that sin whose meaning she had never known. Earth was so beautiful to her, and the smile of God so near her, that her heart ached for those who dwelt in pain, and who denied his love. She longed to make them as herself; she longed to lead them where she knelt.

Alone, leaving her attendants without, she came into the dark and wretched shealing. She had heard from the boy without, that a shipwrecked stranger lay there ill and delirious. Lucille had her father's nature; with all her soft brightness and her childlike delicacy she had a high courage, and an unselfishness as rare as it was elevated. She never had known fear. And she came now into this pent hovel—came to serve and succour the outcast lying there. In the dusky smoke-thickened air, she stooped, as the old peasant rose to her in reverence and wonder, and shook into her lap a bright shower of silver; wealth Strathmore lavished on her, and it ever went to those who were in want. She gave, too, with that generous grace which took all sting from any alms, and made those whom she relieved not her debtors, but her idolators; she gave her charity as widely, and as unconsciously of merit in the gift, as a flower gives its fragrance. Then, while her words still lingered on the woman's ear like some gentle chime of music, she swept with hushed steps towards the dark corner where the strewn grasses were tossed down, and where, on that miserable bed, with sightless eyes and fevered limbs, and lips that murmured wearily words without meaning, Marion Vavasour, homeless and nameless, lay.

They were together;—the innocent and the guilty life; and with the infinite compassion of her youth, Lucille looked down upon her father's murderess, lying there at her feet in darkness and wretchedness, where the rays of the sun did not enter, and the autumn winds made their dull moan about her. Thus they met at last.

"Ah!—how she suffers!"

The soft words stole, wistful as a sigh, from her lips, as she gazed down on the bruised, shattered, destroyed beauty which yet *was* beauty, and survived the wreck of all else in this lost womanhood, this doomed and accursed life. She suffered!—the eyes burning but without light, the lips that moved with senseless words, the weary pain of limbs that could find no rest, and brain that could know no sleep,—in these she suffered with every breath she drew. And beyond these there was a darker, direr suffering still; where the wild thoughts wandered, was over the course of an evil life; where the blind memories went, was into depths of guilt. Sin is sweet in the noon of its power; but it is terrible beyond all terror in the midnight shadow of the grave. And its reflection fell on Lucille with a vague dread; in her young and carefully-guarded life she had never seen the look that she saw now on the face of the woman before her;—that wreck of ruined beauty, that unconscious wild defiance, that lost and broken grandeur which gleamed still through all the darkness of evil and of shame. She had never seen it; it had awe and fear for her, all strange and nameless as it was, yet her first instinct was that of the infinite pity which could shrink from nothing that was human, and could be denied to nothing that was in misery.

She sank down, kneeling beside the wretched bed with all the grace of her own loveliness, all the gentleness of her own nature; and with a musing pain in her eyes gazed down at the woman to whom she had owed the deadliest wrong of all her life, before her life had known its loss. Her heart was heavy with its own first bitterness, with a weary aching sadness that hardly yet knew its own spring; life seemed unclosing about her in all its hidden mysteries, its solemnity of pain; and in the insensible anguish on which she looked, she seemed to see, as by some sudden revelation, how terrible this world could be, which to *her*, until so late, had been one sunny Eden of eternal summer. She touched, with lingering caress, the amber tresses that were tangled with the brown rough grasses of the bed; she laid her hand with cooling perfumes on the brow that burned like fire beneath it; she bent over her with pitying words, whose melody insensibly soothed and silenced the moaning wandering murmurs on the parched lips,

Unconscious what she did, she brought her compassion, her tenderness, her angel ministration, to the assassinatress by whose lie her father perished. And there, in the deep shadow of the leaning rotten roof, she knelt beside her;—her youth, her innocence, her fair ethereal life, beside the bruised, stricken, guilt-steeped outcast, who owed a stoup of water to a beggar's alms.

The day had risen and become noon. Strathmore, who could find no rest, was up, after a few brief sleepless hours on his bed, walking still, scarce conscious where he went, alone in the wild forests and solitary shores of White Ladies. No nearer to his resolve, no closer to decision between the divided duties that had their conflict in him—the duty which bade him guard her life without a cloud, the duty which forbade him to make that life one with his. Choose which he would, he must err to the dead and to her; which error would be the less? That he himself loved, that he himself longed to have the sweetness of her young lips, the love-smile of her eyes, the keeping of her peace and joy, he let weigh nothing in the scale. A haughty egotism had once too entirely ruled him; but now he would have crucified every thought of self with an unswerving martyrdom, and thrust his own remaining years into any depths of woe, if by so doing he could have saved or aided her.

He did not know how the hours had passed; he did not remember how his absence would be noted, since men who have the triumph of eminence, can never have the luxury of solitude. He walked on and on, feeling a strange relief in that ceaseless movement, in that physical exhaustion.

Which must he choose?—the betrayal of his trust in consigning her life to sorrow; or the betrayal of her innocence in wedding her, with the past stifled and buried from her?

Either seemed equally accursed to him.

Wandering without aim, almost without knowledge, he came to where the sea-side cabin stood, with the sound of the waves under the cliffs below, and the great woods locking it in their depths. The group about it fell back at his approach; he looked at them with surprise, recognising those who specially attended her.

"Why are you here?"

"Mademoiselle Lucille is within, my lord."

"Within?—*there?*"

He laid his hand upon the door and pushed it open. For a moment all was hazy and dim before him, coming from the full and mellow light into the darkened shed; then the leaden clouds of smoke seemed to roll back, and beyond them he saw, kneeling there in the gloom, the bright child who was the fitting minister of a godlike compassion, beside the bed on which the homeless exile lay. A sickness of horror came upon him; the darkness whirled before his sight; dizzy, breathless, stunned, he leaned nearer, gazing on them in the blankness of a ghastly fascination;—one glance, and he had known the face of his destroyer.

And he saw them together!—he saw Lucille beside the woman who had tempted him to his crime, and had been, more yet than he, the assassin of her father!

Life seemed to have held no retribution for him until now. Remorse, remorse! where was its use? It was vain as to seek back the dead from their tomb, since his guilt could follow him thus!

He looked on them together, the life of cruelty and sin, beside the soilless youth, pure as the flowers that opened to the dawn; he met the senseless, blind gaze of the eyes in which his heaven once had shone; he saw Lucille, kneeling before that bed of shame, with a prayer upon her young lips —a prayer of *pity!*—and on her face the light of a beautiful mercy, of an exhaustless love. In all the width of the crowded world must *these* meet! One moment, while his gaze fastened there, in what appeared to him an eternity of dim, unutterable horror; in which he saw them in that dark and wretched place across the rolling smoke, that seemed like the pestilential breath of his dead years rising round the innocence of Lucille to destroy her for ever;—one moment, in which a hideous unreality possessed him, and the burning eyes of the woman he had loved gazed without sight or sense in his;—then, with an unconscious gesture, an unconscious cry, like that in which he had once before answered her love and betrayed his own, he stretched out his arms.

"Lucille! Lucille!"

She looked up, rose, and sprang towards him with the fond instinct of her childhood, stronger in that moment of surprise than the estranged pain which was between them. Not knowing what he did, or who beheld him, he pressed her to his breast with unconscious passion, and drew her into his arms, away from that bed of misery, away from the senseless gaze of those haunting eyes.

"My God! what brought you here?—what madness sent you to this accursed place? You—you——"

There was a jarring violence in his voice, a passionate force in the embrace which closed on her, that he was insensible of, that she felt with startled, wistful awe, half gladness and half fear; her heart shrank from it, and yet knew that this was greater love than the gentleness which she had always known. The doubting, wondering look of her lifted eyes, the instinctive movement with which she drew herself from his arms, wakened him to the knowledge of what he did, of what he said; to the memory of how his own words might betray him, of how, before all, above all, *she* must be spared. In the presence of Marion Vavasour his hand had no right even to touch her own! In that moment he could have flung himself down at her feet, and told her all, bidding her hate him, revile him, lay what vengeance and what misery she would on him, so that only there were no secret between them,—so that only she forgave him as her father had forgiven!

He loosed her from him, and his voice was broken and indistinct, while he dared not look upon her face, he dared not meet her eyes, though still he forced her out farther from that place, and nearer towards the pure day.

"I startled you—forgive me! This is no place for you; there is danger here, and evil," he murmured, incoherently.

"Come—come! Do you hear me! Come! You are too young for these dens of vileness!"

"They are only very poor!" she pleaded, softly, while her own words were tremulous, and her heart seemed stirred with the passion that for one moment had vibrated with such force in his. "The people know me well—and—and she suffers so much; let me stay with her a little while!"

He shivered under the gentle words which pleaded with such pity for the outcast lying there. He took her hands one moment and pressed them against his heart, that beat beneath them with loud laboured throbs.

"Oh, my love, my child! your life is too fair to be near mine—or hers—or any that sin has touched! You are pure as the angels; and we——! Come, for the mercy of Heaven, come! *I* bid you!"

A deep flush came on her face, her eyes looked at him wistfully, her lips trembled slightly; vaguely and sweetly, yet with something of pain and fear, she felt that the love which spoke now in his words was another than that which had sheltered her childhood. His will was her law, and with one pitying, lingering, backward glance to where the nameless stranger lay, she went with him, and was borne out by him into the tranquil noon, into the silence of the solitary woods. He knew nothing that he did; he had one instinct only, to force her from that presence as from some pestilential place, to carry her far away down to the fresh waters, into the depths of the fresh forests, anywhere—anywhere—from the search of that burning gaze, from the breath of that destroying life!

She did not move, she did not speak; once she looked upward at him with dark dreaming eyes; that was all; a strange solemnity, half of awe, half of terror, yet sweet beyond all words, seemed to thrill through all her life. She heard the quick, loud beatings of his heart; she felt herself borne on and on by his hand, as if by invisible wings, in silence through the bright sun-lightened forest aisles; alone with him, while the stillness of the great woods was round them, and beyond the glorious freedom of the sea lay flashing in the light.

His arms closed on her as though in their strength to hold her back from the vileness of the past that rose to smite her, his head drooped over her while hot tears fell upon the brightness of her brow, his eyes looked down with a yearning anguish into hers. All his life longed for her; and yet—love between *them!* Love while her father's splendour of manhood had fallen by his hand, and there, beyond the reddened wood, still lived the temptress and companion of his sin! He shuddered at it, he shrank from it as from fresh crime; yet his arms drew her nearer to him; his breath was on her cheek; the moment's instinct was stronger than himself, it shattered every other thought aside, and drove him on unconscious what he did, while all his heart went out to her in passionate pain:

"Oh, Lucille! my child! my treasure! my angel! my lips are not fit for yours; my life is not meet for yours, and yet—— Oh, God!—I love you!"

Her face grew white, he felt her tremble in his hold, she quivered like a delicate animal under a blow, and her eyes glanced up to him with a swift appealing glance, with all the deep and dreamy wonder of a heart freshly startled to its own knowledge. He pressed her closer yet in his embrace:

"My love you have ever had; but *another* love, Lucille;—the love of a husband for the life that is dearest to him on earth——"

His voice, broken into indistinctness, spoke more of tenderness than words can ever hold, and as she heard it, over her brow came a deep changing flush, a soft tremulous light, her lips parted with a quick sigh; a glory touched her life, in which the golden world of sea and sunlight reeled before her sight; her eyes sought his in one fleeting look, and his lips met her own in the kiss which they had never given, often as they had rested there;—the kiss of love. The choice was made;— her life was his for ever.

And there, at her feet, unnoted beneath the tangled grasses and the ivy-coils of the sea-shore, lay one forgotten grave, with the leaves covering the solitary word of record—

"Lucille."

Even while the gladness of morning glanced on the serenity of the waters, and on his own lips was the soft warmth of her first caress, a sudden icy chillness swept through all his veins, and he drew her with a passionate gesture closer to his bosom, farther into the forest solitudes. Their first love-words had been uttered by her mother's grave!

## CHAPTER XVIII.

"Ist auch Diess ein Irrthum, so schont mich, ihr klügeren Götter."

WHEN the night had fallen with its grey gloom of twilight, a shadow came towards the threshold of the cabin by the sea.

The hut was forsaken; the low peat fire burned dully on the hearth, casting a dusky, fitful gleam; on the pallet in the darkened corner the nameless wanderer lay, in blindness, in stupor, in feverish, restless pain. There was not a dog to watch her sleep, or to grieve for her now;—for her for whom once sovereigns had waited, by whom human love had once been gained and spent, and broken, idly and cruelly as a child wastes king-cups in a summer's day.

The shadow crossed the threshold, and the bare mud floor, and came towards her bed in the sullen crimson light; Strathmore stood and looked on her again, drawn there by a force he had no power to resist—the force that makes men their own accusers and avengers. He was alone, and she lay stretched unconscious at his feet.

Once he had said that vengeance had a sweetness which none could ever steal; now he knew that it may bring in its fruition, a pang as deadly for him that strikes, as for the stricken.

His eyes dwelt on her one moment in a long shuddering gaze, this life that was his own crime, incarnate, and ever pursuing him.

Was *this* the loveliness which had seemed immortal in its deathless splendour? Past him there floated, as in a dream, all the dazzling hours of her youth and his. The woman *he* had loved was dead; dead long years ago in the grave where their youth lay. *This* was not she; no more than the yellow faded leaf that, scentless and withered, is trodden in the dust and drifted down the wind, is the rose that yesterday swung in the light of palace-gardens! No more— no less!

He stood and looked on her under the black leaning roof of the hovel, while the sullen blasts poured down through the broken thatch, and the dull flame threw a weird flickering flash over the bed of straw and rough sand grasses. Those who have seen what they have cherished lie still and peaceful in the calm of death, have known an anguish that is mercy beside what he knew now. For he had loved her; with a love that would have given his very life for hers ungrudgingly; a love that now, in all its cheated crime-stained hate, still lived in passionate, hungered misery for all it once had been!

His vengeance had made her what she now was, and now, beholding it, he suffered in it as much as she. That sun-crowned glory of his past!—it was gone for ever; gone like the bloom from these white lips of pain, for whose kiss he once had staked his soul; like the lustre from these dull tangled tresses, whose golden light had once made all his world; like the empire from this ruined life, whose beauty lay before him bruised, shattered, torn, and perished for evermore. And a great agony came on him, mightier than vengeance, vaster than hatred, deep as remorse. He had loved her as never now could he love again—he had loved her, paying down the peace and guiltlessness of his whole life at her word. And freshly, as though dealt but yesterday, the blow of her faithlessness smote him; he could not look on her; he could not breathe near her; he staggered from her where she lay, and felt his way blindly and feebly out into the evening air—down into the core of the woods, where no eyes beheld him;—down to the silent shores, where no step came, and the grey sea stretched in solitude.

He had thought his strength as iron, and it was weaker than the reed. He had thought to mould fate like deity; and an outcast's life, saved by the wanton caprice of the waters, rose in his path inexorable as destiny.

Hours later on he returned to White Ladies by the side-door of the western wing. His step was slow, his proud head stooped and bent. Strathmore, to whose nature defeat had once seemed impossible, was vanquished, broken, netted in, in the meshes of his own past acts; and while an innocent life loved him and was pledged to his, the darkness of his own left him no fitness for its pure presence.

Marion Vavasour was once more in his fate; so near him that his own peasants sheltered her, that the woods of his own lands shut in the wretched shed where she harboured. And he could do nothing; he could not thrust her out from the beggars' charity she was given; he could not drive her from his home, and forbid those who succoured her to give her the pile of straw and cup of water that alone kept existence in her. Lord here though he was, and free to command what he would, he could not exile an outcast from the cabin of the poorest that lived upon his land! His hands were bound. She must haunt him as she would—there was no refuge. One thought alone remained to him. Lucille must leave him; she must not stay where the murderess of her father had once been in her sight, had once been *pitied* by her tender charity! What he had said to her, even in its sweetness, even in its first soft and forgetful moments, weighed heavily on him, with a sense as of evil committed, of danger drawn down on her. What right had he to her love? What right had he to have bound her life with his! Fear, misery, the instinct to save her from her father's destroyer, and a resistless longing impulse to tell her how he loved her, and take her to his heart to shield her there for ever, had hurried him in one unconscious instant into what had all the day through—what even still—seemed to him a sin and an impiety against the dead and her. The die was cast; yet none the less did the gain of her love seem crime in him, did the future that must unite their lives seem darkened and forbidden.

As his steps wearily paced the length of the long corridors, at a distance he saw her, alone in the conservatories, lying under the clusters of oriental foliage, with the great palm-leaves drooped above her, and the brilliancy of autumn flowers clustering at her feet. The white light shone on her, and on the careless grace, the dreaming joy, the abandoned happiness, the childlike rest of her repose, pure and without a shade; happiness so deep and new that it still trembled at itself, was still told in all her attitude, in the very droop of the lashes over her musing eyes, in the very smile that lingered on her parted lips, in the very flush that even in solitude was bright upon her cheek.

He had erred? Surely not, since she was happy through him!

As he approached, she started and raised her head; the light which would never dawn there save for him chased the thoughtfulness from her eyes; the colour deepened in her face; she sprang up, then paused with the wild, shy, delicate grace of the deer—in that moment she was so exquisitely fair! Doom to grief and loneliness that fairy child in the years of her earliest youth? It would have been as brutal as to stifle the young bird in the first music of its song, as to slay with a blow the trusting fawn as it looked up with earnest, lustrous gaze, and caressed the hand it followed!

He stretched out his arms to her, and forgot all save that her life was his to treasure and to guard:

"Oh! my child, my love, my darling! God send that

all pain falls on me; that none comes to thee through *my* love!"

With his accustomed measured step, Strathmore crossed the great length of the withdrawing-room, and approached the place where his mother sat alone; she looked up, and as the light fell upon his face, she saw a change on it, a great softness that changed its melancholy and its resolve.

Her thoughts were weary, the farewell of her young grandson had filled them with his grief; but in the presence of Strathmore she ceased to remember the sorrow, bitter but innocent, of youth, and a sudden fear fell on her: that look upon his face told her much.

Her son stood before her, and his words were very brief:

"Mother,—let the past be buried for ever. Lucille will be my wife."

"*Yours!*"

"Yes. Why not? Why not?"

His voice was defiant, almost fierce, as though challenging the power which should dispute his will and sever them.

"Why? *You* ask that, Cecil?"

She had risen, and fronted him; in her eyes the pitilessness which he had inherited with her blood, on her face the coldness which in her earlier years had been unchastened and unsoftened.

The words struck Strathmore keenly as a knife; his head bowed, his lips quivered—this man bent silent and without defence before the sternest and most unsparing cruelty of words which rebuked him with his sin.

"Have pity!—for her sake!"

His voice trembled in its humbled prayer; and his mother's heart smote her for the stripes with which she had struck him where he was defenceless. She laid her hand softly on his shoulder, her face no longer stern, but blanched with a great horror.

"Forgive me, forgive me! But, oh, my son, it cannot be, it must not be——"

"It *shall* be."

She knew the tone of old; the inflexible will of the Strathmores of White Ladies, than which iron were easier to bend, fire were easier to cross; and she was silent. This marriage! She shuddered from it as from some great sin, from some inevitable evil; yet—she had no power to avert it, no power to arrest it; she could not turn traitress to her son, she could not unfold to the life which was centred in his, the history which would be its surest death-blow?

"It shall be—who shall prevent it?" said Strathmore, and his voice rose slightly louder. "My own peace I would sacrifice, my own life I would give up—what I had suffered would have mattered nothing—but hers I will never surrender. That course is right which most shields her. I swore to keep her years from every grief; I will redeem my oath. Shall *I* strike her? shall *I* curse her? Where would be the atonement I vowed to her father? Would he bid me destroy her young life? Would he see expiation to himself in her misery through the very love which he bade me foster? To whom, had he now been living, would he have given her so gladly as to me?"

The swift, imperious, resolved passion in his voice ceased suddenly, his lips quivered again; he thought with what gladness and what faith Lucille, drawing closer the bond of their brotherhood, would have been trusted to his keeping as to the friend best known and best beloved, by the man whom he had slain, had he been living now!

His mother looked at him; and her courage failed her to pierce by one added sting the wound laid open so deeply and bared without defence. She knew that his decision, once declared, was unalterable; she could not dispute it, or persuade it, and there was truth in what he said, that to consign to bitterness the young and joyous years of Lucille, were to cancel all that had been done as obedience to the dead, and leave worse than unfulfilled the office bequeathed him. Yet —he her husband—he!

She shuddered, and her hands locked close upon his arm.

"Strathmore! Strathmore!—wait. If she should ever know——"

His face grew whiter for the moment; the thought froze his very heart.

"Know! She *cannot*. No living soul could find a trace of her birth."

Her hand leant heavier on his arm, and her voice was sunk to a tremulous whisper:

"But is crime ever buried? It sleeps, but it is never dead; and oh, my son, my son! its prey is so often the innocent!"

He laughed—a hopeless laugh, bitterly, bitterly sad.

"What! even *you*,—my mother!—deny that my guilt can reach atonement! Then remorse is a fool's travail, and the sinner must live for ever in the hell he has made to himself! It is a harsh law—still—not harsher than *I* merit."

The despair in his voice recoiled back on her own heart, and her eyes filled with tears, the slow, salt tears of age.

"Cecil, my son, my son! would *I* condemn you? Remorse is holy to God, sacred in man. The prayer of my life is that yours may be blessed. But—but—I confess it, for *you* to wed her——"

"Peace!" broke in Strathmore, with passionate force. "We have said enough. My resolve is taken; my hand is pledged; Lucille will be mine. Let us never speak again of what we have spoken to-night. Seek her, the innocent child! rejoice with her, give her tenderness, give her love. Henceforth you must show her that she is more to you than she has ever been."

With these brief words of command, rather than of entreaty, he bowed low with his distant and punctilious courtesy, and left her presence; his mother knew that what he had chosen was irrevocable.

"You love him so well, my darling?" she said, softly, that night; and as Lucille's head was raised for one swift moment, and her face uplifted in its shy joy, the aged and world-worn woman who looked on her ceased to wonder that he bade the dead past lie sealed within its grave, and sought to shield for ever in his own bosom the dawning life which had known but the cloudless sunlight of childhood till it awakened to the richer, deeper lustre of its future.

Yet the shadow of the past was on her; and she dreaded it.

On the morrow he left for Paris, and Lucille, with his mother, quitted White Ladies.

He could not wait there, could not have *her* stay there, while in that cabin on the shore Marion Vavasour lay, tendered by beggars' charity!

## CHAPTER XIX.

### "And Unforgiving, Unforgiven."

It was twilight as Strathmore paced slowly up and down one of the deserted allées of the Bois de Boulogne, while the fallen leaves were strewn beneath his feet, and the shades of the night drew on: he waited for Valdor.

The fiery Henri Cinquiste, rarely given to prudence, had now a value and sweetness in his life too great to let him risk it rashly; and he was proscribed in Paris, and could only venture out when evening fell. Strathmore waited for him, pacing the long aisle under the red-brown boughs, hanging stirless in heavy air;—the same allée where, in the years that were gone, in the amber sunlight he had watched the speeding of his vengeance as the Discrowned had passed through her long pilgrimage of insult and of outrage.

In the twilight a man's form came swiftly towards him, and he saw in the rapidity of the step, and the look, which by the still lingering light he could read upon his face, with what joyous and fearless hope Valdor came to the meeting.

For him he felt the deepest pity he had ever known; Strathmore now grieved sincerely and unselfishly for the grief of another. The tenderness of his own love for Lucille had softened the coldness of his heart; it had made him humane—it had made him compassionate. He was in no wise blamable towards Valdor; on the contrary, he had fulfilled his word, and acted with the strictest justice and generosity in his dealing with the cause of his absent rival; and yet he felt something of self-reproach for the hope which, in honourable though erroneous belief, he had been the one to confirm, and which he must now be also the one to destroy.

With glad eagerness Valdor came up to him, and Strathmore held out his hand with the generous cordiality of his earlier years; but, as he met his eyes, the coldness of a sudden and unlooked-for dread came over the French Noble: he saw in them a look wholly new there—the look of *pity*.

"Tell me the worst at once, Strathmore," he said, quickly. "I cannot bear suspense. Is it——"

Strathmore, in the simple impulse of a genuine sympathy, turned from him as he answered, and his voice was gentle and mellow:

"It is I who am to blame, though, God knows, I believed honestly what I told you. Forgive me; I misled you, you misled yourself, Valdor."

He did not look upon the face of the man to whom he was compelled to deal so deadly a wound, but he heard the quick, sharp catch of his breath.

"Is there no hope?"

His voice was husky and inarticulate; that which answered him was tender and compassionate.

"None. I grieve that I ever deceived you."

They stood together under the yellow autumn trees, and, looking on him now, Strathmore saw how keen and mortal was his pain. Valdor had forgotten all in that moment, save the bitter, sudden desolation which struck down all the tender and vivid hope that he had cherished, until it had become well-nigh as sweet to him and as sure as certainty.

He turned, and walked swiftly up and down the allée with his head bent for some seconds; he could not bear that another man should look on what he felt. His belief had been so strong that his love was returned!—and the hot ardour of a Southern's passion was blended with the chivalrous tenderness in which he held her, till the thought of Lucille had become the core and the soul of his life.

He paused suddenly before Strathmore, and in the gloom his cheek was pale, and his lips worked painfully, while in his eyes and his air there was a hot and haughty defiance.

"She loves another?"

Strathmore looked steadily at him, and in his gaze there was a deep compassion still; he grieved honestly and generously for the pain before him.

"She does."

"Who is he?"

There was menace in Valdor's answering glance: his own sudden sharpness of anguish made him unjust, and his fiery anger rose in revolt against his unknown rival.

Strathmore looked at him, and spoke with a rare and singular sympathy in the gentleness of his voice; the young love of Lucille lay warm in his heart, and made him more merciful to all men, specially so to those who had sought her in vain.

"Valdor, hear me first. What I said to you I honestly believed, or I had never spoken it. I thought that Lucille loved you. I told her word for word what you desired me. I did your cause every justice—you know me, and you know that I should do so. I give you my word of honour, that I dreamt as little as yourself that I should have now to tell you what——"

"*Who* is loved by her?"

The question broke fiercely and swiftly in upon his words; suspicion flashed on him, for the glance of her rejected lover saw the altered look which had come upon Strathmore's face since the night when they had parted beneath the palms, a look of light, of rest, of relief, of something that was *almost* happiness.

"I am."

"You!"

They faced each other in the twilight, and their eyes met. Strathmore's face was calm, filled still with much of compassion, and free to all scrutiny, for to Valdor's cause he had done his duty honourably and fully, and he deserved no reproach at his hands. Valdor's was deeply flushed; there was danger in it, and the tumult of a jealous passion.

"You! God in heaven, then you lied to me!"

Strathmore's face grew dark; the lightning leapt to his eyes for a second—only for that,—he could make extenuation and have patience here, and there was nothing harsher than a proud and just dignity in his look and in his words:

"In a calmer moment you will see you do me injustice. It would not be possible for any man who knows my name to accuse me of cowardice or dishonour. I kept my word to you strictly; it was an after hazard which revealed to me what when we parted I dreamt as little as you."

"She loves you!—*you!*"

There was something almost of terror and incredulity, mingled with the jealousy, with which he stood before Strathmore in the gloom of the early night. Strathmore bent his head; some passion was rising in him, and he would not allow it rein; with the soft touch of Lucille's lips in their first kiss, gentleness had stolen into his heart, and wakened compassion in him towards those who suffered.

"And you—you return it? you allow it? you will wed her?"

A haughty anger passed over Strathmore's face:

"Assuredly. I shall become her husband."

As he spoke the words, the winds, slowly rising, swept up with a hollow and melancholy moan through the dying leaves of the autumn trees.

Valdor looked at him, the blood staining his face, his breath thick and laboured, his words stifled in his throat:

"*Her husband!* Never, if I live! You have betrayed me, and you shall renounce all thought of her!"

Strathmore's teeth clenched, but he strove to hold down his wrath, and he succeeded; it was with a melancholy and proud forbearance, the more worthy that it was so alien to his nature, that he answered now:

"Those are strange words, but you have a right to feel bitterly, and I must wait till with reflection and time you do me more justice. I can but give you my word that I acted in honour and honesty to you, while I had no thought that her love——"

"Her love, *hers!* I swear to Heaven you shall renounce such an unhallowed, unnatural, forbidden union," cried Valdor, wildly and blindly, with imperious command. "Strathmore! listen to me. I may never wed her, but neither shall you. I forbid such a marriage, I arrest it; you shall renounce it to-night and for ever!"

"You! Are you a madman?"

He spoke calmly yet, but the forbearance was passing from his soul and the pitying tranquillity from his face, though the meaning of the words he heard did not as yet dawn on him, for he deemed the secret too safely buried to be ever brought to light; no living being knew Lucille as Erroll's child.

Valdor drew nearer still to him, his hot blood up, his eyes lit with dangerous menace, his pain blinding him to all memory, save that the man before him was his rival, who had robbed him of what he loved.

"*I* arrest it, *I* forbid it! By the God above us you shall never be the husband of Lucille."

Strathmore's arms were folded with his habitual attitude across his chest, and his eyes looked steadily into the face of Valdor, in the deepening of the night.

"*You* forbid it?—and how?"

"I shall tell her that you were the murderer of her father."

The words broke, abrupt and hideous, on the silence,— Strathmore started, his face grew white in the grey gloom, and into his eyes came a terrible hunted agony; was he ever to strive towards peace, and ever to have it shattered from his grasp? He lost the strength, the memory, the calm which might still, at cost of truth, have baffled his accuser; any who had looked on him then would have pitied to their heart's core the man whose haughtiest pride, whose humblest remorse, were alike powerless to wash out and to atone for a repented past: any,—save one who loved where he loved!

"You—you——" he gasped; then his voice died, his dread, his anguish were less for himself than they were for her whose death-blow would be the knowledge of his crime.

Valdor looked on him *without* pity, for the evil spirit of a jealous passion possessed him, and while it reigned darkened his heart, and drove thence all compassion, all mercy, all generous chivalry to his rival.

"Ay! Here, where you slew him, I swear she shall know that the hand which she would caress as her husband's, took the life which gave her own. Will she wed you *then?* Ask yourself!"

"Wed me—you would be her death!"

His voice was filled with a fearful misery, for it was her life which hung in the balance and not his alone. He had no thought to mislead the man who thus accused him; for his strength had broken down before the sudden danger, and the nature of Strathmore, when the world had not warped it, was instinctively truth; truth, be temptation, or cost what they might.

"Her death! Better that than marriage with her father's assassin!" broke in Valdor, bitterly, in his despair he grew cruel and reckless. "If you would spare her, renounce that; swear to me that never, whether I live or die, shall Lucille be your wife, or I arrest your union at any cost, by letting her know you as you are. She is the daughter of Erroll; she shall hear how he fell by the hand of the friend he trusted more than a brother!"

Strathmore quivered like a woman who is dealt a brutal blow; he was struck where his strength was paralysed, he was wounded where he had no shield. In the reality of his remorse, he held the vilest words which could scourge his sin but his due chastisement, to be taken in silence and submission; and here he had no force, no defiance, no power, for *she* was menaced! And for her he stooped as for himself he would have never done.

He stood before Valdor, his head drooped, his face livid, his hands outstretched in the first prayer of supplication to which he had ever bent to any living man.

"Your words are bitter, but *I* merit them; were they a thousandfold harder I should have no title to resent them. I, 'a murderer!' I am at your mercy, so is she; I would not ask it for myself, but for her—for her."

His voice dropped inarticulate, with strong effort he commanded it, and spoke again, lifting his head with the dignity natural to him, touchingly mingled with the self-humiliation so alien to his nature.

"You have my secret; measure my thirst for expiation by the vileness of my crime—it is as great, greater it could not be! She was his trust to me; in her peace, her life, lies my sole power of atonement to him. For the love of God, spare me *that!* By your power, be generous! By your tenderness to her, do not deal her her death-blow! She is innocent, would you strike her?—destroy her?—curse her soul with that deadly tale of vilest guilt? Not as rival to rival, but as man to man I implore you. Have mercy—not to me, not to *me*—but to her!"

Not in the most victorious hours of his powerful oratory had his eloquence been so true as now, when it lay but in the broken, hollow words of a great agony—his haughty nature bent and stricken, his guilt confessed, his soul laid bare.

Alas! he who else had been swiftest to be touched and won by the prayer of a proud life laid subject, here was blind, and steeled, and without pity in that hour, for—he loved.

"Renounce your marriage, and she shall not know her father's blood is on your hands."

In the gloom of the night the words fell from the lips of the man who had his secret; and Strathmore learned the bitterness that lies in mercy denied to extremity.

"Renounce! I cannot! *My* peace I would surrender, *my* life you should have to torture as you would, I have no claim to pity, no right to joy!—but I cannot give up hers, I cannot leave her forsaken, insulted, her youth embittered, her life more than widowed! My God! it is *her* happiness that is my solitary atonement to her father. Wreck that! by my own hand, my own consent! Are you brute or man that you ask it? Would you be nearer her love because she were divorced by me?"

The blood stained Valdor's face, and on it came no pity.

"Renounce her!" he said, fiercely, "or she shall know you as you are!"

"You are resolved?"

"Yes, by the God above us!"

"So be it—do your worst!"

Then Strathmore lifted his head and stood erect; he pleaded no more, and on his face, calm now, the look of iron pride, of chill tranquillity—the look which was evil—had returned. It was his special and unhappy fate that whenever he strove—strove earnestly—towards better things and gentler thoughts, there circumstance arose and turned him backward into darkness, and denied him to rise into the purer light.

In the night which had now only descended they fronted one another, the fiery menace of his foe met by a cold and fathomless defiance; and in Strathmore's eyes, although the memory of him whom he had slain yonder in the poisonous gloom beside the old deer-water, still lay like a sacred chain binding down his passions, there was a glance dangerous to the man who had driven him to extremity. Then, without word or sign, he turned away from him and went slowly through the avenue, with his arms folded on his breast, while Valdor, with swift, uneven steps, swept onward, whither he cared not and knew not, into the dark sear woodland of the deserted place.

Fear need have followed him close as his shadow; he had wronged, and denied, and stung to extremity, when it was abased, and unveiled, and suppliant, a nature which never forgave.

## CHAPTER XX.
### Evil done that Good may come.

THE knowledge that Valdor held the secret which, once told, must part for ever Lucille's life from his, left Strathmore stunned like a man felled by an unseen blow on the brain. He had believed that no living soul could find trace of her birth, and the stroke fell suddenly and without warning, paralysing the hand which had deemed its strength strong to all control of circumstance. He was wound beyond escape in the folds of fate, as the Laöcoon in the serpent coils. And the sickening sense of *powerlessness*—the most terrible torture, I think, which this world holds, certainly the most terrible to one whose will is forcible, and whose habit is to rule —tightened about him, and stifled his very life.

He lost all sense, save that of an impotent despair, in which he tore at his bonds and writhed beneath the retribution of his past; a maddened, feverish agony, under whose goad all the evil of his nature rose, a giant in its desperation. His own life he would have flung down a prey to any fate that could have seized it; but hers!—there was no sin that Strathmore would have shrunk from to ward off from her fair and sacred innocence the dark curse of his buried crime.

It left him no more than the sheer wild instinct of self-preservation, such as that on which men and brutes act in a moment of supreme and hideous peril. His calm had been shattered, he had lost that keen acumen which in statecraft placed him beyond rival—that cool, clear wisdom which led him, unerring, to men's every weakness and every impulse. Else, had he judged more truly of his foe; else, had he known that—his swift Southern passion once bated—justice and mercy would have revived in Valdor, and his hand would have withheld the blow which could not have avenged him, save by striking at the one whom he loved most gently and most chivalrously. It was not in the nature of the French Noble to be merciless or cruel; a generous repentance followed swiftly on every thought or act of passion—it did so now.

The jealousy of a love which, at the very moment of its sweetest hope, had been denied and dashed to earth, had goaded him for the hour into hatred and resolution inexorable as those of the man they menaced. He saw in Strathmore but the rival who had robbed him; he wronged him, in the hot haste of a bitter disappointment, by the belief that he had betrayed the embassy entrusted to him; he grasped, in the desperation of his love, at the revenge which would sunder her for ever from the lover who stood before him. And for the hour Valdor was blind with that passion which makes men devils; and was without pity for him who had been pitiless.

But, as the grey morning dawned, and the day rolled on, through whose dreary length he was chained to his chamber for the sake of the cause which he served, lest his presence should be known in Paris, the selfish spirit left him, and the nobler regained its hold. The bitterness relaxed, with which he had been drunk as with raki, till humanity was deadened by it, and no thought was left him but revenge; justice came back to him, and all the softer thoughts of a love which was essentially pure and true arose, and made him shrink from a vengeance which must strike at *her*. His heart smote him for the mercilessness with which he had been steeled to the prayer of the proud nature which had stooped to plead, and to the remorse which had been laid bare before him in its anguish for expiation. He saw that, as great as had been the crime of this man, so was his repentance sacred; his conscience recoiled from undoing the labour of such repentance, from destroying the innocent with the sin of the guilty, from smiting him who strove towards a just atonement with the deeds of his own past.

He knew how Lucille loved Strathmore, for he had studied that love, and feared it, till a false hope had blinded him with its traitor-sweetness. He knew now how the man whom the world called heartless and conscienceless, had been scourged by the flail of remorse, and had centred his sole power of restitution in one young frail life. And the nobler nature wrestled in him with that which was more evil, and overthrew the baser. "His remorse is holy—it is not for me to touch it. Had she loved me I should have reverenced his secret; because her love is his, shall I turn traitor?" This was the true instinct of a gallant heart; and as the long brown autumn day ended and night stole near, he rose armed with such strength as men may best bring to meet the bitterness of cheated hope and joy dashed down for ever, and went out into the falling twilight to say this, and this only, to him whom Lucille loved.

And as he felt the first cool rush of the evening wind, and left the solitude of his chamber for the chilly yellow night, a shadow stole towards him, and he was arrested—a State Prisoner.

In the stillness of that midnight Strathmore stood beside the tomb where deep in the stainless marble was carved the record of his crime. The white autumn mists were heavy on the air, the winds sighed among the long grass that blew above Erroll's grave, and the gold-leaved boughs of the dying trees swayed over the stone where he was lain in the dark dank earth—forgot by all save one.

Strathmore stood there beside the resting-place of the man whom he had slain in all the noon and glory of his manhood; and his heart was sick with the deadly pain of the past, and with the burden of the future. For evil had seized *both*. And the sin-taint from that which was gone, breathed over, and reached, and poisoned the fair years ungrasped.

He knew that the past, once told, would be as surely

death to her as the touch of poison or the breath of pestilence; he knew that Lucille, living but in his love, would be smitten more gently by the fellest disease that ever seized the loveliness of youth, than by the words which should bid her see in him who sought her with a husband's tenderness the destroyer of those who gave her birth. It was not his own passion, his own peace, his own joy; not the shelter of his crime, or the years of his future, or the desire of his soul which was at the stake and in the balance—*these* he would have given up a prey to any fate, a meet sacrifice to any vengeance that befel him; what were in jeopardy were *hers* —his trust from the man whom he had loved as David loved the son of Saul, whom he had slain as Cain slew the son of Eve.

She must be spared.

This was the sole thought, the sole sense that was left him. He had been denied mercy. And, swift as naphtha to flame, under the torture, all the worst in him leapt to life. With that denial his resolve was taken, blind, and knowing neither how nor when its way would be pioneered, but fixed and inflexible—the resolve to silence at any cost, at any peril, the rival whose knowledge of his secret menaced Lucille. Alas for him! Strathmore had not yet learned that it is not given to man to mould the shape and way of fate at will, and that to do evil that good may come, is but to add sin to sin, sepulchre to sepulchre.

When he left his foe in the still autumn night his will was set, forged to iron in the fires of an agonised and imminent terror. Crime itself looked holy in his sight if for her, and all that could save *her* was justified to him. And he had ever in him too much of the passionate imperious Cæsarian choice: "Let him murder, but let him reign!"

Yet, it had been truly said of him, "A bad man sometimes, a dangerous man always, but a false man—never." He recoiled from the sole means of preservation which rose within his grasp as he would from some dastard poison with which he had been tempted to still the foe who held his secret. Strathmore, guilty in much, and cruel where his will was crossed, had no taint of the traitor in him. Great crimes might stain him, but baseness or perfidy had no lodging in his nature. His creed of honour was lofty, knightly, unsullied—the creed of the stately nobles whose blood was in his veins—and an act that even drew nigh the vileness of betrayal was loathsome, and had ever been impossible to him.

Yet here, in the blindness of dread, in the suddenness with which he saw Lucille threatened, and knew that he must either silence the lips which could breathe his secret, or see her life destroyed—here, there rose but one means of salvation for her, and to shield her he grasped it. Anything, I have said, looked just to him which should be done to save the innocent from the burden of his guilt; all, that for himself he would have withstood, grew to him a resistless tempting, a sin righteous and imperative, when it stood out before him as the sole force by which he could rescue her from destruction by his own hand—the hand pledged to her as her husband's.

The ordeal was fearful to him. His soul recoiled from evil, and, "as the hart panteth for the water-springs," thirsted for peace—peace of heart, peace of conscience. And it escaped him—ever, ever. He was driven on and on unceasing—forced to sin that the innocent might be saved, forced to do evil that good might come.

His influence was not seen in his work; none knew that his mind had conceived it; silently, wisely, with a master's finesse, with an unerring skill the web was woven, the mine was sprung, by means the subtlest yet simplest; a word, a hint—nay! scarce so much—and the State hounds were set on the slot of Henry Cinq's Royals. Strathmore had known the projects of that too frank and too chivalrous party; a thread dropped which could not be traced to him, a suggestion lent which could not involve its speaker, a counsel given which was but the well-advised warning of a foreign minister to a friendly court; and he who had been so rash in the bitterness of cheated love as to menace one who never spared friend in his path, and never aimed save to strike home, was flung into a State prison, where the loyal heart would consume in silence, and the knightly spirit would break in solitude, till the cell should be changed for the galley bench of the Bagne or the malarious swamp of Cayenne.

Strathmore had wrought the ruin of the man who had braved him—wrought it with the subtle, yet passionate and unfaltering will with which his race destroyed whatever was bold enough, and mad enough, to cross their road, and oppose their power. But his soul had revolted from it, and in it he had endured for Lucille what for no other stake he would have suffered. He would have refused to save himself by such a cost; he paid it to save her. He, whose honour his foulest enemies could not impeach, knew himself false to the man who had placed faith in him; the cowardice of betrayal tainted, in his own sight and his own knowledge, the act by which his rival and his foe had been given up to a doom not less inexorable, scarce less cruel, than the grave; for the single time in a long life, which, unscrupulous, pitiless, and darkly stained, had yet never been soiled with one unknightly taint, he knew himself a traitor to his trust, a traitor to his creed.

And he stood there beside the tomb of the dead man for whose sake he had done this thing.

"Traitor! traitor!" said Strathmore, in his teeth, and in his eyes was a terrible wistful misery as they gazed down on the black grass that grew thick above Erroll's grave. "I only needed to be *that!* Heaven help me! I said her life should be before my own. So it has been, so it shall be. It is done for *your* sake, in *your* trust. Oh, God! surely for you, though not for me——"

Not for himself—never for himself—but for the dead whom he loved, and the hallowed life that he guarded, surely, he thought, the work of his expiation would not fail at the last!

Following the consequence that links one sin on to another, he had plunged headlong down into additional crime; as a man, having once set his foot into the loose quicksands, is drawn step by step, lower and lower, powerless to wrench himself free from the devouring mass, sinking farther and farther, locked in and sucked downward till he is lost for ever, while the sun is bright above-head, and the horrors of the grave yawn for him alone—for him by whom one false step first was made.

In the very hour when all his heart ached with its yearning for a purer life; in the very moment when he had taken to himself the treasure and the trust of another existence to be bound in his own, in the very instant when all that was vile in him seemed to have fallen away, and he had sworn to consecrate such years as might remain to him, to unremitting effort to assoil his life, and give it such worthiness as he could still reach, to be in union with Lucille's—in that very instant temptation had again assailed him, and he had fallen beneath it; crime had again come ready to his hand, and he had stretched out his hand and taken its iniquitous aid, its shameful succour. Were the idle myths of superstition true, were the fables of benighted priests real, he asked himself, with cruel self-mockery and self-reviling; and had he sold his soul to some fiend of darkness that he could never make his escape from sin, but always seized it and became one with it like this? Was he devil-possessed that he could never resist the guilt he loathed, but was forced down into it, and dwelt, as though he loved it, always in some deeper depth of its pollution, some closer bond of its fellowship and communion?

No man living on earth could have hated him, as he hated himself. No man have thought his infamy so deeply damned, as he himself knew it to be. The act that had made him a murderer, was scarce so vile in Strathmore's sight, as the act that made him a traitor!

He had saved her—but at what a cost! For her he would have given his life at any hour; but he had given far more now.

His oath had been to sacrifice all things past, and present, and future, to the keeping of her father's trust; and the fulfilment of his oath had become more than the sacrifice of mere existence: it was the acceptance of a long and living martyrdom —the martyrdom, not of renunciation, which guiltless may bring strength to its own torture, but one that could have no such solace—the martyrdom of shame! Shame! none the less, but the more, because like his doom, it was unknown and unchastised by man.

Traitor!

The word sounded in his ear night and day; it lay like a curse upon his name; it mocked him in his memory with every honourable phrase that others uttered to or wrote of him; when he went among his peers he knew himself not fit to have place near them; when their unstained hands met his, or their frank words applauded him, he knew that if they could tell the infamy that was upon him, they would leave his presence as they would leave any blackguard's who had robbed their treasuries—he had been false to all the dignity of his order, to all the honour of his manhood. He knew it; the open scorn of Europe could not have made him know it more terribly. Strathmore—in all his guilt a man who held, with all the loyalty of a proud nature, and the ingrained instinct of a patrician creed, to the most stringent laws of honour; a man who, in all his worst errors would never by nature have become false, but who would have cut off his right hand rather than have sullied his lips with a lie, or betrayed the meanest thing that crawled if it had once trusted him—suffered in the consciousness of disgrace, in the enforced shame of this sin so alien to his every instinct and his every act, a torture which beggared all that life had ever brought him.

It might have been less terrible if he could have suffered openly for it; for with every time that he took the world's homage, every time that he moved amongst his own order, he felt himself afresh a traitor against it and them—letting them honour what *he* knew dishonoured. His nature, more-

over, was one to give itself up without appeal to all the
chastisement that was his due; and here no hand chastised,
no voice upbraided, and no judges stoned him; what he had
done was unknown, unseen, and he was compelled to go to
what *was* joy, even all darkened and tainted as it was; joy
that he was conscious by every justice should never have been
his. He had to go to the sweetness of Lucille's tender words,
to the caress of her young lips, to the beauty of her reverent
and happy love; he had to go to all these things that make
earth while they last an Eden, with the knowledge in his
heart that turned them into bitterness. It was this loveliness
waiting for him as reward for the treachery he had wrought,
this happiness given to him as recompense for his sin, that
made him seem to himself a thousand times more loathsome.
If he had done this thing to save her, while giving her to
another's arms in his own sacrifice, he might have forgiven
it to himself in some faint measure; but now although no
thought, no memory of self had prompted him to it, although
it had been done simply and solely *for her*, the joy that came
to him through it made it beyond all pardon in his sight. And
it had a tenfold anguish, striking him back into the darkness
of accumulated guilt at the moment when some beam of light,
some ray of peace had strayed in on him; when with the love
of Lucille he had vainly dreamt of regained tranquillity, of
joy that would come to him out of her joy, of a purer happiness that might still be his, of a better life in which his later
years might take their fairer hue from hers, and be spent
with her in the effort towards nobler things. This hope, this
dream, had come to him with the treasure of her innocent
affection; it was gone for ever now. He almost dreaded the
gaze of her eyes; he almost shuddered from the touch of
her lips.

For the sin that he had sinned for her was heavy on him;
and he had gained her by the crime of an Iscariot.

There is no guilt so terrible to him by whom it is done
as the guilt that is *abhorrent* to the nature which yet stoops
to it.

Late in the fall of an autumn evening he reached Silver-rest to meet her for the first time since he had done this last thing for her sake; in so utter yet so erring a sacrifice. The twilight was darkening over sea and land, though here in the sheltered south, flowers still blossomed and woods were still in full leaf. A little while,—and when he had parted from her, in the sweetness of her love he had thought that there might still be in some sort peace for him, and pardon for his past; he had thought that the future might still bring him some blessing, through her, and through the trust so loyally, so passionately obeyed. *Now*—he shrank from her presence; he had not right or title to one shadow of the tenderness she gave him; he felt that what he had done for her must, soon or late, bring its own punishment, that in *his* embrace even her own angel-like beauty must be tainted, her own fair God-given life be doomed and destroyed with his!

All the wild untamable nature in him suffered now;—suffered, flinging down like film the philosophy of his creeds, the languor of his world, the egotism of his habits; suffered with the dumb agony of an animal, the blind pain of an untutored barbarian. Nature was stronger even now than all the force of intellect, custom, sophism, and reason.

He believed at last in his own utter weakness; he believed at last that he could not command oblivion.

He paused now, as he went to where they told him that she was, in the stillness of the twilight, on the wooded shores of Silver-rest. He longed for her with unutterable longing, yet he dreaded to see her as he had never dreaded any thing on earth; a chill tremor passed over him, and he stopped to still the beating of his heart. He would have gone to the scaffold like Montrose or Derwentwater with unmoved serenity, without his pulse quickening its throb one instant;—now going to one who revered him almost as a deity, and for whose sake he had wrought the iniquity he loathed, he shook like a woman in every limb, and paused, as in the days of Hellas, the guilt-stricken paused before the threshold of the sacred temple they dared not enter.

Yet;—he must smile on her as though no chasm lay between them; he must look down into her trustful eyes; he must take her life into his own; he must become her husband. Was it not for this, this only that he had sinned?

In that moment he recoiled from his offered joy as he would never have recoiled from death. In that moment—once again—to lose her, or to wed her, seemed alike an anguish passing his strength. The brown still depths of leaves enclosed him, there was no light about his steps, the lull of silence was oppressive, the chiar'oscuro of the falling evening was only broken by the deeper blackness of some towering rock that lowered through the gloom; he paused there, hearing only the beating of his own heart; the darkness was like the darkness on his years, that had no place beside the bright spotlessness of hers. Then, with a sudden gesture, almost of despair, he dashed back the boughs, that parted them with that black barrier, as his own acts parted them in his own sight. He saw her there; in a flood of warmth from the setting sun that found its way about her, and bathed her in its halo, as, in the Old Masters, the Children of God are bathed in light; the crimson shafts of the red rocks slanting upward till they were lost in hanging wreaths of mist; the scarlet and golden foliage encircling her; at her feet the violet waves of the calm waters; and full on her face the lustre of the dying sun's rays as they poured down from the west. Coming from the shadow of the gloomy woods, he saw her in that glory of radiance, pure as her life, radiant as her smile, divine as her innocence. What place had he beside her? With a great unconscious cry, that in that moment forgot all that must be sealed and silent for her sake, he threw himself before her ere she knew that he was near; there, at her feet, in that sunlit luminance that never now could touch his own dishonoured life, emblem of the peace and beauty he had for ever flung away; his arms about her, his head sunk in a suppliant's entreaty, his burning lips upon the hands he clasped.

"Oh! my child!—my treasure!—my darling! I have come

back to you, but my life has no fitness for yours. And yet—oh, God!—I have given you more than my life; I have suffered for you more than a hundred deaths; I have denied you nothing; I have lost for you all I had left on earth. Love me, for the pity of Heaven! love me, come what will! It is for you that I have sinned, for you only that I live——"

The wild words died almost in their utterance, stifled in his throat, as he knelt before her, his head bowed, his arms thrown round her in the passion, less of an embrace than of an agonised prayer and supplication. The last, only, reached her ear; the last which told her it was for her alone he lived, and which implored her tenderness. Vaguely, with a great terror, mingling with the dizzy sweetness of his sudden presence, she felt that he suffered, she saw that his life had a misery in it untold, unconfessed; and the love, greater still than all fear in her, and far deeper than her young years, gave her its truest instinct;—she had no thought of herself; she only felt that *he* suffered. Her soft lips, with a tremulous hesitance, met his in their first self-offered kiss, her eyes with a dark dreamy lustre gazed into his own through tears that rose but did not fall; her voice was broken with a deeper music than it had ever known:

"Ah, my lord! my love! have you yet to learn that my life is yours, and that your death will be mine?"

The words were few, and very low; but there was an accent in them that told that this, and nothing less than this, was the love she bore him; in the golden light and scarlet foliage that circled her, the radiance from the western skies shone in her eyes and bathed her still in its bright aureole, as though loth to leave a thing so fair to the cold shadows of the night. Looking upward he saw her thus in the warm glory from the evening rays;—sin should not have been *her* saviour! He knew it now.

He had sacrificed to her all he valued upon earth; he had beggared himself more utterly than poverty could have beggared him when, for her sake, he had lost Honour;—at the last, would even this be done in vain?

"Evil done that good may come." Rash and unhallowed work which tampers with the Unseen, and sows the poison-seeds that the golden fruit may bloom;—at the core of the fruit will not the poison ever be found?

Yet if the cause of any earthly life could have justified that touching of unfolded destiny, hers would have been that one; hers which he deemed he had done justly to spare at *any* cost, as he looked on her in her loveliness, and met the sweet, shy, half-veiled joy of her fair eyes.

His approaching marriage was made public, and the world saw nothing save that which was most natural in it. There was, true, some wide disparity of years between them; but then he had altered so little in person from what he had been at thirty, and had an eminence of so brilliant a fame, that the world felt no wonder that in his maturity of prime and of power he should have fascinated, and been fascinated by, the beautiful youth of his ward. Once pledged to it, on the impulse of a moment that had been stronger than himself, he hastened his marriage with the least delay that was possible —hastened it with a restless, fevered impatience that shared far more in the disquiet of dread than in the softer anxiety of passion. The knowledge that one lived who knew his secret filled him with a ceaseless and bitter fear ever gnawing at his peace; *he* was silenced, from the grip that held him, Valdor would never again be free to come forth and lift up the veil that hung before that ghastly past; yet, that this secret should be in the power of one living man, however that man were stricken powerless, filled with the deadly unrest of an ever-conscious, never-banished dread, the heart which, through a long life, had never learned before what it was to *fear*. In Lucille's presence this was lulled, in her absence it fastened on him resistlessly with a haunting, nameless terror. For Marion Vavasour, too, lived!—of her he could learn nothing, save that she had recovered in the peasant's hut that had given her shelter, and had gone from White Ladies; gone none knew whither;—she lived, though lost in the desert of the world. Danger had risen once; never more could he feel secure it would not rise again, not again to be thus grappled with and hurled down before its touch could reach Lucille. It was this which made him hasten his marriage to its earliest; he felt that her life was unsafe until placed beyond the power of man to sever from him, until guarded by him with the title and the power of a husband.

It was still but autumn, not a month from the hour when he had first betrayed to her his own love, when he stood with her the night before their marriage-day, looking on that life which still seemed to him too pure for the grosser touch of passion; with which his own was well-nigh to him as much profanity, and desecration, as the love of other men had seemed. There are lives in their first youth, ere childhood is wholly left, ere womanhood is one-half learned, which look too heaven-lent for *any* love, even the noblest and the best. Lucille's was one.

Without, that night, the seas ran high, and dark waves were flung against the granite headlands, and winds were wild among the tossing gorse; but where they stood in solitude there were warm scented air, and delicate bright hues, and flowers in all their summer blossom, and she neither saw nor knew the darkness of the night. His kiss was on her lips, his voice was in her ear.

"And you are happy?" Strathmore murmured, as he bent over her. Restlessly, wistfully, incessantly he asked this of one who took all her joy from him—the question whose answer he knew so well! But of that answer he was never weary—never weary of watching as he did now the rich lovelight in her face, the gladness in her smile, while she nestled closer in his breast as to her best-loved, best-trusted shelter, half shy, half ashamed still, in the awe and beauty of her new and wondering joy.

She was happy—happy through *him*. Strathmore asked no more than this, and asked not this for his own sake. For, in his remorse, and in his expiation, the haughty arrogance of his nature was smitten down, humbled to lowest depths;

and where he stood, on that marriage eve, with her lips against his cheek, and her life sheltered on his heart, he bowed his head over her with an unspoken prayer:

"For her sake—in his trust—oh, God! that I may have power to keep her thus for ever!"

And in his heart a voice spoke—that voice so often stifled, so often disobeyed, so often rebelled against as weakness, that voice which men call conscience. "Why was evil done that good might come? Sin added yet again to sin is but barrier piled on barrier between a soul and its atonement."

It was noon on the day of the solemnisation of his marriage, and Strathmore stood among some of the proudest of his order, speaking on the trifles of the hour with his habitual soft, low, slight laugh. The accustomed serenity was on his face, the courtly smile upon his lips, the languor in the cold, harmonious music of his voice; they saw in him but one of themselves, a subtle statesman, a consummate courtier, pursuer of a lofty power, reaper of a ripe ambition; *they* saw no change in him. But in his heart was the restless fever of a passionate disquiet, born from the gnawing consciousness of traitorous infamy wrought that good might be its offspring.

"God is my witness no impulse of passion, no vileness of self-pity, no thought of my own peace actuated me—it was for her, for her alone," he told himself perpetually, and said aright; for passion he would have trampled out, self-pity was a weakness that was unknown to him, and his longing to fulfil the trust of Erroll was holy, sincere, and without taint, though its fruit and its action were error. Yet a terrible unrest was on him; a sickening dread possessed him—he who had feared the laws neither of nature nor of man. Was the darkness of his own life fit to blend with the pure dawn of hers? Was a hidden sin such shield as should have guarded her?

He thrust thought from him, and it would return. He bade the past be buried, and it rose again. He strove to behold but the fairness of the future, and the dead years swarmed around and mocked him. He was master of all men save of himself!—and as he stood there, in his easy and courtly calm, on him were a foreboding, a fevered and nameless fear, unseen of men.

As Lucille came into his presence these were forgotten, and when he looked on her, he remembered nothing but the young love that was his own.

They who were gathered there were world-worn, languid, cold to much, indifferent to all; men and women who wore the purples of the patrician, and had long forgot the creeds, even where they still kept the years, of youth. Yet there were none among them who, seeing her on her bridal morning, were not touched to something of mournful and unbidden tenderness at sight of that fair and opening life. They did not know why they felt thus, they did not seek to know; thus, long ago, they might have felt, looking on the dawn of an early shadowless day, rising in summer light, conscious themselves how soon that day must die, scorched by noon heats, and sunk in shadows of the night.

The low, sad lulling of the seas, beating on the sands without, sounded audibly through the stillness in Silver-rest. Without, the autumn day was wild, and fitful, and tempestuous, while the grey curlews flew with startled cries over the surf, and the yellow leaves of the scattered gorse were whirled upon the wind. But within, the chambers were filled with delicate colouring, with fair women, with the gleam of diamonds and sapphires, with the scent of a myriad of exotics, while the light fell warm and mellow about Lucille, and on the white coronal of the virginal and bridal flowers. As he bowed before her, and, leading her out, took his place beside her, the courtliness of his habitual manner, softened and tinged by the infinite tenderness he bore to her, no memory was on him then save of her beautiful youth, as her eyes drooped, full of shy dreamy lustre, and her face flushed in her soft awe, in her sweet shame. Her heart was subdued at the weight of its own joy. What had she done, she thought, that she should share his life as no other had ever shared it;

that she alone, of all the world, should be thus loved and blessed by Heaven and by him?

The words of the marriage ceremonial commenced, while the ocean filled the stillness with the plaint of its mournful melody.

"I require and charge you both, as ye will answer at the dreadful day of judgment, when the secrets of all hearts shall be disclosed——"

The syllables fell slowly and solemnly on the hushed air, charging the confession of all sin or knowledge which could sever the lives that would be bound in one;—and he who heard them, while on his soul was the secret which uttered would part their lives for ever, stood silent: the words rolled onward, echoed by the melancholy burden of the seas where they broke, wave upon wave, on the distant shore.

He was silent; and what other lips could tell the crime of his buried past? None there. He had said, "Let the dead past bury its dead," and the dead speak not.

Once only his face lost its enforced look of calm and grave tranquillity; it was when her hand touched and lay within his. Then the ritual which was uttered was lost on his memory; the scene that was around him grew unreal; the surging of the seas beat and throbbed through his brain; his eyes shrank from the young loveliness beside him, and his voice, as it pledged her a husband's vows, sounded hollow in his ear. What he saw was the upward gaze of the dying man whom he had slaughtered, what he heard were the faint broken words, which, even in death, had *forgiven him;* and for one instant on his face came that look, hunted, terrible, guilt-stricken, which had come there when in the mists of the sunrise in the years long gone, he had read the message of the dead, the message of pardon, which had written him out for ever in his own sight a murderer. In that hour it was not Lucille of whom he thought, it was not Lucille whom he saw; it was the friend whom he had loved and slain.

The moment passed; Strathmore recovered the control so rarely broken. His hand closed upon hers, his voice fell

serenely on the silence, he bowed his head beside her, and
unarrested the marriage words rolled on through the quiet
calm, that was only filled with the dreamy lulling of the seas.
His love was pledged her as her husband's. His hand closed
on hers as the guardian of her life.

"Those whom God hath joined together let no man put
asunder."

On the deep stillness the words were uttered which bound
their lives in the bond which the world would not sever, nor
death annul.

And with her face flushed, as with the glory of her future,
and luminous with the angel-light that Dante saw upon the
face he loved in the Vision of the Paradiso, Lucille looked
upward in his eyes—his Wife.

## CHAPTER XXI.
### The Roses of the Spring.

IT was the early springtide of the year.

The broad sunny waters by Sheen lay cool and tranquil
in the light; the woodland was in its first glad freshness; the
glades and gardens sweeping to the edge, and the white
glistening walls of villas through the trees, were warm in the
noon brightness; and it was restful and lovely here, in a bend
of the stream, beechen-sheltered, and with mossy islands
breaking the wide river, and drooping their willows lazily
into its waves. Down the stream floated a boat shaped like
the Greek feluccas, a graceful water-toy, with sails like the
silver seagull's wings, and gold arabesques glistening on its
white carved sides, and azure cushions piled up on its couch;
—the nautilus-barge of a Nereid were not more daintily fair.
And on the shore, under the sheltering trees, a woman sat
wearily watching its course, half in apathy, half in fascination. She was tired, travel-worn, haggard, heart-sick,
where she sat, resting drearily there, looking out with sunken,
sun-blind eyes blankly over the stretch of the waters; and she

gazed as though bound by a spell at the joyous sweep of the vessel: they were in a contrast so strange—she, the bitter, hopeless, beggared woman, crouching in the shadow, and that bird-like boat winging its way through the light, with the sun on its snow-white sails.

And she thought of her past, when her course through life had been proud, and patrician, and cloudless, and in the light of a noontide sun, like the course of that boat through the waters!

Nearer and nearer glided the Greek barge, while on its cushions lay a young girl in the first years of her youth, the awnings of azure silk above her head, a pile of hothouse roses lying in her lap, the sunlight falling on the fairness of her face, bright with a softer glory still—the glory of a life without a shadow, of a joy without a wish. She who sat on the shore looked and noted her with envying, evil gaze; she knew nothing of her, but youth, joy, peace, the purples of the aristocratic order, the gladness of a loveliness gracious and beloved, these were accursed and abhorrent in the sight of the Outcast:—they had once been her own, though now there waited for her but the sepulchre of Age, the grave of Beggary.

Nearer yet floated the fairy felucca, as though bearing a Water-Fay to her river home, to her golden throne reared in the snowy bell of the lotus-flower;—floated till it was moored at a landing-stair close to where the solitary wanderer sat, who never moved, but gazed still, with the stupor of weariness at the toy-barge and its freight, as its young Queen rose from her azure nest, and passed over the carpets her attendants threw down before her feet, with a group of girl-patricians like herself, sunny as the morning.

Her white and delicate skirts almost swept the dust-stained dress of the lonely woman where she sat; and she looked down on her compassionately, pausing with that generous and loving pity for all who sorrowed and were in need, that was the divine instinct of a nature which, in the fulness of its own gladness, would fain have decreed that none should suffer. Of her she had no recollection.

"You are ill?" she asked gently, while the odour of the roses that filled her hands was wafted to the travel-tired wanderer.

"I am very weary!"

The words had a heart-sick depth of misery, and the voice which uttered them was strangely contrasted with the want and desolation of her loneliness—sweet, rich, and full of music still.

The contrast struck upon the young girl's ear, and she paused, while her fair eyes, in whose depths the sunlight lay, gazed down on the hollow, sunken, haggard face at whose look she shuddered, even while it touched her to yet deeper pity, for there were in it something of fearful beauty, of wild grace, that nothing could destroy save death itself.

"Let me aid you," she said, stooping, while she dropped some gold into the wanderer's lap, the sweet and gracious compassion of the words robbing the alms of all bitterness that might lie to poverty in the charity of wealth. "This is but little; but if you come up to the house, we may be able to relieve you more."

The woman looked upon her, still with a blank stupor and an evil envy blended in her; and the sun shone on them—together; the wanderer, with the darkness of desolation and the shame of many years upon her, and the young girl, with the sun bright on her fair and fragile loveliness, on the fragrant burden of flowers that she bore, on the light gold of her perfumy hair, and on the beautiful smile that was less upon her lips than in her eyes, in their deep and happy radiance.

She moved to pass onward from the Pariah who crouched there in the beechen shadow; but as she moved she saw the look, which had flashed with something of proud, shrinking pain as the gold had fallen into her lap, fasten on and follow, with wistful, thirsty gaze, the blossom and the fragrance of the roses;—such a look as an exile gives on a foreign soil to flowers he remembers in his native land, whither he can never again return. With an impulse and gesture of exquisite grace, she gave the rich clusters to the lonely and travel-worn wanderer.

"You love flowers? Take them, they will comfort you."

While the softness of the pitying words still lingered on the air, in charity more angel-like than the grudging charities of earth, she went onward with her fair, bright group of girlish aristocratic youth, soon lost to sight in the foliage of the villa woodlands; and Marion Vavasour sat in the gloom beside the reedy waters, with the roses lying in her lap, and their dreamy fragrance heavy with the perfume of the Past.

They were the flowers of her sovereignty, the flowers of her symbol; she had loved them with the poetic and artistic fancy which so strangely mingled with her panther cruelty, her murderous wantonness; a thousand buried hours lay coiled for her in the shut leaves of the moss-laden buds, a thousand memories uprose for her with the rich sweetness of their odorous dews, her youth, her loveliness, her power, all the golden glories that were for ever dead were sepulchred for her in the closed core of those scarlet roses.

Beggared by the arrest which had spared her liberty, but had confiscated all that she possessed and had banished her the city; beggared more utterly yet by the wreck of the vessel in which she had been bound for the New World; she, who had been more cruel in the days of her triumph than was ever beast of the desert goaded and ravening for prey, had sunk to the lowest depths of misery, of keen and bitter want, of wild and impotent despair; and, still denying God, believed at last in Retribution.

And she sat there looking blankly and blindly down on the fresh fragrant roses that the compassion of a soilless life had laid upon those hands crime-stained as the murderer's palm; and she drank in, as with a desert-thirst, the fragrance that bore to her the perfume of her Youth, the fragrance of the emblems of her Past!

A step roused her: she looked up, wearily, from her stupor;

"Who was it gave me these?"

He who was passing, an old ferry-boatman, paused:

"An angel on earth a'most, God keep her! The great minister's young bride. He's cold as ice to look at, but they do say that he just worships her."

"*Who* is she?"

There was a terrible hurrying eagerness in the quiver of her voice.

"His lordship's wife, I tell ye, the Lady Cecil Strathmore."

"Strathmore!"

The boatman had passed onward, and he did not hear the echoed name, in whose dry, stifled cry ran the intensity of hate. From where she sat in the heart-sickness of fatigue and of privation, she sprang up as a panther springs from its lair at scent of its foe and its prey, her limbs once more instinct with eager life, her form quivering with passion. She dashed the roses down on the wet sward and trod them beneath her feet, till their beauty was ruined, and trampled from all likeness of itself, even as was her own. She flung out into the river depths, with loathing gesture, the gold that had been given by that tender and gentle pity; in want and weariness, in poverty and despair, footsore, and with none to give her bread, a wanderer, and knowing not when night should fall where she should lay her head, she cast out to the waters' waste the alms that were of *his* wealth!

The insanity of a blind, reckless, cruel hate possessed her; the hate, long-chained, baffled, powerless to find its vengeance; the hate which was athirst to coil itself with deadly poison-folds about the life that was omnipotent and honoured amidst men, and hiss back in his ear the words by which he once had doomed her: "Such mercy as you gave I give to you—no more!"

At last, at last, she had learned where to strike; and though her hands were empty now, some weapon, that would deal the death-blow to his life through what he loved, would not be long unfound.

To that reckless and tigress lust, what were the gentleness of the youth which had paused to pity her suffering, the divine compassion which had succoured the stranger and the desolate?—to the soul that was seared with evil and envy, and the deep guilt of murderous passions, they were but as oil to the burning, but as fuel to flame.

When the night fell over the river-maisonnette, which had been one of the bridal-gifts of her husband to Lucille, and where they came at the close of most weeks, that in the world she had now entered she should not wholly lose the freshness and the solitude in which she had dwelt from infancy, and which had made waters, and woodlands, and the sweep of free forest winds, the life of her life, Marion Vavasour, unseen, made her way through the aisles of the gardens, stealing with noiseless footfall, as the cheetah through the jungles.

Her youth for ever dead, her loveliness for ever lost, no end left for her but beggared misery and wretched age, and the death-bed of the homeless and the outcast, she had but one goal, one passion, one future—revenge; and like the cheetah she could crouch, waiting with untired patience for the hour when her spring could never miss. Love she had never known, save for her own beauty, her own guilty power; but hate, the cruel, cowardly, wanton, vengeful nature of Marion Vavasour—a woman in her wickedness as in her weakness, in her crimes as in her cowardice—knew in its deadliest and most ruthless desire. Not with philtre or with steel had she any thought to destroy what she hated; her hand would have shaken *there*, for her heart would have shrank from the physical peril that would have recoiled on herself; true to her sex, she thirsted for a more cruel and a more craven vengeance; she longed to destroy by some subtler torture—to say to him, as he had said to her, "You shall live to suffer!"

She made her way, shunning detection, through the still, cool avenues and gardens, where the starlight was trembling in the white spray of fountains, and the linden-leaves were filling the night with their odour. She had no purpose, no object, save to watch as the snake watches what he dares not attack; save to feed, by looking on its goal, the hate which fastened full as brutally on the young life which had been filled with merciful compassion for her loneliness and poverty, as on his which had bade her perish in the darkness of the waters, and left her to sink downward to her grave.

Her eyes gazed round as she moved onward; the scent of the air, the gleam of the statues among the foliage, the voices of the nightingales thrilling through the silence—they belonged to her Past!—and the soul of this woman, hungering for her lost life, knew no passion but to destroy those who now dwelt in the paradise from whose gates the flaming sword of a pitiless vengeance had driven her forth to the desert. She stole on, shrouded by the fitful moonlight, till she found her way to a marble terrace, where some of the windows still stood open to the night; and, sheltered by the ilex shrubs, Marion Vavasour crept nearer and nearer, and gazed into Lucille's bridal home. Kneeling there, she could see the long vista of the lighted chambers, which had a few moments past been filled by the guests of the Cabinet Minister, a small, choice gathering, the roll of whose carriages still echoed through the still night that was stealing into the Sabbath dawn. The dank dews fell chill upon her brow, her limbs were stiff and weary, she had no clanship save with the great outcast multitudes, whose name is legion and whose portion wretchedness;—and she gazed upon the light and luxury and beauty, the rich colouring and delicate hues, and gleaming marbles veiled in the warm clusters of countless blossoms, where what Strathmore loved, lived in his honour and his shelter, in the grace of earliest youth, and in the purples of grandest power.

A sickly and deadly envy shivered through her veins, and she stretched nearer and nearer, as the reared snake darts from out the shadow its hooded head and poisoned barb.

She, kneeling there without, saw Strathmore in the light within;—and where he stood his head was bowed, while on the coldness of his face was that fond warmth which never came there save for one. They were alone, and Lucille leaned against him; her arms were wound about his neck, and while his hand caressed the light wealth of her hair, her eyes looked upward into his with that love which was the holiest and fairest thing which had entered in with the ambitions, the passions, and the remorse, of an unscrupulous and erring life.

They were so near, that she who watched without, could see the look with which the eyes that had spoken their mute merciless doom to her when he had loosed her to the fury of the seas, gazed down on the young loveliness gathered to his bosom; so near, that she could hear the voice which had bade her perish in the devouring waters, soften to more than woman's tenderness, in answer to the fond words whose happy murmur had filled the silence:

"Ah! if it were not to wish you less honoured and less great, I should wish we were always alone, and that Lucille never lost you to the world?"

"Lucille never loses me to the world, for never is she one hour from my thoughts, though the world claims my time and my presence."

And as those answering words echoed on the stillness of the midnight to the ear of the hidden watcher without, she saw at last the single place in his armour of proof where, if one poisoned arrow ever pierced, the mailed and kingly life must reel and fall; and a whisper hissed from her own blanched, fevered lips, "He loves her—he loves her!"

Through the stillness there trembled the low sigh of that perfect joy which, like the hush of noon, is silenced by its own intensity, as Lucille looked upward to his face which, cold and changeless for all others, to her ever wore that gentle tenderness which, so long hers from her guardian, was a hundred-fold hers from her husband.

"Ah! how beautiful it is to live!" she murmured; and the words of happiness which had never known even a dream of pain, of love which lent its own divinity to all existence, stole to the strained ear and thirsty hate of the woman with whom to live had been to sin, and who had but one seared and cruel passion left—the passion to destroy.

"Thank God it is so for you, my darling!"

"For *us!*"

"'For us'—yes. For me while for you."

She nestled nearer to his heart, while her voice was still hushed in its deep dreamy sweetness.

"I wish there were no suffering for any? I cannot bear to think that there is so much pain on earth; can you? I saw a woman in want to-day; I wish you had been with me. Her face has haunted me ever since; it looked so *lost*, so full of evil, yet so full of weariness. Why is it that some faces look like that?"

"Do not seek to know, my child!—you could never even dream."

"She grieved me, too," pursued Lucille, while the light from above fell white and soft upon her where she leaned against him, her head resting on his breast, the pearls woven in her shining hair, the costly laces of her delicate dress trailing on the floor, with bright flowers flung here and there upon them. "She sat so haggard and so desolate by the river all alone. It must be so terrible to be *alone!* I thought the very poorest had some one to love them?"

"But she was left less desolate when you had seen her, Lucille?"

He knew that her nature had no pleasure greater than in giving rest and succour to all who were in need, and he let her spend his wealth as widely as she would in charity; every fair and gracious mercy traced to her, every blessing that fell on her from the lives she aided, rejoiced him.

"I am afraid nothing could help her very much," she answered him, musingly, in the voice which had become to him the sweetest music that earth held,—it was so full of joy! "She looked so longingly at my roses; they might have been the faces of familiar friends! I gave them to her, for I thought they might comfort her if she loved them as I do."

Over his face passed a shadow of startled fear, of disquietude, heavy though nameless; he knew not why nor what he dreaded.

"Your roses! It was strange that a beggar cared for them, Lucille?"

"Why? Perhaps they recalled to her some happier past. Do you know I think—I fancy,—she is the same woman I saw ill at White Ladies, one of those who were shipwrecked, she whom you found me with, that day;—you remember?"

He shuddered, and drew her to him with a gesture of passionate tenderness.

"Do not speak to strange people, my darling," he said, rapidly and uneasily. "You are too young to discern whom it is fitting you should notice. Let none, save those I sanction, ever have access to you."

She raised her face, illumined with her tender and beautiful smile:

"Ah! I love to have anything to promise you and to obey you in!—I wish you gave me more, then you would know how Lucille loves you."

He bowed his head, and kissed the lips which had so sweet an eloquence for him, and drew her with fond care from the breath of the night breeze as it swept through the opened casements; his frame, firm knit as steel, and braced in his youth by desert heats and ocean storms, felt even the slight chillness in the summer wind, since it might have danger for the early life he cherished.

And she who watched without with burning, jealous eyes, while the darkness brooded over her hiding-place, where she crouched as a serpent coils beneath the leaves, saw him lead Lucille through the long vista of light and warmth, of renaissance hues, and tropic foliage, until their forms passed from her sight, and she heard the distant closing of a door falling behind them. Yet she knelt there still, sheltered by the leaves, and with her face looking out into the starlight, haggard and lit with a terrible baffled passionate desire, ravening for its prey; knelt there until the light died out from the windows, and no sound stirred the silence but the gentle lulling of the river, and all was still in the hush of sleep.

The night was serene, the winding waters murmured in tranquil measure on their way, the stars shone down in holy solemn peace; and as the poisonous snake steals, dark and noiseless, through the gentle night where none behold its pestilential trail, Marion Vasavour stole through the dark shelter of the leaves, looking backward, ever backward, to where were sleep, and rest, and soft dreams only stirred by as soft a caress, while like the death-hiss of the snake gliding to destroy, the whisper hissed from her set lips: "He loves her!—he loves her!"

## CHAPTER XXII.

### "Sur l'Avenir Insensé qui se Fie!"

THE light of a fire, made of wood of aloes brought from the East, and filling the air with its incense-like perfume, shed its flickering brightness over a room luxurious as any palace chamber in the Arabian Nights. Hangings of azure silk, arabesques of gold, rich-hued Guido heads, and delicate white carvings, art-trifles of rarest beauty, and flowers scattered in profusion everywhere, bright in hothouse blossom, were lit by the fire-gleam into such a mingled mass of colouring as artists would have worshipped in its chiar'oscuro. Not less would they have loved the face on which the fire shed its glow; the thoughtful brow, the spiritual eyes, the lips on which was a dreaming smile. There was a light upon her face that had never been there, there was a perfection in her loveliness that it had never before reached, as Lucille leant back in a low chair, gazing into the bright wood embers, while a large greyhound lay stretched at her feet, and the warm glow played upon her gold-flecked hair, in the twilight of the spring day which had grown chilly in the great squares of patrician West London, six months after her marriage.

She was alone, but her reverie was sweeter than the companionship of any save of one, and her thoughts were fairer dreamland than any poet's song or romancist's story could have told her. Joyous, and without even passing shade, as her caressed and guarded youth had been from the days of her earliest memory, it seemed to Lucille that she had never known happiness until now; now that she was his own, of his name, in his home, unsevered from him, and dear to him as no living thing had ever been.

It was growing very dusk, but the half-light, the uncertain lustre crossed and deepened by the shadows, suited her imaginative and meditative nature. Had her own life known a touch of twilight, she would have learnt to find the twilight hour unendurable; her days were full of sunlight, and she loved the weird poetic pause between the day and night.

Suddenly the greyhound rose with a deep bay, shaking his silver chain, Lucille lifted her head in eager listening gladness; a step they both knew echoed without, the door opened at the far end of the chamber, the portière was flung back, and Strathmore entered. In an instant she had crossed the vast length of the apartment, and had thrown herself into his outstretched arms; her face flushed with delight, her eyes gazing into his as though they had been parted not for hours but years.

"My darling! my darling!" murmured Strathmore, as he bent over her; and in his eyes as they looked down upon her it might be read that in that moment at least he was happy; it might be seen how deeply this man could love, who, by a fatal error, had believed himself as cold, as he was, of a truth, inexorable.

He led her forward to where the fragrant aloes' flame flung out its ruddy heat upon the hearth, and as he sank into a couch beside the fire, she threw herself down at his feet, resting her bright head against him, while his arm was still about her. For the first time in his life his home was sacred and welcome to Strathmore; before, it had been to him but a residence in which to sleep, to dine rarely, save when he entertained the world, to keep the state and pomp requisite to his public position, and to give his ministerial banquets and receptions; now it was dear to him, for it was also hers.

"What, you were all alone, my child, and in the twilight, too?" he said, fondly, as his hand caressed her hair.

She looked up, while the firelight shone in her eyes and on the radiance of her face.

"I would always rather be alone when you are not with me. It is solitude without you wherever I am, and if I am *quite* alone there is nothing to break my thoughts of you."

"Lucille! you should not love me so well."

She looked up, still with a smile which spoke beyond words.

"Love is all I have to pay you in. I cannot give too much."

"Pay *me!* I am the debtor."

Her caresses, her tenderness, her infinite devotion to him, were ever new, ever sweet to Strathmore; with any other he might probably have been satiated and wearied before now, with Lucille he was never tired of gazing on the fairness of her face, and he could never hear too many of her fond words. He had loved her ere he had wedded her, he had loved her far more since.

"As I said the other night, if it were not to wish you less great, I could wish we were always alone," she whispered him, while she lay at his feet, making a bright artistic picture with the greyhound at her side on the soft, rich-hued skins upon the hearth.

"I could wish, too, that I had never to leave you," he answered her, tenderly, his hand still wandering over the light gold of her hair. "Well, we will be alone for a time; there is nothing that needs me imperatively now, and we need not go to the Queen's ball till late. You shall have an hour or two to yourself, Lucille."

Her face beamed with delight.

"Ah, I am so glad! I feel how proud and glorious it is to bear your name when I am with you in the world, but I love better still to be with you alone. Others are your companions as well *there;* but I am the only one who shares your solitude."

He smiled; the intensity of her affection for him, too great in its usurpation of all her life and thoughts, never alarmed him, as it might well have done, for her: he only saw in it the fulness of her happiness through him, the completeness with which her happiness was merged in and dependent on him, and thus also in it the completeness of his atonement to her father. The cool and daring nature of Strathmore was not one to fear the fatal adversities of chance. Accident is chiefly dreaded by women; by men rarely, by Strathmore never. When the sin that he had sinned to Valdor for her swept over him with a remorse scarce ever lulled, he strove to thrust it aside; he would have taken fresh guilt to his soul to have spared Lucille one passing touch of the knowledge of sorrow.

Lucille leaned nearer against him, while a warmer flush rose to her cheeks.

"There is something I want to ask you—may I?"

"May you!" he repeated, with a smile. "My own darling! have you need to ask that? What is there I ever refuse you, Lucille?"

"Oh no, no! Nothing that I could beg you to give or to do; but this is different—something I want to ask you of yourself."

"Of myself? Say what you will, my love."

He thought she alluded to political matters, for Lucille's intelligent and highly-cultured mind rendered her very far in advance of her actual years; and all childlike, guileless, and poetic as her nature was, she embraced and entered into his career with a depth of comprehension and of sympathy which made her no unfitting companion of a politician's life.

"I have never asked you before; but I think you will tell me now—now that I am so near to you," she said, softly, and half shyly, while the colour deepened in her face as she spoke the last words. Her reverence for her guardian had been so interwoven with her life, that it was still inseparably mingled with the fuller, freer, and still fonder tenderness she bore him as her husband. "I want you to tell me"—and her voice sank very low, while her arm stole round his neck—"to tell me of that cruel woman whom they say that you once loved?"

Strathmore started violently, as if a snake had stung him; a look of terror and of horror glanced into his eyes. As the firelight shone upon his face and hers they were in strange contrast; the one worn, pale, blanched with a great fear, and dark with all the memories of the past that flooded on him with that single question; the other bright and fair in all the loveliness of earliest youth, its delicate colouring flushed, her violet eyes beaming, humid and eloquent, as her shining hair brushed his cheeks.

"Of her!—of *her!* My God! What do you know of her?"

In the passionate agitated words, to which a ghastly dread gave the first sternness, the first harshness which had ever tinged his words to Lucille, the cool wisdom of the statesman was forgotten, the truth betrayed; he had not remembered with what ease her question might have been eluded, her innocence blinded and misled.

Lucille looked at him; her eyes startled and filled with wistful pain, her colour faded, her face full of self-reproach and sorrow. She saw that he was wounded—and by *her!*—and she heard in his voice the first accent of anger that had ever fallen on her ear. She did not know how far removed from anger, how far worse than his worst anger could have been, were the memory and the dread which gave his words their first and momentary severity. She threw herself on his heart with loving, broken whispers of regret and grief; it was the first time pain had ever risen up between them—the first time she had ever known the misery of his displeasure.

"Forgive me!—do forgive me! I meant no harm; I did not know! Oh, for the world I would not grieve you!"

The tears that shone in her eyes, and quivered in her voice, recalled him to himself; he shuddered—already must his accursed past fall on her, and bring sorrow to her even through him!

"Lucille, my darling! I have nothing to forgive. You have done no harm—*you* have not grieved me. You have asked me nothing but what you have a right to ask. It is only—only——For God's sake tell me what made you say that then—what made you speak of her?"

Lucille lifted her eyes to his, in which he read every thought, mirrored as in a glass.

"I only heard of her what Lady Chessville and Lady Castlemore said, long ago, last year at White Ladies; and——"

"I know, I know," broke in Strathmore, hastily, for his mother had told him of that conversation. "But why should you——"

"I could not tell you what made me think of her then; but I often do, because—because I have longed to ask you if it were true she was so dear to you, and if it is from any memory of her that you cannot bear the roses, and call them the flowers of sin? I longed to ask you if—if you regret her *now*, and if you loved her better than you love Lucille?"

Her voice shook a little in the last words, and her head was bowed on his breast as she whispered them; of restless jealousy, of evil curiosity, her radiant and ethereal life knew no taint nor shadow. But now and then she heard a sharp quick sigh from Strathmore; she saw a darkness come over his face when he thought her eyes were not upon him; she was awakened by restless murmured words in his broken sleep; and Lucille, who lived but for him, had wondered, dreamily, vaguely, as she had wondered when she had gazed out on the moonlit abbey-lands of White Ladies, whether the regret of that dead, nameless passion was still on him—had wondered who she had been, this traitress who had deserted him, yet whom he had perhaps never forgotten or replaced. In her true and childlike instinct she had not kept the fear by her in silence to brood over its pain; she had brought it at once to him.

She felt him shudder from head to foot, and his hand tremble as hers closed upon it. To speak of Marion Vavasour to *her!* and yet to the trustful innocence of Lucille he could not lie.

His voice was hoarse as he answered her, with a harsh impetuous passion vibrating in it that she had never heard there, yet which, like his violence on the sea-shore when she was a young child, she knew instinctively was not violent to her.

"For the mercy of God, do not speak of her! I loved her —yes!—with such love as you cannot dream. Heaven forbid that you should! Let my past be!—my present is yours. My name, my home, my heart are yours; do not taint them with what is accursed, with what is unfit for your lips!"

Lucille lifted her head, and looked up in his eyes with that gaze with which on the sea-shore she had looked at him in her infancy; her eyes were wistful, startled, but, beyond all else, full of a deep and yearning tenderness for *him*. Her lips quivered, her colour rose; his grief was hers, and his wrongs her own. She clung to him closely, her heart beating thick and fast.

"Was she so faithless to you, then—this wicked woman? Oh, how could any one whom *you* loved betray you!"

"For God's sake, hush! Her name on your lips!"

The words were muttered in his teeth, as he rose hurriedly, putting her from him, and paced the length of the chamber, the twilight only broken into darker shadow by the warm flashing gleams of the fire which shot across it, hiding his face from her. It was agony to him, this torture of her innocent questions, of her fond sympathy, of her tender grief at his wrongs! His self-control was destroyed, his calmness and his strength shattered down, all the darkness of the tragedy hidden from her came back upon his memory, all the inexpiable brutality of his guilt towards Erroll seized him as in the first fresh hours when he had stood beside the bier where the dead man lay stretched in the summer sunlight, with Lucille's unconscious words! He could not look upon her face while she spoke to him of the assassinatress of her father.

Unwitting of the blow she dealt him, she, who only knew that she had grieved him, and had called back to him some past that was bitter in its remembrance, sprang to him with the soft rapid flight of a bird, and threw herself again upon his heart.

"Forgive me! forgive me! I did not know that I should grieve you—I, who would give my life to spare you pain! I had no right to ask what you had not told me of yourself. I was wrong, very wrong."

He pressed her closely to his bosom, her words of self-reproach seemed to him to heap coals of fire on his head. If she knew what that past was he "had not told her"!

"You asked nothing but what you had a right to ask," he said once more, while his voice, like her own, was broken. "Leave me a moment, my own darling—a moment; I will speak to you then."

Her eyes turned on him wistfully, beseechingly, but not to obey him never crossed the thoughts of Lucille; it was the unquestioning obedience, never of fear, wholly of love, which she rendered him. She left him as he bade her, and stood in the light of the fire with her head bowed on the white carved marble. Her face was very pale, the tears hung heavy on her lashes, her heart was touched with the first pang that she had known since the marriage-day which had given her to Strathmore. She thought how he must have loved this woman that her mere memory smote him thus, that for her sake alone he had shuddered at the mere scent and sight of the scarlet roses.

His step echoed on the silence of the chamber; the twilight shadows hid his face as he walked up and down for some minutes; then he approached her, and his features, while they were yet worn and weary, had recovered their serenity, and he drew her to him with his accustomed tenderness as he stooped and kissed her.

"My precious child, you have but asked what it is surely

your due to know," he said, gently and gravely, with that perfect self-command which never, save for a few moments, deserted him. "You have a right to ask everything of me; I have a right to answer; and I rejoice at nothing more than that no thought even which passes through your mind should be concealed from me. Confide in me freely—never more so than when your doubts are of me."

Lucille lifted her head in eagerness, her cheeks flushed again, her eyes full of love.

"They were not doubts of *you*. How could I doubt you ever?—what could I doubt you in? It was only that I doubted——"

"What?" he said gently, as she hesitated.

"That—that," whispered Lucille, softly and swiftly, "that you have never loved me as you once loved *her*."

A quick shudder ran through him; but his self-control, freshly reconquered, was not lost again.

"You thought truly, Lucille," he said, gravely. "In you I love innocence—in her I loved guilt. Is there matter for envy for you, there, my guileless child, who cannot even dream what such guilt is?"

Lucille's face grew awed and wistful while the thoughtful shadow which was ever more or less upon it deepened, but a beautiful light shone in her eyes.

"Ah, then,—I am dearest to you?"

"God is my witness, yes—a thousand-fold! And now, while I acknowledge your right to ask of me what you will, I, too, would ask one thing of your love. The past is dead; when you bid me look on it, you bid me look back upon years that are accursed in my memory." His hand, as he spoke, trembled where it rested on her shoulder, but his voice was calm and sustained. "The history of my madness for—for her of whom you speak, I could not tell without such suffering as the opening of old and deadly wounds brings with it. I ask of you to spare me that. If you bid me endure it, I will; what you demand to know I will not refuse to answer; but you love me, Lucille--I think you will not force me to dwell on a past that can have no rivalry with you, a name that it would but pollute your innocence to learn. Am I wrong?"

"No, no! I will never ask you one word again!" she murmured, passionately. "*I* bid you suffer! Oh, my lord, my love, would Lucille be so little worthy you? I was wrong to say what I did. All I longed to know was that you loved me too well ever to regret another. I know it now—I want no other knowledge!"

Tears so rare in Strathmore's eyes, rose in them as he heard her words. He had judged aright her tender, generous, and lofty nature; he had known the chord to strike to make her young heart vibrate and echo to his will, but it touched him to the soul; though from all love, though in all justness, he was still deceiving her, and his eyes were softened to a deep gratitude, as before some divine and holy thing, as he bowed his head, and let his lips rest on hers.

Thus that danger passed—passed, leaving no shadow on Lucille's life. When once her fear was unfolded, it fled. She knew that she was alone in his heart; that knowledge, as she had said, was sufficient for her. He had wished his past unasked of; she banished even thought of it from a mind which best loved to mould itself by his law, and by his wish.

She was the incarnation of shadowless youth, fair as the dawn, in those hours which he had promised her they should spend alone, as she played, like the child she was, with the greyhound on the hearth, and sang in music like the gladness of a forest bird, and threw herself at Strathmore's feet, while the fragrant aloes' flame gleamed on her face, and she told him of a hundred poetic thoughts, and fairy fancies, and pure ambitions, that lived in him and saw in him the glory of their dreams. The evil of his past had touched, but glanced harmless off her, leaving no memory and no trail behind it. If her life could but be kept thus!

*If!*—vague, disquiet, nameless dread had fastened on him since those innocent questions, which had sought unwittingly to unveil the tragedy, whose truth, beheld by her, would be death, like the unveiled face of the Medusa. The past was on him, like a fixed and recurrent dream; and while the night brought Lucille sleep as light, as soft, as smiling in its dreams as the rest of infancy, his own thoughts, sleepless and wandering through the darkness of dead years, went ever to one memory alone—the memory of Marion Vavasour.

## CHAPTER XXIII.

"*Dios Consiente, pero no para Siempre.*"

A SCORCHING noon burnt the vast sandy plains around Marseilles, and the great pine forests beyond Grateloup, and the blue glittering sea had no motion along the whole line of southern shore, from where the olive woods of Monaco sloped down to the waters in the east, to where the chesnuts and the vineyards of the Western Pyrenees were withered by the intense and cloudless sun. The heat was unbearable, rare even for the Midi, and it was most stifling, most pitiless, most hateful, in its blinding glare, and its burning, breathless oppression on the dreary stone bastions, and the stone-locked harbour of Toulon, where the galley-slaves of the Bagne were toiling under their burdens, and working in long files under the lash of their *gardes-chiourmes*.

Hard, merciless labour, the toil of beasts of burden, dragging up the sloping planks the ponderous trucks of building-stones, or panting, like horses overladen, under the chains by which they were fastened to the timber, or the iron, or the loads of gravel that they brought along the fortifications in the parching desert-heat. Toil, terrible and bitter to be borne to the limbs inured by every hardship, and to the sinews, coarse and strong as oak fibres, of the Auvergnat or the Nantais; of the Cevennes charcoal-burner or the Paris felon, who had burrowed from birth with the rats in the Catacombs, and held his fête in the vile saturnalia of the Quartier de l'Enfer.

Toil, by the sweat of the brow, and to the uttermost limit

of strength, to those begotten in wretchedness, born in misery, reared in starvation, and braced to hunger and to thirst, to outrage and to crime. But tortures that were like the protracted throes of one long living death to the hands that were soft as women's; to the limbs that were enervated by luxury; to the lives that were accustomed to every delicate indulgence; to the pride that had never stooped to any living man, and now wore the fetters of the galley-chain as haughtily as it had worn the orders of a noble; to those who were thrown with common felons, their only sin that they had chosen the losing side, and had been Patriots instead of Placemen, or in lieu of prudent and purchasable creeds, which could have altered with the wind, had chosen, in an unheroic age, the chivalrous code of a hopeless loyalty. The red shirt and *bonnet vert*, the coarse food they would in other days have seen their dogs turn from in disgust, the irons that ate into their flesh, the nights of misery on their horrible beds, the ton weights under which the hardiest cattle would have broken down, the deadly labour under the long burning days—all these they shared with the common criminals of the land which they had only loved too well. And even these were mercy beside that fell companionship which lashed them side by side with the hideous pollutions of great cities, with the brute greed which had taken life for a copper coin, or a toss of brandy, with the vilest guilt and with the lowest vice that made manhood deformity and the world a hell.

One of these—waiting, as he had been waiting well-nigh for a year, deportation to Cayenne—manacled to a gaunt Liégois, who had been sent to the galleys for arson, was dragging a load of sand, fresh dug from the excavations, the ropes that fastened him to his burden cutting his flesh as his shafts cut a galled horse, the sun scorching to blisters his bared shoulders, the irons locked upon his ankle and his wrists, his taskmaster behind him to revenge each laggard step, each pause when in the heat he sickened and reeled under the weight, with a sharp scourge of the lash as to a disobedient hound.

Bound with criminals, and sunk lower than the dogs, stripped to the waist, and weighted with fetters, with his hair shorn away, and the sweat of an intolerable travail on his brow, the Aristocrat was still distinguishable from those with whom he was companioned; the hands which laboured with the pick-axe and the spade no suns could brown, the neck round which the cord was passed that harnessed him to his truck no indignity could bow, the proud silence which every outrage, jibe, and blow tried beyond human endurance, no insult and no torture could break. Namelessly, strangely, but with a chasm of difference between them that no unity of suffering, of labour and of bondage could bridge over, the Noble stood out apart from the Criminals with whom he was condemned to herd; never made like them, never made one of them, by any outrage, by any misery. For all else than this, Raoul de Valdor would have been unrecognised, and passed as a stranger, by those who had known and loved him best, as he toiled here, a political *condamné* in the Bagne of Toulon.

A yacht had come into the Toulon harbour, driven there overnight by a tempest, and at anchor that glittering, sickening, torrid day; while not a breath stirred the drooping sails, not a touch of coolness came over the lake-like waste of the Mediterranean; not a cloud, ever so slight, broke the painful steel-blue glare of the hot skies.

The yacht had been wintering about the Morea and the Levant, idly and purposelessly, for to the young man who owned it it mattered little whether he were under the skies of the East or the West, beneath the shadow of Mount Ida, in the Ægean, or of the frowning pine-crowned crags that overlook the Danube; for the glory was gone from his life, and he was in those years which refuse to believe that although one sun has set to-day, another will rise with the morrow. He cared little where he went or what he did; and he strolled listlessly now through the Bagne, hearing little what was said by those who showed him over it, though his heart was stirred to a keen, unselfish pain as he saw the crime and the wretchedness locked in, in the vast stone jaws of that merciless trap. He, with liberty, youth, health, and "all the world before him where to choose," felt that the grief which overshadowed his life because one desire of his heart had been forbidden him, was egotistic, rebellious, and unworthy of manhood, when he looked upon the hideous mass of crime, the intensity of human misery, the lives, loaded with fetters and labouring like beasts of burden, which were about him in the bastions of Toulon, doomed beyond escape until death should come and loose them from their chains.

"Good God! is that creature a man?" he said, as he pointed out a Caliban with the frame of a giant, but with a face so loathsome in its mastiff-like brutality and its low dogged, sullen ferocity, that it well seemed to belong to those "lower beings beneath humanity," which the Spaniards of Columbus, Ojeda, and Nicuesa, expected to find in the Terra Nuova.

"A Nantais, who cut his father and mother's throats for a little matter of gold the old people hid in a pitcher," answered his conductor, carelessly. "They found him guilty, with *circonstances extènuantes*."

"What in Heaven's name could they be?" asked the young Englishman, as he moved hurriedly with an uncontrollable horror from the place where the parricide was.

The other shrugged his shoulders:

"*Une phrase de paille, monsieur!* We do not love capital punishment. The executioner is your pet across the Channel; he is not so with us."

The young man was silent, his blue eyes ranging thoughtfully over the droves of men chained together for such incongruous causes, for such disproportioned crimes. Something of that profound melancholy and despair which comes over men of great minds when they reflect on the complexity, the vastness, and the diverseness of evil, and see no way which can sever justice from cruelty, or ally mercy with necessary vigour in the law, weighed even on his naturally careless, unmeditative temperament. His gaze rested on the face and form of the Parisian Noble, as he laboured along the plank with his truck-load of gravel. Lionel Caryll had known him well; scarce twelve months before they had spent months together at Silver-rest and at White Ladies, but his eyes looked on him without recognition, so utterly was Valdor dead in the Galley-Slave of the Bagne. Yet that nameless air, that look of "blood" which still lingered, attracted Caryll; he gazed at him long and with compassion.

"He has committed no crime!" he said, involuntarily.

"He has committed the worst, monsieur," said his guide, laconically.

"Impossible!" broke in the young man, with that frank impulse natural to him. "What is he accused of that such a man can be here, with common felons, with assassins, and with parricides?"

His conductor stroked his moustaches, and smiled amusedly; he had seen many such men there, seen them live and die there.

"That one conspired against the government."

"What! For a mere political difference of opinion; for a——"

"Chut, monsieur!" said the polite but prudential functionary, with a smile, "that is not the way we talk in France."

"May I speak to him?" asked Nello, attracted by the pale, proud, weary, yet unconquered look of the condamné.

His companion hesitated:

"Yes, monsieur, if you wish it," he said, after a pause.

It was out of rule, but he was himself a considerable person in the Bagne, who could accord such liberties without suspicion or correction, and he knew that the young Englishman was highly connected with several houses of the British aristocracy. There could be no danger, and he called the prisoner to him roughly and imperiously, as he would have called a dog.

"Don't do that, I will go to him," said Nello, quickly,

wounded, half with anger, half with pain, as he felt, almost with a personal mortification, the harsh shout of the callous custodian to the man whose single crime had been that patriotism which, deified by us as we read the pages of classic history, is damned by us in our own day, if shaped in other form to that in which we choose to mould it for ourselves.

As he moved, Valdor obeyed the command, the Liégois incendiary, with whom he was coupled, following him perforce; obeyed, as one too proud for a petty and a vain resistance, and of too knightly a nature to show that the miserable outrages of an inferior's tyranny had power to sting or gall him. But the blood had risen to his hollow cheek, and his head was lifted with a certain grandeur as he approached his taskmaster; the man was great in his fallen might, In his captive's fetters, as he had never been in the days of his rank and his brilliance. There is a majesty in Adversity, though it is a king to whose purples the mocking multitudes will not bow down; for the world worships and censes only the sovereign which it calls Success, even though oftentimes its crown is tinsel, its path is infamy, and its treasuries are theft.

As he drew nearer, his eyes fell on Lionel Caryll, the colour deepened in his face, and a look of terrible pain came into his eyes. The last time he had seen the youth had been the night when he had believed that Lucille loved him.

Nello, with the chivalrous courtesy to misfortune of high breeding and of a gentle nature combined, lifted his hat, and bowed with a smile as engaging as he would have given to the proudest potentate in Europe, and with a deep respectful pity spoken in his glance, while the Bagne official stood by smiling in his sleeve, and thinking, "What eccentric animals they always are, these English! *Saluer un forçat!* Bah!"

"Monsieur," he began, hesitatingly, "pardon me that I have taken the liberty of asking to speak with you. I am an Englishman, Lionel Caryll, and if I could have the honour to serve you in any way——"

"Lionel Caryll! and you do not know me!" said the *condamné*, with a smile of such resigned melancholy that it pierced to the heart of the young man.

"Know you?" he echoed, wonderingly, while his eyes dwelt on the haggard, wasted features, the weary, lustreless eyes, and the browned gaunt face, shorn of beard and hair, of the forçat before him. And as he looked, slowly and incredulously, remembrance and recognition returned on him, he grew pale as death, and recoiled in horror.

"Valdor! Merciful Heaven!"

"Even I!"

There was an intense pathos in the simple words in which the late brilliant and chivalric Noble acknowledged his identity with the prisoner of the Travaux Forcés, in whom the friends of his lost life could find no trace by which to know him!

"Gracious God! how came you here?" murmured Caryll, while his voice shook with emotion, and the dank dew gathered on his forehead in the shock with which his youthful and fervid nature was struck at meeting the man whom he had known and feared as a dazzling courtier and a powerful rival, now weighted with irons, and leashed with a criminal in the convict works of Toulon.

"I suffered for my cause. Many better men than I have done as much, and more," answered Valdor, briefly.

If he knew that one whose hand was without mercy to strike, and whom in one mad hour he had threatened when the haughty soul of Strathmore was flung down before him in the humility of supplication, had been that which, unseen and indirectly, but none the less surely, had sent him to his doom, Valdor was not made of that nature which could have told this to Strathmore's young kinsman.

Nello gazed at him blankly, and with a paralysed horror still; it seemed but yesterday that he had envied this man all his versatile fascinations, all his courtier's graces, as they were together, where they gathered round Lucille in the lighted drawing-rooms, or shot over the deer park, or rode through the forest aisles of White Ladies. And now they met here in the white blinding glare and the stone-locked prisons of Southern France!

It was very terrible to the warm young heart of Lionel Caryll, whose sympathies were all quick, and whose compassion had not been worn away by the constant claims upon it which years bring with them. He could have shed tears like a woman at the sight of the man before him, while all his English blood was up in hot revolt at the tyranny which bound the political offender in the same brutality of chastisement, as was incurred by the vilest criminals, by the fratricide, the incendiary, the poisoner, and the assassin.

"Merciful God!" he cried, passionately, "can such things be? What! only because you held to the creed of your ancestors, and wished to win back for your King his legitimate throne, the country that was once ruled by Henri Quatre flings you here with the vilest criminals upon earth!"

Valdor gave him a swift glance, which counselled him to hold back his indignant protest, for the overseer of the Travaux Forcés was looking suspiciously at the young man's flushed face, and heard all the fiery words, as Nello spoke in French.

"*Dios consiente, pero no para siempre*," he answered, in the Spanish proverb, with a mournful and restrained dignity, which perhaps, more than anything else, showed how captivity and degradation had worn away the hot impulsiveness and the brilliant insouciance of the French Noble, while at the same time they had brought out in him a grandeur which had not been there in the days of his fashion and his fortune.

"God's vengeance should fall here, then!" muttered Caryll, in his teeth, too ardent and too full of impulse himself wholly to obey Valdor's sign, though he had seen and rapidly comprehended it. "How long are you sentenced to this iniquitous, accursed misery?"

"For life. I am one of the *déportés* for Cayenne."

"Cayenne! Why, it is death itself, they say, those pestilential swamps! Is there no hope possible?"

"Hope does not enter here," said Valdor, with a smile more unutterably sad than the most bitter lamentations could ever have been.

The young man ground his heel into the hot sand on which they stood with a mute passionate gesture; he was by nature generous, sympathetic, and ready to do battle for any wrong, however foreign to him, and the constant action of Lucille's mind upon his own had lent him some of her unselfish and fervent pity for those who suffered.

Valdor looked at him, and even on his sunburnt face the blood rose as he leaned forward for the moment, forgetting that he was in chains.

"Tell me," he said, hurriedly. "Tidings of the world never reach here more than they reach the dead in their tombs! What of Strathmore!—of——"

Caryll knew the name before which he paused. With the rapid instinct of a lover, he had seen that Valdor also loved her, though of what had passed that night under the palms he had known nothing. His heel ground the sand under it with a fiercer force than before, his eyes fell, he half turned away.

"My uncle has wedded Lucille," he said, briefly; and, while he uttered the words, all the anguish which that marriage had cost him in its first hours tightened afresh about him: he forgot the Bagne of Toulon; he forgot the men before him, and the stone walls around him; he only remembered the love of his youth.

Valdor answered nothing; he had known well enough what the answer would be, though perhaps, as with us all, until certainty fell like the axe of the headsman, he had, without knowing it, hoped against hope. He was silent; he had learnt of late to endure; but a grey pallor overspread the dark bronze of his face, and the heavy iron fetters that bound him to the Liégois criminal shook against each other as though struck together by a sudden blow.

"Is she happy?" said Valdor, after a long silence, while his voice was very low. The thoughts which were passing within him were little dreamed by the young man beside him —thoughts of the dark tragedy which had ushered in and still overhung the life of Lucille.

Nello's face was still half turned away, and was flushed with the keen pain which the subject brought him. He answered, however, with frank truth, as it was his nature to do, and moreover, since the night in which he had seen Strathmore's coldness broken and his pride levelled by the community of suffering, he had felt to him as he had never done before.

"Happy? Yes. At least they tell me so; I have not seen her since—since before her marriage, but I know how great her love was for my uncle, and that he would give his life to spare her a moment's pain."

"He is so dear to her?" asked Valdor. The chains he bore, the misery he endured from one dawn to another, the sentence which devoted his whole life to a fate beside which the Noble's death upon the scaffold had been mercy, were scarce so bitter to him as that question, for what he loved and had for ever lost, was in the instant of its asking.

"Her life is centred in his," answered the young man in his teeth, for he had not yet learned to speak calmly of what had struck him a blow that for the time had withered all the beauty of his youth. "If harm befel him to-morrow, I believe it would be Lucille's death."

Valdor was silent, his head drooped, his lips grew very white where he stood, while the massive irons that linked him to the Liégois trembled as they hung from his wrists. Gazing down upon the yellow glare of the sand, he thought how wide and fearful a vengeance was in his hands upon the man who had consigned him here if liberty alone were his! Liberty! He shuddered as the word merely passed, mute and colourless, through his mind; its very memory was mockery, whilst around him were the white inexorable walls, the galley-gangs, the fettered criminals of the Toulon Bagne.

The overseer, tired of the conference, and afraid of allowing a foreign visitor longer intercourse with one of the *galériens*, broke in, turning to Caryll:

"Monsieur, it is out of rule for a stranger to speak with a forçat! I can permit the interview to last no longer. *Au travail, numéro six cent quarante-cinq! Va-t-en donc, animal; vite!*"

Passionate words of rebuke, remonstrance, and unavailing wrath, rushed to Caryll's lips, while his blue eyes flashed with longing to seize the official in the strong grip of his right hand, and hurl him down into the midst of the excavations beside which he stood. But a meaning, warning glance from Valdor arrested him, as he whose whole individuality was lost in "numéro six cent quarante-cinq" bowed with his old grace, and with that majesty which calamity nobly borne ever confers.

"M. Caryll, I thank you from my soul. The sight of your face has been like water in a desert to one who is shut in a living grave, and to whom the world is dead."

Then, without resistance, or without sign that he had even heard the brutal voice of his taskmaster, he moved away to the plank where his labour awaited him. Swift as thought, Nello followed him with eager words of pity, sympathy, and indignant grief; but a hundred lynx eyes were on them, and the glance of Valdor mutely warned him, as he would serve him, to fall back with those generous but rash words unuttered, while from his own lips a single phrase was whispered, so low that the young man could barely catch it: "*Doucement!—et conciliez Lavigne!*" Lavigne was the government employé who was conducting Nello over the Bagne.

His senses, quickened by the keenness of sympathy, and by the desire which Valdor had divined, to serve in some way, though he had no knowledge how, the man whom he had suddenly found in such terrible captivity, Nello caught the cue rapidly, though vaguely; he fell back, letting Valdor and the Liégois return to their toil, and turned to the official with as much carelessness and courtesy as he, no good hand at diplomacy and deception, could assume on the instant. He accounted to Lavigne for having known the political offender by his having met him at his uncle's house. Strathmore's name was too familiar in France not to be well known even to the Toulon officer, and was in a great measure a voucher to him that no harm could result from the young Englishman's recognition of "Numéro six cent quarante-cinq;" and Nello obeyed, as far as he could bring himself to do, Valdor's whispered injunction, "*Conciliez Lavigne*," by entering with apparent interest into the official's explanations of the working and the regulations of the Bagne, and by inviting him to the inspection of his yacht, and to luncheon there on board with him. Most surely Caryll, with not a little of the pride of his family in him, with an honest hatred of wrong and a heart sick at the tyranny to which he was witness, had never so stooped, but that a warm, eager, indefinite longing was already on him to loosen by some means or other those cruel fetters with which a man innocent of all crime, save a mistaken cause and a quixotic loyalty, was flung amongst thieves, bondsmen, and assassins.

When he had quitted the Bagne, and sat at evening on his yacht-deck, seeing the sun go down in all its golden glory in the Mediterranean waters, and musing on the mass of misery and guilt where the galley-slaves, when night closed in, would lie down manacled and side by side, in worse beds than kennelled dogs, the young man's thoughts revolved incessantly and restlessly round a thousand vague, wild, chivalrous, impossible plans for Valdor's rescue. He could see no way to it that was feasible; he could devise no scheme, however rash and reckless, that it was possible to obtain a chance to put in execution, but his nature was sanguine, his heart was generous, and he came of a bold race, who let nothing daunt them or oppose them.

Strathmore, in England, little dreamed the projects that floated through his young nephew's mind, till they settled into a matured and resolute will to liberate the condemned man, if daring or skill could find any means to do so, as he leaned over the side of his vessel looking at the stone bastions of Toulon, where they glared red in the ruddy sunset light. How, when, at what risk, and by what measures he could not tell; but to free the French noble was as resolved in the youth's heart as though the Eumenides of Greek fable had place and sovereignty in human life, and had appointed him the chosen instrument by which the evil which had been deliberately wrought should recoil on the life that had begotten it.

When the sun had sunk and the stars had come out, he still leaned there, looking down on the phosphorescent water, musing on this thing; while in the Bagne of Toulon the prisoner, lying in the cramped misery which makes sleep torture, and denies even the merciful oblivion of slumber, and the restoration of lost joys which dreams may bring with them, thought of Lucille gathered to her husband's heart,— thought of the vast and awful vengeance which was his upon Strathmore *if—if* he had but LIBERTY!

And the yacht stayed off Toulon.

## CHAPTER XXIV.
### The Symbol of the Dying Flower.

SUMMER in the heart of the great city—mockery of the name! Summer! with the incessant roll of traffic, never ending from the dawn of one day to the dawn of another; with the loud beating of steam-presses throbbing and thundering through the nights; with the glory of the skies in azure warmth or starry stillness, shut out from sight by the great wilderness of roofs; with the dense heat of the noon burning on arid pavement, on whirling dust, on grey, gritty, barren walls; with the brightness of the sun shining on toiling crowds, on panting horses, on thronged narrow thoroughfares filled with noise, with stench, with reeking heavy heat; on dark, noisome courts, where, when its rays steal in through some broken chink or loosened shutter, they find men labouring and lusting for gold, with their eyes blind to the day and their souls lost to heaven. Summer! with the only bird a prisoned lark in some garret window, that shakes its dust-covered wings and strains its parched throat in song that is but a long quiver of agony, while its beak plunges into the dry sear sod as though in some wild memory of the fresh woodland grasses far away. Summer! with the only flower a sickly drooped plant, whose leaves hang lifeless, and whose blossoms are colourless with smoke; with the only living water the ink-black, poisonous river, forest-thick with masts; with the only murmur through the day and night the toiling of the weary feet of crowds who have forgotten what green fields are like.

Summer!—it is a terrible and ghastly thing in the pent alleys of a great city, and Marion Vavasour, when she stood leaning her arms on the sill of her narrow window, and gazing down into the noxious street below, sickened at it as under a physical torture. Beauty, colouring, poetry, luxury, they were the life of this woman's life; her eyes longed, her heart thirsted for them, as the lark's for the woodland shadows, as the flower for the light of the sun and the sweetness of the morning dew. Years of evil and of infamy could not trample this out of her nature; she had been born for all the luxuriance of power, all the delicate lustre of sight, and scent, and touch, and ever-changing scenes, which are the prerogatives of wealth; she lived in *them*, without them she perished famine-stricken. The heat, the noise, the dusty glare, the barren, vulgar hideousness of the life about her were bitter torture to her, the death to which she had sunk in the whirling ocean had not been one tithe so accursed to her, as the living death in which she dwelt. Proud, she was steeped to the lips in degradation; a poetic voluptuary, her life was sheared barren of every memory of beauty; once a patrician and a ruler, she lived now a pariah imprisoned in want and misery. Vengeance could not have been more subtle and complete.

Where she looked down into the hot, vile unsightly street,

with its crowded wretchedness, and its narrow strip of sunny sky left between the high pent roofs as though in mockery of all the glorious world beyond, laughing in loveliness and light, that was lost and unknown to those who were dwellers here, her thoughts wandered to her dead and golden past.

The hours of triumphs, the homage of courts, the rich perfection of her peerless loveliness, the days of her glad and splendid sovereignty, they floated before her in memories tangled and lustrous like the glories of a dream. A thousand summer days, a thousand summer nights, the perfume of Southern climes, and the fragrance of luminous seas flashing in phosphor light, whilst the air was balmy with flowers, and filled with music from palace-stairs, gleaming marble white through deep odorous thickets of myrtle. The murmur of love-words whispered low, and the radiance of her own resistless beauty, with the gold light on her hair, and the proud challenge in her eyes, and the throngs of princes and of courtiers waiting on her steps, that swept like Cleopatra's over rose-strewn paths:—they drifted past her, the phantoms of dead years, and a dull, sickly sense of unreality stole on her, looking on that glorious sun-lighted, diamond-crowned vision of her youth.

Had hers ever been this fair and sovereign life? Was she what the world had known as Marion Vavasour? The soft grace, the rich lustre, the divine fragrance of that bygone life, were they all dead for ever? Could the light never come back to her eyes, the laughter to her heart, the beauty—her loved, lost beauty!—to her face, for which men had deemed the world well lost?

And the ceaseless ebb and flow of the black river-tide, and of the surging throng in the weary glare below, seemed to beat as answer on the stifling air,

"For ever, never! Never, for ever!"

Yet among the living, as though condemned ghost-like to wander without rest among the world that knew her not, and in which she had no place, Marion Vavasour was dead!

She gazed down into the colourless dust-strewn street, while the air was filled with stifling odours from which she shrank, and up from the river swept pestilential vapours in the arid noon, in which the pale leaves of the garret-flower drooped, and the caged lark sat huddled and blind, with wings that hung nerveless, and a little life without song. And, as she gazed, through the weariness of her beggared years, one human passion rose, still sweet, still unexhausted, still the right and the lust of the outcast as of the monarch—the passion of revenge.

The hatred which had destroyed her, was scarce so cruel and so pitiless as the hatred that she bore; for men at their worst never reach the depths to which a woman sinks when once unsexed, and cast into the fathomless sea of unlicensed evil; the tigress is more cruel than her mate. Men strike at what they hate; women, more subtle and more merciless, strike at what is best-beloved by the life they would destroy. It is the difference of the sexes; one tramples out under an iron heel, the other poisons unseen and with a smile.

Vague, shapeless, hopeless, her vengeance rose before her sight; she knew now where to strike—but how?

Sunk amongst the lowest, destitute, and banned from every household, how could she sever two lives, lifted far above her in the security of rank, and power, and peace? How could she learn the force to forge a bolt to reach and pierce the kingly mail of the patrician and the statesman? She had seen where the single weakness lay in the steel-clad strength of the man who had denied her mercy; but her hands were empty, she had no weapon with which to strike. All that brutality could have compassed, all that a serpent subtlety and an insatiate thirst could have schemed and been slaked in, she would have done; but her power was paralysed, whilst her passion to destroy burned but the fiercer for its impotence.

"He loves her!—he loves her!" the words that had been hissed from her lips in the night stillness as she had looked on them, broke from them now, as though in them she felt the whole measure of her hate were gathered, as though in them lay the mystical incantation at whose summons vengeance would rise incarnate, to be her minister and slave. She hated Lucille as that which is evil ever hates what is pure; the compassion which had pitied her, the sweet graciousness with which the young girl had smiled on her and offered her her roses, were but memories which made her savage greed the thirstier to destroy her.

She knew nothing of her save what rumour, floating to her as rumour floats amongst the masses of those above them, told; that she was a young, highborn girl, of whom many idle stories wandered downward through the ranks of society, till even the lowest caught and retailed them, touching her gentleness to all who suffered or sought charity, and her husband's devotion to her, rumour's hundred tongues outlying one another in what they babbled of the beauty, the luxury, the brilliance with which it was his pleasure to surround her, and of the idolatry in which he was said to hold one whom he had wedded when the world had deemed him bound solely to power and ambition.

This was all she knew; but it was more than enough to overfill the measure of a deadly hate, sole lingering passion of a ruined and ruthless life, which, driven out itself from every fairer and every holier thing, loathed and panted to destroy all beauty that lived in another, all light that shone on other lives.

Strathmore had been her slave; in his passion, in his crime, *she* had been his temptress, even as she had been his destroyer; and a burning, poisonous jealousy consumed her, twisted in with the lust for her vengeance. She hated him with a hate unutterable; but a thrill of thirsty *envy* ran through her when she knew that this young and graceful loveliness was in his home, in his heart, in his life.

If the vain and sensual nature of Marion Vavasour had ever loved, she had loved—for a brief while—the man whose mad devotion had been lavished on her in that imperious force which wakes the heart of women in their own despite;

the cruel tyrant had valued most the costliest toy she most utterly, most brutally destroyed; the sweetest, richest hours of her rich, sweet past had been those in which Strathmore had lain subject at her feet. She had believed that love was for ever dead in him, and rightly; the feeling which he bore to Lucille was too pure to bring the passion he had known once, and once alone. But this *she* did not know; she only knew that in another lay the joy of his life; that to another was given his kiss, his thoughts, his riches and his tenderness. And the poison of a fierce and brutal jealousy was in her—the jealousy of a woman who hates, and who has lost all that makes womanhood human.

"He loves her!—he loves her!"

The thirsty words were on her lips as she leaned out, looking on the heavy, sultry street; in them she seemed to feel the prophecy and surety of her vengeance. Yet how touch those who dwelt as far above her now as the skies were above the wretched companions of her infamy? How, with the impotent hate of an outcast, reach and sever the lives surrounded with the might and the purple of power?

The serpent is powerless as the dove to harm, unless it can wind its way in to wreathe around and breathe its venom on the life it would destroy. She had the will, the thirst, the passion to strike, and to strike without pity; but her hands were empty. It was hopeless.

Where she leaned, the flower on the pent, dark casement was blown by the wind against her lips; she shuddered from its touch; she thought of the rose—rich, fragrant, dew-laden—that she had drawn from its leafy nest of foliage on the terrace at Vernonceaux. As that scarlet, odorous rose, had been her life in the Past,—like that withered, prisoned flower in the closeness of the sunless, noxious garret, was her life in the Present! The poetry which still lingered in this woman's nature made her lean over the yellow faded leaves drooping there in the sickening air, and see in them companions to her fate, and caress them with a weary hand—the hand that once dealt life or death at pleasure, and was touched with as

reverent a kiss of homage as that which queens receive.
Susceptible, impressionable still, a thrill of terrible joy ran
through her, as at some symbol and metaphor of vengeance,
sure, if slow, as she saw gnawing at its roots the poisonous
fungi—they were to her an omen and an augury.

"Ah!" she whispered to the flower, with the graceful,
imaginative fancy which once had been her softest charm,
now warped, usurped, and darkened, and made evil like herself, "they have shorn you of beauty, of fragrance, of glory,
of life. No sun shines on you, and none think you fair. You
are dead, and the world will give you no place—but you hold
what will poison still!"

"Was any one ever so happy as you make me?" Lucille
asked him, with a sigh of joy, as she leaned against him, in
the lateness of that night, looking upward at the stars, while
there stretched below the casement, the winding waters and
the dark woodlands of the home that had been her bridal
gift. She did not know why, for all answer, he pressed her
closer to his heart.

"Thank God!"

"And you!" she murmured, while her eyes looked upward into his, "with all the glory and the greatness of your
life, you never forget Lucille."

"When I forget Lucille, my life will have ceased!"

His head was bowed over her, and his voice was sunk to
that deep tenderness which changed so utterly the chill
languor of its habitual tone, and was never heard save by
her. She was an exquisite child to him still, with all her
soft caprices, her poetic earnestness, her fairy fancies that
were law to him, her unsullied innocence that was hallowed
to him, and only became tenfold the fairer, tenfold the
fonder, to his sight and to his heart through the changed
ties which made her young life one with his.

The keenest remorse sleeps often and long, as the deadliest serpent lies dulled, and still, in peace through many hours; and in the happiness of Lucille almost he found his own, for in her he saw his atonement and his expiation.

She lifted her head with a fond caress;—those kisses of Lucille's lips seemed to purify his own; remembering them, callous words had not seldom been checked, a pitiless sneer not seldom been foregone. He strove—as far as his nature could—to *be* what she believed him.

"How beautiful the night is! The day smiles on us, but the night always seems fullest of God's love and pity!" she said, while her eyes gazed up to the still starlit skies with that meditative love of nature which beheld "God in all things," and found poems in all, from the lowliest flower to the darkest storm.

He smiled tenderly on her;—to comprehend this was not possible to him; in his youth he had never known it, in his mature years it was yet farther from him; but in her it was sacred to him from disdain, safe even from a jest.

"You see beauty in all the world, Lucille! If these chill, lustreless nights of England are so lovely to you, what will the Southern ones be—the nights of Baiæ, of Sicily, of Greece?"

Where they leant against the balcony in the moonlight, he spoke of all to which he would take her some leisure time, when the pressure of office should relax and leave him free; of hours on the Mediterranean, where the lateen-boats were filled with fragrant freights of violets or olive-wood; of luminous waters, with the golden orange fruit and purple grapes hanging above the waves; of nights in the Carnival time, when from some lofty casement she would look out on the Roman throng and on the dome of St. Peter's, studded and circled with light; of moonlit evenings, floating down the soft, grey Bosphorus, with each stroke of the oars leaving a trail of phosphor gold, and the snows of Mount Olympus towering in the lustrous radiance of the stars. Of scenes and hours which he drew from the memories of a long life, accomplished eloquence and facile words supplying that poetic temper which, so vivid in her, had never, even in youth, existed in him, so that its absence could not strike coldly or harshly on her, as she listened to the mellow music of his voice, and the graphic painting of his words, and let her thoughts float over the golden glories which steeped that rich dreamland, her future.

And in such hours as this—letting memory drift from him, and the fevered ambitions and bitter contests of his world be forgot, while his thoughts and his words took their colour from hers—Strathmore himself was *almost* happy. "Almost"—for the great lost soul of the man could never wholly cast aside the burden of its sin; and the light of his life, that "light which never was on land or sea," had died for ever for him when Marion Vavasour had betrayed him, and Erroll had fallen by his hand.

## CHAPTER XXV.

### Quæstores Paricidii.

It was far past midnight in Westminster, and as the Minister, whose sweeping and polished eloquence withered like an ice-blast all it smote, passed out from the House, after a great field-night, the approaches were hemmed in by a crowd breathless to see and eager to welcome him. Successful, but never popular; firm rooted in the confidence, but holding no place in the love, of the nation; wondered at, but scarce understood, in a country which deifies the Commonplace, and calls its best Man of Business its best Statesman, the subtle and profound intellect of Strathmore was little comprehended; his genius was state-craft, his aspiration absolute dominance; born to rule, to command, and hold an undisputed sceptre, he was as little capable, at heart, of sympathy with the English nation, as the English nation with him. Solely beneath his sway, they would have been ruled with the steel of a Sulla at home, but they would have never been degraded and ridiculed abroad. The hand of the tyrant might have been iron, but it would have grasped a sword never to be bribed into its sheath by an appeal to a trader's instincts.

Thus, England had little comprehension of him, and as little love; but the spirit of his policy was essentially the spirit which ennobles the blood of a country, and gives her the fear of her foes and the faith of her allies; and although this is the spirit which of all others is most lacking in the politics of the nation, and is deemed by her most costly and "idealic," there are hours, now and then, when the blood stagnant in her veins is roused by it, as the war-horse which has long worn the girths of the huckster's saddle, and borne the trader's pack, still rouses to the trumpet-blast of the charge, and scents the battle afar off with eager, restless memories of glory gone.

This night had been one of them, and for once the old grand temper was awake in the country, and it recognised its exponent in the man, who, if his hand were iron, would at least uphold with it the might of England, and not put it behind him for the gold of a shopkeeper's bribe, to be slipped into the closed palm.

As he passed out into the night the crowds pressed closer and closer, and cheered him to the echo: that night in the autumn of the bygone year, when he had given his life to the peril of the seas for the sheer sake of those perishing in the storm, had brought his name home to the hearts of the people with a warm human sympathy, which the aristocratic exclusivism and the rapid brilliance of his career had banished, rather than won. It had made his name loved by thousands whose eyes had never rested on him, and whose lives could render his no comprehension. It was in the hearts of the people now, and they were stirred as by one impulse; their shouts of welcome echoed to the night, roused by something higher than the trading interest, nobler than mere popular clamour; it was homage given, unbought and unbidden, to that which was loftiest, truest, grandest in Strathmore's nature.

For the moment he was moved to something holier than mere lust of power, to something warmer than the mailed pride of ambition, as he bent his head to the assembled multitudes; it was not the patrician who acknowledged the acclamation of the populace, it was the man who recognised the sympathy of his brethren.

He sank back in the solitude of his carriage, with a new and softened light within his eyes, and a weary sigh of rest after conflict.

He had done evil, but he had done also good—good, he hoped, wide, lasting, wrought for his country and for the sake of millions, who yet lay in the womb of the future. Might not this suffice to wash out the blood-stain on his life?

Scattering the people clustered in the narrow ways, the carriage moved forward in the clear light of the summer moon. The cheers rose deafening on the air; the masses swayed and surged in the fitful shadows; the great stone piles pealed back in echo the name the multitude hurled in honour to the starlit skies—"STRATHMORE! STRATHMORE!"

As the waves of a sea part and roll back, so the waves of human life swept aside with their mighty murmur, and, as it had risen from the sea-depths, with all its lost and evil beauty, known through all the change of years and ravages of a dishonoured life, so there rose to his sight, from the waving crowds and flickering shades of night, the face of Marion Vavasour. For a moment seen, and in a moment lost. Yet in that moment they had looked on one another, and an eternity could have told neither more.

The new and better light died out from Strathmore's eyes; a great anguish tightened about him; a dread, such as had seized him when he had seen her face in the yellow autumn mists of White Ladies, clenched upon his life, withering all hope, all peace, all future unborn years. The temptress and companion of his sin was that sin's avenger.

"Atonement!" The lurid cruel eyes of the woman for whose beauty he had steeped his soul in guilt, mocked at it, and drove him out from rest, as the Furies drove Orestes, even when remorse had brought him weary, and worn, and sick unto death, to lie, if but for one brief hour, at the foot of the altars of God.

It was long past midnight.

His face was haggard, and his step had changed from its firm and stately tread to one slow and weary, as he passed through the halls and corridors of his ministerial residence, through the glow of white light, rich hues, delicate marbles, and clustering foliage. He had come from a proud success, with which Europe would teem on the morrow; he had come from the homage of the peoples, rendered as by one voice to him as the upholder of the honour of their nation. Yet it was not as a victor that he returned, and had the world beheld him in his solitude, it would not have found one memory of its triumph remaining with the man who, but a few seconds before, had spoken in the name of England the grand challenge which would uplift her ancient fame in the sight of a listening world, and who now came, as the guilty come into the presence of the innocent, with the knowledge and the burden of a dead sin alone with him, and upon him.

He passed through the silent chambers into Lucille's, where the aromatic silvery lamplight was soft and shaded, burning low.

Early in the evening he had returned with her from a state gathering, and had bidden her go to her rest; for used to the child-like simplicity and even tenor of her years at Silver-rest, she was too young to be much in the restless vortex of that great world, of which her loveliness and his name had made her at once a queen—a queen as guileless and unconscious in her child-sovereignty now, as when her crown was of the woodland violets, and her wealth of the ocean shells, by the sea-shore at Silver-rest.

She had obeyed him; she had no will save his, the gentlest guide, the surest guardian her life could ever have owned, since he had bent the iron of his nature like a reed, and changed his very character, until all its coldness, egotism, and ascetic indifference to all which weaker men hold dear, were lost in tenderness for her. Listening long for the echo of his step, she had sunk to sleep, with words of prayer for him the last upon her lips. He moved through the long space of the chamber, and stood beside her couch, looking on that rest to which the night brought no evil memories, and whose dreams were pure and joyous as the dreams of infancy.

Her bright hair fell unloosed about her, a flush was on her cheeks, for the night was warm, her head rested on her arm in all the grace of profound repose, and that unconscious and dreaming youth smote him tenfold with the bitterness of guilt as he stood looking down upon her in the shaded silvery light; was his heart one on which it should be hushed, were his lips those whose kiss should wake her from her slumber?

Once more in the shadows of the night the eyes of his temptress and destroyer had looked on him, rising up from the surge of the multitudes as she had risen from the surge of the waves, forbidding him peace, claiming him hers by right of their dead sin, by right of their mutual guilt to the life which had been slaughtered by the lie of the traitress, and by the hand of the assassin. What place had *he* beside the rest of innocence? It were juster that he were driven out to dwell with the lost, and the accursed, in the shame and the hatred of all things pure and sinless, of all lives loved of God.

As though even in sleep conscious when he was near, Lucille stirred, and awakened, with the light in her fair eyes, and the smile upon her face with which she had awakened from the sleep of childhood in her dead mother's bosom, and had looked upward to the gaze of him whose crime had made her desolate ere yet she knew her loss or felt her wrong. Her low cry thrilled his heart with its waking welcome, the flush of a beautiful gladness deepened the warmth of her cheeks, her arms were thrown about his neck, while her lips breathlessly whispered sweet, eager questions for his honour, his triumphs, his greatness, all dear to her, as the life to which, in *her* sight, they gave the sanctity of the Patriot and the grandeur of the Ruler.

The voice which answered her quivered slightly; the lips which met her caress were cold; the face which bent over her was dark and worn with the memories which thronged about him in the hush of night. The colour died from her cheek, the light was quenched in her eyes, the shadow of his own fate fell upon her.

"You suffer! You are ill! What is it—what has grieved you?" she asked him, in the rapid dread, the vague terror of any evil which menaced him.

He drew her closer to his heart, and the dissimulation, the self-control which were alike his nature and training, did not desert him now.

"Nothing, my own love. I have been speaking two hours, and the debate has been a tempestuous and lengthened one, till for once I am weary and fatigued; that is all."

She did not doubt him: that his lips would have spoken other words save those of truth, she dreamed no more than she dreamed of the blood-stain on his life; but the eyes which took all their joy from his gazed wistfully upward to the face which, waking from her slumber, she had seen, not for the first time darkened and careworn, with the resurrection of a guilty past, the futile yearning of a great remorse.

"All? You are sure it is all?" she asked him, wistfully. "You would not keep anything from me even in love? You would not withhold even a thought? You would let Lucille share your pain as she shares your glory?"

His heart sickened, his conscience shrank under the tender words; his eyes, fathomless and unrevealing beneath every gaze and every torture, fell under the questioning appeal of those uplifted to him in their innocence, unconscious of the anguish that they dealt.

Evil should not have been the salvation which had saved her; guilt should not have been the secret of the heart on which hers leaned! A quick shudder ran through his frame; he drew her to him with passionate force.

"None would have loved you as I love! None could have been to you as I am, Lucille?"

"Ah! No, no. Why ask?—you know that so well!"

And as she clung to him, her bright hair falling over his arms, her eyes full of such liquid light as painters give to the pure and happy eyes of angels, she heard but in his words the tenderness of her husband's love, and had no knowledge in them of the sleepless dread of that remorse which strove to lull its suffering, and to find peace where no peace was, with the remembrance of her guiltless life, blessing and blessed by him.

## CHAPTER XXVI.
### The Outcast by the Gates.

LIGHT, and colouring, the coolness of water, the shade of leafy depths, the fragrance of flowers, the green belts of sloping lawns, and the sparkling spray of fountain columns tossed aloft among the brilliance of blossom and the lofty heads of trees, all she thirsted for were here, where Marion Vavasour stood looking through the iron tracery of gates, as the prisoner through his bars gazes at the world to which he can never go forth again. They were the lodge-gates to the grounds of the Thames villa of S. A. R. le Duc D'Etoile, filled with the choicest gathering of England at a brilliant fête, that was simply called a garden party. Where she stood, crouched down against the iron scroll-work, in the dust of the highway, she could see the velvet slopes of turf, the pyramids of bloom, the glimpse of white distant terraces through the breaks of stately avenues—she could hear the swell of far-off music, even the low murmur of a laugh when a group swept near—she could breathe in the rich fragrance of flowers and of perfumes—she could look, in one word, on the life of her Past.

A few years since, and he who was host there had led her through the salons of the Tuileries, bending to her word in homage, seeking no empire so precious as one smile from the lips that poets hymned, and the eyes that recalled all the glory of Helen's. A few years since, and she had been of them, with them, omnipotent by right of every sovereign grace—unrivalled, were it only by the light of that *angelico riso* which played upon no other beauty as it played on hers.

*Now* the Prince d'Etoile would have passed her by unknown;—and she stood without his gates among the outcasts of the great highway, one with the roofless, nameless beggars, who, in the whirling dust and summer scorch, crouched among the trampling hoofs and crowded wheels to look with hungry, wondering eyes through the bars at these stray glimpses of the life, so unlike theirs, that their sight could not grasp, nor their fancy realise it. Her hands were clenched upon the bars, her brow was pressed on the cold iron; she saw the blent light and shadow, with the sun-gleam on the lawns, and the glimpses of blossom and of colour that glanced between the trees; she hungered for her life that was lost for ever; she stood an alien and an exile looking on the things that knew her no more!

The white wand of a lacquey struck her on the shoulder with a sharp reprimand; the same action, the same words with which, in the years that were gone, the chasseur of the Marchioness of Vavasour and Vaux had used to the Bohemian Redempta. There is a wild, wanton Nemesis at times in human life. She started at the blow and the indignity; for the moment she forgot that she had no longer the power to *resent*—most bitter loss of this world's losses!—and turned with her old superb grace, with her old proud patrician rebuke.

In the carriage, whose way she stopped, its occupant leaned back among the cushions alone, bowing, something haughtily and distantly, as the throng, gathered about the gates, lifted their hats to salute him. As she raised her head she met his eyes; he knew her; a quiver passed over his face; he shrank visibly, irrepressibly, as though a knife had struck him; and his carriage swept on through the ducal gates, leaving her without in the dust and the throng of the parched highway.

A moment before, full of the projects, the contests, the purposes, and the successes of power, of the attitude of the session which hitherto had been in all its triumphs his own *aristeia*, and of the far-stretching foresight and matured calculations of the ambition which had been from his youth, and would be to his death, his master-passion, Strathmore, at sight of her, forgot all save his past, its dead guilt leaving its weakness in the life in all else strong—its buried crime claiming him slave, who in all else was ruler. Leader and chief, master of men, and moulder of circumstance, he could not purchase or enforce oblivion—he could not choose but bow, conscience-stricken, before the eyes of an outcast in the throng! He had loved her, he had sinned for her: she was in his life for ever, its burden, its retribution, its destroyer.

All his past came back, with that one look from the sleepless eyes of Marion Vavasour.

While he joined his own world, while he spoke the courtly nothings of the day, while he chatted with princes and with peers, and moved through the brilliant groups of the gardens, her memory was on him, and the sense of a remembered crime, fresh as though born of yesterday, upon his life.

A few lengths of leafy avenue, a few stretches of sward, and he looked on the fairness of Lucille's face, in its first and loveliest dawn of youth—youth without a shadow, without a fear, without a soil. The centre of a group whose polished homage she still heard with naïf surprise, and still turned from with graceful carelessness, she stood on the broad white steps of a terrace, where a thousand blossoms encircled her in their luxuriant colours, like a young Angel of the Flowers. Against her leant a handsome boy, a little heir of the house, who looked up at her with loving eyes, while she smiled down upon his beauty and wound a wreath of half-opened lilies among his golden locks, as much a child as he, as joyous and as innocent. She was a picture, soft as a poet's dream, in the haze of earliest summer; yet he looked on it with a shudder: he saw it through the darkness of his past. A brief while, and he knew that she would smile thus upon the laughing eyes, and toy thus with the sunny hair, of a child born to his race, and bearer of his name,—and he from whom her child would take existence, had been the destroyer of her father!

Thus ever his own sin recoiled and struck him, in his gentlest thoughts, his purest hours.

Strathmore, to whom fear was unknown, and in whom the common weaknesses of men had no place, dreaded with untold horror to see the eyes of Marion Vavasour fasten on Lucille; he felt as though the very air must tell his secret when she passed the woman whose lie had made him slay the man whom he had loved.

In his vengeance he had bidden her go forth to the fate that waited her; to live as they live, who trade in beauty, to die as they die, craving a crust. His bidding had been obeyed, the condemnation to which he had sent her out had become hers to the uttermost of its law; and now—the Outcast he had made was in his path, stronger than his strength, more powerful in her abject wretchedness than he in his haughty eminence, an Até that dogged his steps, and rose, haunting and abhorred, between him and the light of the summer sun, between him and the holiness of innocence. Where he stood, with a calm smile on his lips, with serene and witty words at his command, flattered, honoured, sought, a courtier, a statesman, no ambition beyond his grasp, no rank but what could be his at his will, his thoughts were filled with restless, fugitive schemes to banish from his sight, and thrust out of his world, that nameless beggar at the gates!

A homeless wanderer was more powerful than he; he had

had his vengeance, whose sweetness he had once said coul
never escape him, but its fruit was his also, and of whateve
it brought forth must he eat.

An hour later and his carriage swept with swift and siler
roll over the turf, and under the pleasant shadow of the tree
in the warmth of the setting sun. Lucille lay back besid
him, her bright, rapid words broken with sweet melody c
happy laughter, her face turned to him, radiant with the ga
softness of her father's smile, while she told him a thousan
brilliant, airy trifles of the world that was so new to her, an
of which she saw but one phase,—full of graceful beaut
and harmonious as music to *her*. And he heard her while h
thoughts were heavy with deadly memories, he looked on he
uplifted eyes while his own restlessly sought the face of th
woman to whom he was for ever bound by the indissolub
bondage of a mutual crime. He dreaded the gaze of h
traitress, as he had never dreaded the close presence of deat
when the waves beat him down, and the cold, curled mass c
the reared waters buried him beneath them—he dreaded fc
it to fall on the one beside him, as men dread the breath c
a pestilence to pass over what they love.

The carriage swept on through the green avenues ar
the sunlit freshness of the park, along the side of glancir
water, and with the low gladness of mirth on his ear. Su
denly Lucille's voice dropped, her laugh was hushed, over h
face stole the earnest sadness of a deep compassion; sl
leaned nearer to him, and her hand stole into his.

"Look there! That is the woman to whom I gave n
roses. How weary, how wretched, how *lost* she looks! Cou
wo do nothing for her?"

And he heard the pitying words spoken of her fathei
murderess!—he saw her eyes fill with a divine tenderne
for the woman whom he had loved with a madman's pa
sion, and sent out to a vengeance great as her guilt and b
own!

By a ghastly fascination his glance followed hers into tl
throng about the gates through which they passed, and I

saw, fastened on Lucille's face, a look like the chained and baffled panther's, thirsting for her prey; a look that sent through all his veins an icy shiver.

Lucille turned pale, and her large soft eyes, which rested on the outcast with such mournful pity, filled with a startled fear like those of a young fawn, as she leant farther back in the barouche, and her hand unconsciously closed nearer on his.

"How strangely she looks! She frightens me!"

For his life, for her life, he could not have answered her, while upon them was the gaze of Marion Vavasour quoting the past, claiming the future, by right of that mutual, unexpiated crime which had destroyed the guiltless. His face grew white, his courage shrank from Lucille's exclamation, he shuddered beneath the clinging touch of her hand; and the woman who watched them saw that even now the first hour of her vengeance had come, that even now she had pierced through the single weakness of his mailed strength, and forced him to *remember*.

A moment more, and the carriage swept on through the light and shade, leaving the homeless wanderer in the throng; and he saw but his own memory of the woman he had worshipped, of the woman who had betrayed him, with the diamonds crowning the gold wealth of her hair, and the lustrous, languid light in her antelope eyes, as she had been in the glory of her youth, in the sovereignty of her beauty, on the night when, at her tempting, he bowed and fell, knowing nothing save the sweetness of her kiss!

Lucille looked upward at him with anxious wistfulness.

"Are you in pain? Are you ill?"

Life could not have held for him a more bitter pang than lay in her question!

But he was long used to wear the impenetrable armour of an unmoved serenity, and live beside a guiltless life without a sign of self-betrayal. His voice had its accustomed calm as he answered her, and his eyes met hers with their old tenderness, if in them there was a deeper and more weary melancholy.

"No, my dear one, it is nothing—save heat, perhaps, and I am somewhat tired. But,—Lucille,—do not look at those unhappy outcasts again; you cannot help them; the vastest wealth could not avail to succour all the wretchedness of a great city; it only agitates you, and is injurious for you, my darling, and, as such, pains me."

Those who had best known his past, could not have heard in his words or in his voice the betrayal of anything save solicitude for her; still less could she have done so.

She looked upward at him with a smile that was earnest and almost mournful.

"I will not, if I can help it; but when I see any who look so hopeless as that, I wonder why life is so beautiful for me and is so stricken for them! Why is there so *much* misery? All would love God, and do good, I think, if they were happy?"

"A beautiful and simple code of ethics, my child!—if you could give the world your innocence and your faith, it might be true."

"But is it not true?" pleaded Lucille, while her thoughts travelled wistfully over the mysteries of evil and of pain which were vague and strange to her dawning life, which had been one long, cloudless day, under one guardian care since her birth. "Love is born of gentleness, and gentleness, I think, would win the harshest and the most lost to *something* better. Perhaps if even that woman we saw just now had been shown mercy when she first suffered, she might not be so utterly callous as she looks? How strangely her eyes fastened on me, did you see? Why was it?"

How could she know that every one of her words was worse than a dagger in his heart?

"Why, my love?" repeated Strathmore, wearily. "Why? Because those who are lost and evil, hate all that is guileless and pure! Because her life is guilty, and yours is sinless!"

As the night follows the day, Marion Vavasour followed the lives she hated. Having once seen that her sight and her presence had power to pierce him to the quick, she never released him from it; wherever one of the people could follow a man of rank and eminence, she followed him; secretly, so that no other noted her, but surely and constantly, until that vigil, veiled but unceasing, grew intolerable to him, with that torture which he had dealt out to her, when, before the stroke of his vengeance fell in the sight of assembled Paris, go where she would his eyes were upon her, seek escape as she might his silent presence was ever near, mutely quoting to her the Past, mutely menacing the Future.

When he left the Lower House, or drove out of Downing-street, he saw her: when he passed from State ceremonies he met her eyes, where she stood amidst the crowds which thronged the approaches of the palace, and were trodden by horses' hoofs, and driven asunder by the whips of lacqueys. Leaving the fond words and lingering farewell of Lucille in the brightness of morning, there, near his gates, in the sunlight, would be the form of the woman whom his vengeance had driven out among the lost, nameless, hopeless multitude. Going from the closeness of contests, from the struggle of parties, from the question of peace or war, weary with the heated pressure of lengthened debate, or the success of a hard-won victory, his pride was stricken, his victory was embittered, his strength beaten down, his greatness made miserable and worthless in his sight, by the guilt that was brought back upon his memory as he saw the face of his temptress in the midnight gloom, or in the greyness of the breaking dawn.

Her presence—almost *felt* rather than actually seen—grew intolerable to him; the sight of that haggard face, with its thirsty eyes and its wreck of womanhood, its fearful relics of grace and of beauty, lingering there as though in hideous mockery of what she once had been, became feared by him to whom fear was unknown, with a nervous and unconquerable dread. He strove to bury his past, to live it down, to wash it out with the assoiling of atonement, to steep it to oblivion in the fair life that he cherished and guarded, and force it into silence under the grandeur of a dazzling and ambitious career,—and Marion Vavasour was for ever before him, the haunting wraith of those dead years, the avenger, as she had been the temptress, of his crime.

He could not free himself from her; he was powerless here. Wealth, station, command, were impotent to force out of his path the woman who dogged it; eminence and authority were of no avail to put away from him the pursuant presence of an outcast. Life was hers as it was his, and where she came was common to the poorest as to the proudest, the broad and crowded highway of the world. True, he could have given her into arrest as a vagrant, but that he dared not do; he knew the menace that spoke in her eyes, he knew that from her lips enough might be told of the past that bound them, and of that hour in the solitude of the sea-storm, when his hand had loosed her to the grave, to crush and break for ever with its horror Lucille's love and life.

She knew not the vengeance which she held thus unconscious in her hands, but *he* knew it; and it chained him from every act which might have otherwise released him from the woman who, under the scourge and agony of his denial, had prophesied the hour when he should ask in vain of earth or heaven the mercy he had refused. Now and again wild, dark, baseless thoughts drifted through Strathmore's mind, for his nature could not wholly change; but they were each perforce abandoned, each fraught with too close danger of waking the very evil that he feared. The sense of weakness and of dread tightened upon him, worst tyranny of all to the man to whom feebleness and fear were craven things, unknown and unpitied; a baffled impotent hopelessness began to gnaw into his life as it had done when he had first learned that Valdor had unearthed his secret; a sense of despair grew on him; atonement was a madman's dream, since guilt was deathless thus!

He dreaded, moreover, lest Lucille should note the constant vigil of the woman to whom she had given her roses; lest she should question him of it in her ignorance, whilst he, powerful in wealth, in rank, in command, would be powerless to drive out from her the presence, and ward from her the gaze of the one in whom she saw but a beggared wanderer of the People. When he was not with her, he sought with almost morbid solicitude that she should never be alone. His own days, claimed and absorbed by public life, he provided that all her hours should be so filled with a succession of pleasures, entertainments, and companionship, that in his absence no space should be left for her to spend in solitude, that she should never observe how closely the outcast to whom she had tendered her flowers watched her when she drove from her own gates.

For Marion Vavasour, in the strange caprice of a hopeless hatred, which grew the more bitter because each day as it rolled by brought her but a more vivid sense of its own utter impotence for vengeance, never wearied in following the young girl whom she longed to destroy not less than to destroy him. Day after day, night after night, she spent the long hours watching and waiting for one glimpse of Lucille.

Under the park trees, where those more homeless and more wretched yet than she had slept through the summer nights, and lay in the dry long grass in the sun, staring blankly at the delicate glittering throng of the life with which they had nothing in common,—scarcely their humanity —she saw her sweep by through the light, whilst men checked their horses, and the crowd without the rails turned to gaze after a loveliness that touched all those who looked on it, who bore it away, rather in their hearts than in their thoughts, as men who have looked on a face of Titian, or a dream of Delaroche, bear its memory away into the heat and noise of the busy streets and the avarice and struggles of their narrow lives, and are the better for it, though they scarce know why. In the stillness of a Sunday noon she would steal down and hide amongst the hanging foliage,

where she had been given alms from Strathmore's wealth,
and watch, from the distance, where Lucille wandered among
the aisles of her rose-gardens, or rested near him where he
sat, as they believed unseen, under the shadow of cedars or
acacias, whilst he listened to her words with the smile upon
his lips that was—for the moment at least—a smile of peace
and happiness. In the heat of a summer day, while the
pavement was white with the driving dust, and her temples
throbbed with a dizzy pain under the incessant thunder of
the street traffic, she heard the long shout roll down the
ranks "for the Lady Cecil Strathmore's carriage," and saw
her passing from concert, or déjeûner, or drawing-room, as
her outriders made way for the stately equipage, while the
woman to whom power, and luxury, and homage had been
the very core of her life, envied these, the outward symbols
and privileges of rank and wealth, more hungrily than worthier and fairer things. In the depth of midnight or in the
breaking dawn, one amongst the ever-toiling crowds whose
feet know no rest, and whose ebb and flow are like the unceasing roar and murmur of a sea, she saw her, beside Strathmore, passing from some palace dinner or court ball, the
bearer of his name, the sharer of his honours, while she herself stood there, in the gas-glare and the hurrying throng,
alone in the vast inhospitable city, with no life waiting her,
no companionship, no shelter, but those she shrank from and
abhorred;—since the haughty patrician, the proud aristocrat,
the delicate, refined, poetic epicurean, still lived in Marion
Vavasour's nature, and could not perish until death itself.

Thus—day after day, night after night—a ferocious,
poisonous hate grew up, and strengthened in her, for the
young life that was made one with his; strengthened the
more, because powerless to injure; and he knew it, yet he
could not thrust her from his path—he could not force her
from the earth in which she had common right to dwell.
The tide of human life was beyond his control, and had swept
them together even whilst furthest sundered by every social
barrier. She lived, and in her lived also his buried crime;

here the proud statesman had no power, the negligent man of the world no shield, the polished courtier no armour, the "iron hand under the silken glove" no weapon;—he knew his sin, and lived in feverish, broken, shapeless expectation, lest its retribution should rise, and pass over him, to smite the life that was sheltered in his bosom.

"I see that woman so often—that woman to whom I gave my roses!" said Lucille, wonderingly, once, while with a gesture that was almost fear she shrank closer to him as their carriage drove from the French Embassy through the midnight streets.

"You allowed her alms, my love; it is sufficient to make her follow you. Notice her no more."

He kept his voice calm and indifferent, and the reply was given without hesitance, seemingly without effort; but instinctively, unconsciously, where she leaned against him in the darkness of the night, he drew her closer to his heart, as though she were menaced by some near and physical peril.

As his eyes had met those of Marion Vavasour, in the flickering light of the lamps, while his carriage had flashed past the place where she stood, and her gaze had travelled from him to rest on the face of Lucille, to the memory of both had returned the words that Redempta the Zingara had spoken, long years before, when they who had become each other's curse first met under the summer stars, by the Bohemian waters:

"There shall be love; and of the love, sin; and of the sin, crime; and of the crime, a curse; and the curse shall pursue and destroy the innocent."

The curse already had destroyed lives that were guiltless; —was yet another still demanded?

## CHAPTER XXVII.

Thalassa! Thalassa!

IT was on the close of a burning day in the hot Midi; a day of intolerable glare, of destroying drought, of parched, stifling, cholera-laden noxiousness under those brazen skies, within those relentless walls of the Toulon Bagne. The horrible heat had made even the *gardes-chiourmes* heavy and listless, and they had suffered a few of the *forçats*, unchidden, to drop down, gasping and powerless, like panting hounds; nature wears itself out, and humanity is remembered now and then, even in a convict prison.

At one part of the fortifications a brace of galley-slaves was working, a little asunder from the rest, on a sandy level facing the sea, with a single overseer near them; brandy, and the heat, and the sand glitter, made the *garde* sleepy and inattentive; while heavy bribes from a young Englishman, who had of late been much about the Bagne, had something, yet more than the sultry air, and the fumes of the *petits verres*, to do with his unusual lack of vigilance and the separate post of labour he had given to the political *déportés*, on that stretch of sand excavations lying in front of the stirless summer sea. They were kept late at labour there, for the new stone curtain and redoubts that were to be erected at that point were pressing, and the government had directed that no time should be lost, but that separate parties of the *galériens* should be told off, to continue the works night and day until they were completed.

The *forçats* were of less value than the brutes whose toil they bore, and to whose labour they were harnessed; it mattered nothing how many hundreds of them might wear out, drop down, and perish in that giant travail—if they died by droves so much the better, there were the less expenses for the exchequer.

The hot day faded, the twilight fell lightly, rapidly, without stars, for the skies were black and stormy. The *garde-*

*chiourme* lit his lantern, the prisoners toiled on, with spade and pickaxe, deep down in the sand and gravel, with their backs bowed and their limbs weighted with irons, and their breath like blown and worn-out horses in that unnatural and herculean toil to which their lives had no habit, their limbs had no use; while scattered all along the sand level were the chains of convicts, with the crack of the overseers' whips sounding on the silence, and the glitter of the lanterns shining down the line in the descending twilight that would soon be night.

And beyond, on the water, the yacht lay at anchor, with a blue light, that she had hung out for many nights past, burning at the mast-head, to prevent, as it was understood, her being run down in the darkness by the *chasse-marées* and other vessels that came to or past the port of Toulon, trading from Italy and the East.

The *garde-chiourme*, with grumbling imprecations, turned to re-light his lantern that had gone out, setting it down on a block of granite while he adjusted its wick, growling coarse Bas-Rhin oaths at his prisoners for not doing their work quicker; it was a signal, though no word had ever passed between him and them; a slight risk made worth his while to bear by Lionel Caryll's rouleaux of gold pieces, with which he could purchase his escape from his hateful post, and buy the little strip of land in Alsace, which ever since his boyhood he had vainly coveted. His back was turned; with a wrench the *déportés* tore asunder the irons which had been all but filed through, and only hung together by a link, sprang up out of the pit in which they worked, and fled, fleet as hill-deer, over the sandy surface in the grey of the falling night, their footfall noiseless on the loose and yielding earth. Busy with his lantern, he did not, or seemed not to, hear their stealthy and sudden flight. When he turned the full blaze of his light on the gravel-pit, and, looking down, found the yawning hole untenanted, and raised the hue-and-cry, the *condamnés* had had three minutes' start—a priceless treasure in that race for liberty and life.

The alarm was given. Force, brutal and omnipotent, was out like a sleuth-hound after those who sought that most begrudged and costly thing on earth—their Freedom.

The bastions swarmed with soldiery; the *gardes-chiourmes* poured out with hunters' fury, petty tyrants who had lost their slaves; the shots rang on the still night, all Toulon was astir; two *forçats* had escaped, two men out of whom all sense and sin of that daring vice of Liberty should have been crushed and drilled in the granite walls and under the iron chains of the life that had lowered them to beasts, and robbed them even of their Names. The Bagne was in tumult, the hell-hounds tore out on the search over the wide sand level stretching to the sea, the bullets hissed through the air, the gendarmes hurled themselves, armed to the teeth, on the track of the fugitives. Inside the Bagne they would have been recaptured at once; outside the walls there was one chance, for that one chance was the Sea.

The Sea!—incarnate liberty itself, that held out freedom to the bondsmen. The shots seethed past them and fell round them, scattering the sand in their eyes and ploughing the ground at their feet, their ankles plunged into the loose soil, the yells, and shouts, and curses of the alarm were borne to their ears on the wind, their limbs were dragged down by links of the hanging chains, their strength was impoverished by toil and misery, a fate worse than death was close on them, with every second that brought their pursuers nearer and nearer ere they could reach the grey line of the gleaming water, longed for, panted for, so near and yet so far! Across the line of sand, yellow and level in the fitful shadows, with the severed fetters clanging like the trailing irons of escaping slaves, with the press of the close pursuit hunting them down, with the sound of the seas and the roar of the following multitude, the crash of the gendarmes' tread, and the hiss of the plunging shot deafening their ear and giddying their brain, with life and liberty beyond, and behind a doom more dread than death, they fled on through the heavy, breathless night.

They reached the water edge; the loose, fresh-raised sand embankment overhung the sea by some eight feet, the waves surging and churning below under the lash of the rising mistral. With that might, which desperation alone can lend, they cleared it with a bound of agony, and fell with a low, sullen splash and plunge into the dark waters.

A volley, fired by those in pursuit, thundered down the shore; the balls hissed and shrieked as they cut the water, while the oaths of gardes and gendarmes yelled furious upon the air. One, as he rose to the surface, was shot through the back; with a scream that echoed over the sea, he bounded out of the water in the reddened light, then sank never to rise again. The other dived, and the storm of balls passed harmlessly above him; ere he had leaped, he had torn off with such convulsive strength as is born of a supreme despair, the irons still clinging to his foot. He had no weight on him; he was a fearless swimmer; and there, at the mast-head, burned the signal-light, that to him, and for him, meant aid, succour, welcome, liberty, and all the breadth and freedom of the world. He kept under water, only rising rarely to the surface, and then so cautiously, that in the shadowy sultry evening he was unseen.* Those on the shore had seen both sink when the volley had been fired; they supposed both had been shot down when the death-shriek had rung over the sea. It was of little moment; both were dead instead of both *déportés*. The sea was alive for a while with boats, and lanterns, and men groping with grappling hooks and fishing-nets for the drowned bodies; while torches flung their ruddy glare over the white foam and black, angry waters, and he who lay under the waves, amidst the tumult and the flickering glare above him, knew—with every sound that passed, with every breath, for which he stole upward to the air in stealth and suffocation—the bitterness of death.

---

* In case any resemblance may be traced between the escapes of Valdor and of Jean Valjean, I may observe that the above chapter was written before I read the "Misérables," or knew that there was such an episode in the work.

Then—as though nature herself lent succour from the brutality of man to man, which outruns all the rage of desert birds, all the ferocity of forest beasts—the gathered clouds broke with a tempest of rain, driving, drenching, beating down the flames of the torches, and casting darkness over all the sea. The pursuit ceased, the search was given over;— the dead bodies of two *forçats!* what were they but carrion? At last—at last—he was alone in the sheltering water, and this darkness that to him was more blessed than ever is the sweetest light of summer moon, or gleam of bridal starlight. He rose, and through the denseness of the gloom and the ink-black sheet of falling rain, he saw, beaming star-like, the little azure light. Liberty, life, all the lost glories of his strength, all the robbed vigour of his manhood, swept back with a rush all through his frame. Even in that instant of mortal danger and physical misery, once more he had hope, and he had freedom; they are the twin angels of men's lives.

He swam out to the bright blue starry light—swam with that strength which comes in the extreme hours of our fate, making us "rend the cords even as green withes."

A few brief seconds more, and he stood on the deck; Lionel Caryll had saved him.

"Free—thank God!"

The words broke from both their lips as the wild rain-storm lashed round them; then, without sign or show of life, he fell down at the feet of the English youth, the blood gushing from his mouth and nostrils—his senses blind and gone.

Before the sun rose, the yacht was far on her way down the Mediterranean waters; Valdor was free.

Thus strangely does Circumstance turn avenger in this life.

---

## CHAPTER XXVIII.
### Under the Wings of the Angel.

IT was autumn at White Ladies.

The dying leaves were once more drifting on the wind; the sun set in stormy purpled skies and tawny pomp of tempest light: the seas ran high, and hurled their white foam-crested waves upon the sands:—it was the fall of the year, rich, grand, profoundly mournful, with here and there its summer hours few and fleeting, eagerly treasured, early lost, like the last lingering smiles on dying lips, in voiceless and eternal farewell to all that they have loved and blessed.

It was autumn, and evening; and Strathmore stood on the rose-terrace of White Ladies, while the lingering rays of the sun that had set poured a golden lustre over the crimson foliage, the brown rolling woods, and the river, yellow with the dead leaves of the water-lilies. The fever of an unutterable inquietude was on him—the fever of conscience, which knows no rest. He had left behind, in the rushing crowds and peopled streets of the great city, the face which had pursued him like a recurrent and inevitable fate; but she was in his life, she was in his thoughts, she poisoned all his peace, she accused him in memory of that past that he had sought to crush into oblivion. She had risen out of the surge of the vast throngs as she had risen from the waves; she had returned into his life, she who had cursed it. He did not know what he feared, yet he feared everything—*he!* —who had not known what fear was. Even the idolised life of Lucille had grown torture to him—he dreaded lest his unrest should lend its alarm to her, lest in his sleep dreaming words should betray him, lest in his eyes she should read the secret he veiled. Never yet was there crime which did not sooner or later know this doom!

He stood now looking over the sweep of forest, park, and sea that lay before him in the ruddy fading light. Power, honour, beauty of possessions, riches of heritage, the greatness which ennobles life, the love which softens and endears it—these were all his, and all were darkened, cankered, turned to misery and dread, by the shadow of one dead sin. All that was fair in his sight was poisoned by the past; all that was sacred for him was imperilled by his guilt; all that was dearest to him would be destroyed for ever, if one voice arose to whisper the knowledge his heart held.

His eyes filled with yearning and with pain as he gazed at the west, where the sun had sunk beyond the sea. He thought of Erroll.

"He is avenged—he is avenged!" he murmured, where he stood in the silence of the falling evening, "more utterly than if I had died upon a scaffold, as other murderers die!"

Yes—for the pang of the scaffold is but a moment, and Strathmore's chastisement was lifelong.

Like a promise of redemption, she whom the dead had bequeathed him looked upward in his eyes in the last lingering sunlight, as her hand stole into his.

"Why have you left me? We are alone for a day at the least, and when alone you are wholly my own!"

He shrank from the caressing words: "wholly hers!" while the darkness of the past claimed him, drawing him ever and ever down out of the innocence and light of her presence into its pestilential memories!

He pressed her to him with a passionate instinct, a feverish tenderness, born of a terrible and nameless prevision.

"Lucille!—Lucille! I have never given you an hour's pain—never denied you a single wish? I have made you happy? My love is sufficient for you, and you want no other?"

He spoke as he had spoken when she had wakened from her sleep, in vague, oppressive misery, in restless, irresistible longing to be told, again and again from her own lips, that through her the atonement of his sin was made. Oh, madman! who thought that atonement lay in the happiness of another life, instead of in the purification from passion, the renunciation of evil, of his own!

She looked up at him with wondering pain, and on her face was the look of an unspeakable love—a love beyond her childhood's faith, beyond her joyous youth; spiritualised, exhaustless, "faithful unto death," mournful even in its intensity, as though the tragedy from whence it sprang unconsciously shadowed it, and made it less the offspring of joy than the angel of consolation.

"Oh, my lord—my love!" she said, softly and passionately, while the tears rose up and stood in the eyes where, to him, there ever seemed to lie the sadness of her father's fate and of her young mother's piteous doom. "Have you need to ask me *that?* He whom you loved, knows how Lucille loves you. My life has no thought, no wish, no memory, but what are yours, for is not my life—*you?*"

He pressed her in a close embrace, that she might not see how his eyes filled and his face paled at the reverence and the sweetness of those tender words;—she loved him thus, and of that very love would be her death-blow, if ever from her father's distant grave the truth should arise and be revealed.

A letter she had lain down on the marble gleamed white against the dark and crimson leaves of the autumn roses; the superscription lay uppermost; as his glance, mechanically and without note of it, fell on the writing, he started with a shudder that she felt through all her frame as his arms were wound about her.

He loosened her from him, and seized it—all the golden and purple glories of the sunset reeled before his sight. The writing was that of the man who held his fate—of the hand that he had thought to weigh and fasten down, paralysed for ever, beneath the irons of the Toulon galley-slave.

"That letter!—That letter!——"

The words died on his lips faint and ill formed; even from her in that moment he could not wholly hide the terror that fell on him, passing all cowards' fear of death.

She looked upward, with the swiftness of affection, to notice any shade of pain.

"Why! What is it? Nothing that grieves you? It came just now; I took it from them, and brought it to you?"

"Quite right!" In that instant he had recovered self-command, and his voice was measured and gentle. "It gave me pain at the moment, my love, for—for—it is the writing of one whom I believed worse than dead. Leave me alone to read it. See!—there are your fawns waiting for you. Go, and give them their roses."

She looked at him a moment with wistful uncertainty; his voice was tranquil now, and he smiled on her, yet she could not forget that shudder which she had felt convulse him as she had been gathered in his arms.

"Go, my darling," he said, with a smile—a smile while his hand closed on the letter of the man whom he had thought silenced, as by the silence of the grave! "Go;—I would be alone a few moments."

She looked at him again, wistfully still; then went, for his wish was her law—went with the grace and swiftness of youth, for she had still a child's sure pleasures, her hands filled with autumn roses, her hair glancing in the sunlight, while the young deer trooped to meet her with the delicate chimes of their bells.

And he stood there with the opened letter in his hand, and the prescience of calamity, which had been upon him since he had first seen the face of Marion Vavasour in the summer midnight, become palpable, and fronting him with the work of his own hand. The crimson from the west shone full upon the page, and the words seemed to reel in a scarlet haze before him as he read:

"Strathmore, I am free, and in England. You may have learnt, ere now, that your noble nephew gave me liberty, and regained me more than life. I shall await you to-night on the shore by the monastery church; you will come as soon as the night has fallen. "VALDOR."

He who had been so deeply wronged, wrote with the command of a monarch—he who had wronged, stood with the letter crushed in his hand, without sense, sight, movement; all his life blasted in him.

The blow fell unsoftened, unprepared; the letters by which Lionel Caryll, bound to silence for a while, had at last, from the East, sent the tidings of his rescue of the condemned, had not as yet reached him. The words he read were like the delirium of a dream; the force which had unlocked the prisoner's chains and set him free, seemed unreal, unnatural, as power that should have burst the bonds of death and given resurrection from the grave. This was all he knew; that he who had the secret of his life had risen from a bondage, certain as the tomb, and held a vengeance vast as his own wrong!

As a tiger leaps from the gloom ere its presence is seen or its passage is traced, so his retribution sprang upon him. All was dark round him; unintelligible, untold; the prison gates had been broken, the living sepulchre been unsealed; his wealth, which had sent his young kinsman to wander at will in foreign lands, had been turned into the power which had loosed the fetters, and released the captivity of the man he had betrayed and condemned; the net of his own acts was wound about him; the dishonour which had seemed wisdom in his sight had been forged into the weapon of his own destruction. *His!* not his alone, or he had borne it. It was the life of Lucille that his dead sin menaced. For her he had done this thing; against her it now rose beyond his strength to save.

A stunned silence and tranquillity fell on him; suddenly and mutely as poison kills, all his life was shattered, and all hope destroyed;—there is no resistance in an absolute despair.

He held the letter clenched in his right hand, his face was grey and bloodless as a dead man's, he gazed with a blank stare out at the rose-hued, golden light: the world was unreal about him, the sun-rays glared blood-red in his sight;

he saw the face of Lucille, but it seemed far off—gazing at him with love that was anguish, with eyes that pierced his soul and saw the history there, with holiness that barred him from her and divorced them for evermore, while she floated farther and farther from him, borne away by an angel-band.

Dizziness seized him, he felt his senses failing, his sight growing dim: instinctively he grasped the marble column near, and strove to keep his consciousness, his calm;—she must not know!

"*Not know!*" He remembered that when the space of that night should be passed the knowledge of all would have reached her. He knew that she must die:—the life that lived but in his own, and the yet unborn life that he had given, both perish through his sin.

\* \* \* \* \*

She stood before him, with the fragrant roses in her hand, and the lingering stray beams of light shining in the spiritual sweetness of her eyes.

He shuddered beneath her gaze;—all that was dearest to him grew worse torture than devils frame. A little while,— and she would know him as he was. A little while,—and she would know that his kiss was accursed on her lips, that the barrier of an ineffaceable sin sundered them for ever, that the love she held the truest guardianship on earth was but a vain atonement for a brutal crime.

She came and knelt beside him, she wound her arms about him, she sought his lips with her caresses. Was he in suffering, was he in pain? He was silent to her! Why? He would keep nothing that grieved him from *her*, even in love!

And he had to smile on her while his heart was breaking! He had to look down into her eyes, while he knew that towards them stole the doom of his past! Imprisoned from her sight through all her life, his hidden sin was loosed to rend her from him and destroy her at the last. And in the failing light she gazed upward with her deep, dreaming love, and her lips, with the sinless smile of childhood, were lifted for his kiss!

O God!—the throbs of his heart, as they beat against hers, must tell her he thought the secret they held; on the darkness of his face she must behold the darkness of his soul! She leaned her cheek upon his hand,—the blood-stain there must scorch her. She laid her head against his breast,—the guilt it veiled must scare her from her resting-place.

The guardian of her peace, the husband of her youth, the idol of her trustful life—and through him she must die!

His arms closed round her with passionate anguish, his lips clung to hers with endless kisses,—to him it was as the embrace of death, to him it was hopeless as an eternal farewell.

Yet he held from her all sign;—he spared her while he could all knowledge of his torture;—he sacrificed his misery to her, as he would have sacrificed honour, greatness, life itself, and given himself to an eternity of woe, could he have bought redemption at his cost for her alone.

He left her;—and she had seen no trace of the agony which could have broken its bonds, and flung him at her feet, with tears of blood at every smile her fond eyes gave to his, at every lingering touch her lips left on his own. But where she could not follow or behold him—out in the shadows of the falling night, under the shelter of the leaves—that agony had its way, nature conquered the force that had chained it down and forbidden it all utterance.

He stood and gazed at her through the unclosed casements;—he knew that in life they might never meet again. The light fell around her, flowers in a wilderness of bloom enclosed her, above her, there stretched through the shadows, the ivory spear, and the white wings, of a sculptured Angel, Ithuriel; and upward to the statue's face she lifted her soft, haunting eyes, the eyes where the sadness of the past ever lay beneath the smile of childhood. And she must perish!—she, the redeemer of his life, by whom atonement had come to him, through whom all holier things had touched his heart.

He wondered that he lived!—that dumb, stupefied wonder of despair which seizes those who suffer, those to whom death *will* not come.

He saw nothing but her—the light shed a halo like a glory on her brow; her eyes, looking outward to the night, seemed to look through his soul; and above, where the marble Ithuriel leaned, the white wings of the guardian angel enclosed her, and the white spear banned from her, the innocent and the sacrificed, his love that was accursed, his guilt that had arisen!

And out of the gloom of the ruined cloisters and the hanging screens of ivy, there crept a shadow darker than any on the night; that shadow looked with him upon the innocence that the white-winged spirit guarded; that shadow, unseen by him, followed him as he went down towards the sea.

It was the form of Marion Vavasour.

## CHAPTER XXIX.
### "The Bows of the Mighty are Broken."

THE full autumn moon shone on the silent seas, the grey shades of the mediæval arches, and the stirless boughs drooping above the scattered ivy-covered graves, as Strathmore went through the night; went with his proud head bowed, and all the haughty serenity of his bearing broken and crushed. For he went to the man whom he had wronged.

Valdor leant against a shaft of the ruined abbey, with the light shining on his face; the ravages of captivity and of wretchedness were something worn away, but beauty, strength, brilliance, all the glory of manhood were gone, and gone for ever; and Strathmore shuddered as he looked on him. How could this man forgive? To have saved his life he could have uttered no word, have advanced no step; he paused, and stood silent. All the enormity of his sin seemed to arise and stand betwixt them; all the vastness of the mercy he had come to seek seemed to stretch out, mocking and lost before him. "Mercy!" What title to it had he?—he who had ever denied it.

The night was very calm, and its stillness was unbroken as they met; the one saw the husband of Lucille, the other her avenger and destroyer.

"Strathmore! were *you* traitor to me?"

The words fell at last from the man he had wronged, low, almost gentle, but with reproach profound as that which alone passed the dying Cæsar's lips to him whom he had loved too loyally.

Strathmore quivered from head to foot; traitor he had been, but there was no treachery in his blood. With a lie he could have disarmed this man; with a lie have denied the charge; there was no proof against him save such as his own words should give; no living soul who could have brought this last sin home to him save himself. From him whom he had wronged, moreover, he came to seek a mercy so vast, that the mercy which spares from death is pale to it. But while steeped in so much error, lost in so much crime, he still clung, even in his darkness, instinctively, and at all cost, to Truth. He bowed his head.

"Yes! I betrayed you."

"*You!*"

That one word was all he uttered, but in it all else was spoken; the reproach, too deep for passion, too generous for revenge, of the betrayed who wrote: "It is not an open enemy who hath done me this dishonour, for then I could have borne it. It was even thou, my companion, my guide, and my own familiar friend."

"I!"—he lifted his head, and as the moonlight shone upon it, his face was filled with a terrible despair, and with that which is worse than suffering, and which had never before then reached his life—shame. "I betrayed you—for her sake!"

Viler than he was in his own sight, he could be in no

man's; abhorrent of his sin, the purest could not be, more than he was then; "a traitor!" many crimes had stained, but, in his creed, none had dishonoured him till this. And the tyrant nature in him, sickening at its own evil and its own shame, laid itself bare to the bone, making no plea, seeking no lie, craving no pardon, asking no palliation, save such, if any there were, as lay in those brief words, "for her."

A deep sigh broke from the man he had ruined; he had been dealt an injury so vast, that all the life that lingered in him could not suffice to efface or repair it; he had been flung into a living tomb, and been crushed under a more lingering torture than that which gives death at a blow; his cause had been lost, his manhood had been wrecked, his strength had been destroyed for ever; yet his deep wrong was less before him in that moment than the anguish which struck him like a knife, that the friend whom he had honoured and trusted, whose bread he had broken, and whose hand he had grasped, should have turned traitor to him.

"Better have dealt me death than have done friendship this dishonour!"

The words were brief and simple; wider rebuke lay in them than lies in invective or in curse: and Strathmore shuddered as he heard. None knew their truth more utterly than he; none honoured honour more sacredly than he who had violated it; none held its laws more just and binding than he who had broken through them.

He bowed his head as one who bows before the lash which he merits too deeply to arrest.

"Say what you will! The vilest words you give will never reach the vileness of my guilt. I wronged you more brutally than by a death-thrust; and yet—I sinned for her!"

As he spoke the last words, his head was reared with its old royal dignity of bearing, and through the misery upon his face there flashed the old untamable, inflexible passions which through life had wrecked his peace and stained his soul.

"I betrayed you to save her from my doom. To spare myself a thousand deaths I would have never turned a traitor to a dog that should have trusted me; you have known me, you know that! It was in *his* trust. I had sworn her life should be before my own; I kept it so. I have been true to *him!* You do not loathe me for my wrong to you more vilely than I loathe myself; my sin is not blacker and fouler in your eyes than in mine; and yet,—were it to be done again, I would do it, if so only I could save her! Crime is more accursed to *me* than it ever was to the best life that ever shrank from it. I sicken for peace, for rest, for expiation— oh, my God, for *guiltlessness!*—and yet there is no crime I would not take on me if it could spare her. I owe her all— my soul itself!"

The words rang out on the still night, floating far over the starlit sea; his wild erring sacrifice, his guilty grand defiance flung down before the man who held so terrible a power of vengeance, blent with the heart-sickness of despair, the pathos of a vain remorse, the wretchedness of an utter impotence, of a love that was powerless to defend or save.

He who heard stood silent and motionless, his eyes fixed on Strathmore's face, on which the light of the moon fell. His own wrong, his own love, the memory of all he had endured, the knowledge that he who stood before him was the husband of Lucille,—these were forgotten in that moment; he only saw the depth and vastness of this man's guilt, the passion and the despair of his remorse. All else seemed too poor, too mean, too utterly of self, to be remembered then; all else seemed to float far away into oblivion before the might of this man's misery, the greatness of his hopeless thirst and travail for expiation.

Strathmore met his eyes unflinchingly; criminal he was, but coward never. He stood erect, his face white as death and drawn as with the deep and haggard lines of age. He did not plead; he offered no word more that could have seemed to seek extenuation of his sin; not even for her sake could he stoop to pray for mercy from the man he had betrayed. He knew that she must die—for he knew that the ghastliness of his past, touching her, would slay her, like the breath of the destroying angel.

"You have your vengeance—take it," he said, calmly, while his voice was changed to a hoarse and hollow utterance vibrating on the stillness. "Take it! It is your right. The innocent and the unborn will perish together for my guilt. It is no more than *I* merit."

Valdor shuddered, and the red blood flushed his face; for the moment he had risen above the weakness and the error of man, and had remembered alone pity such as Heaven itself may yield. But he was human—he had loved; with those words he was dashed back to the frailty of humanity and of passion. He saw before him the lover, the lord, the possessor of the life that he had worshipped—the husband of her youth, the father of her child.

A great struggle shook him, like a storm-wind. He turned and paced the long stretch of sward under the ruined aisles, his steps falling in heavy uneven measure on the silence that was only stirred by the sighing of the waves, far down below, beyond the glimmer of the moonlit leaves.

If ever man strove between good and evil, he wrestled with his tempters then. But not for the first time did he come to the conflict, nor for the first time had he conquered. Long ago he had striven to have strength for this hour if it came; and he had strength now.

He drew near and stood before Strathmore in the grey calm shadow of the monastic burial-place, beside the ivy-covered lowly grave on which that solitary word was carved,

### Lucille.

"Could you not trust me in so little? True, I spoke, to you in madness; I refused you mercy in the blind hate of passion; I knew not what I did! But could you not have known me well enough to know that, when that hour was passed, I should regret? Could you believe that, in cold blood, I should have been so vile as to take from you what loved and was loved by you? Could you think that your appeal would not disarm me, that your remorse and your atonement would have no sanctity in my sight? I spoke in haste—I erred; but before the night was passed I had repented."

"*Repented!* Oh, my God!—and I——"

The words rang out like a great death-cry over the silent seas.

"And you—misjudged me! As you misjudge me now. It is not for me to revenge your guilt—and revenge it on the guiltless! It is not for her to suffer because I was wronged—such vengeance would be for devils! Your secret is safe—your remorse is sacred with me. Lucille shall never learn that you were her father's destroyer; she shall never know that she was Erroll's child. I came to say this to you—this only. Friendship is ended for ever between us; but there may be still, at the least—forgiveness."

In his eyes, as he spoke, there was a divine light, and in his voice a divine pity; noiselessly, swiftly, as though to put aside all answer, and to spare him whom he had pardoned from his own gaze, he turned and went through the soft shadows of the leaves, through the twilight of the ruined aisle, through the stillness of the night, away down to where the sea lay. And the man whom crime had not made a coward, to whom remorse had not taught mercy, in whom misery had not availed to bring humility and pity, who had trusted to the strength of his own hand, and the mailed might of his own will, and had been his own god, his own judge, his own law, trembled like a great tree stricken at its roots as he heard the words which *spared* him, the words of that mercy which he had ever denied; and he fell down on the sward, stricken there motionless, prostrate, voiceless, as in the years that were gone he had fallen by the side of the dead whom he had slain. Never had his sin looked so great to him as in that hour in which its vengeance was withheld from him; never had his soul been so near to its redemption as now, when its vileness looked darkest in his sight, and was laid bare in the light of an unhoped deliverance, till he beheld it as it was beheld of God.

Out of the shadow of the arches stole the human shadow that had followed him. With the glide of a snake she swept through swathes of light and breadths of gloom, through tangled grasses heavy with rain, and wide, endless stretches of park land, broken up in hill and dale, with forest-trees and deep deer-pools. As the snake steals its rapid way, so she stole on hers, swift as a stag's flight, passing, as though borne on the wind, through the twilight of the still and silvery night.

She had his secret—she had her vengeance. And ever as she went, with her amber hair loosening in the breeze sweeping from the sea, and something of her lost dead beauty lent to her face in that moonlit gleam, as her eyes flashed once more with the evil triumph, the victorious and cruel lust of the years that were gone, Marion Vavasour murmured ever, till the words were borne in strange wild rhythm on the woodland silence far away, to join the ceaseless lulling of the waves:

"Such mercy as you gave, I give to you—no more!"

Lucille watched for him.

The night was hushed and very soft, with the light of the stars falling over the vast depths of woodland, stretching downward to the sea; and as she gazed upon it, while the west wind played among her hair, and the fragrance of dew-laden flowers rose upward from the grass below, her eyes filled with tears—the tears of a joy beyond words, that trembled even at its own intensity. She was so happy!—she who shared his life as no other had ever shared it.

The murmur of the sea, the low glad belling of the deer, the odour of every blossom that was borne on the wings of the wind, the silver gleam on every leaf that quivered in the moonbeams, these were all poems to her—sweet voices that chimed in with the rejoicing of her life. And where she leaned, with the dreaming lustre in her childlike eyes, and the star-rays circling her fair bowed head, her lips moved in prayer, pure as the prayer of infancy, and as unquestioning in faith. Prayer for all things that suffered; for all lives that needed pity; for all who were weary and travel-laden, and had sinned against the holiness of love; for all the homeless and the desolate, who bore the heat and burden of the day, and knew the shadow of that merciless calamity whose knowledge had never touched her; prayer of that compassion which rises from the fulness and the gratitude of joy, and from the glory of its own hushed gladness remembers and looks back on those who suffer, and pleads for them even as angels plead.

The night itself seemed to grow holier about her, the silence to pause in purer and gentler vigil around the sanctity of those early years, and God's own presence to encircle and to shield the life which knew him without fear as Love alone.

And towards her, through the darkness, with the noiseless swiftness of the wind, stole the shadow of the destroyer.

## CHAPTER XXX.
### "In the Silence of the Night."

HE lay stretched on the dank earth without movement, save for the shudder that now and again ran through his frame. His guilt had been abhorred from the first hour of its committal, but his pride had remained with him unchastened, unbent, untaught, to work its doom by its scornful and blasphemous deification of will and of power. Now this, too, was stricken from his hands—his own weakness had come home to him, he had been strengthless before the recoil of his acts, he had recognised the supreme wisdom of the truth, without which all lives are at best but of warped beauty and of splendid error—the truth which lies in following that which is just, letting result come as it may with the future.

He had been *spared!* The warmth, the redemption, the divinity of that mercy which he had ever denied, had touched him as the light of morning touches the gloom, till all that is dark and impure is bathed in its glory. Mercy,—likeness and attribute of God, which when it comes to earth makes man god-like,—he had always thrust from him; he had veiled his face and closed his heart to it; remorse had never taught him pardon; striving for atonement, he had never taken its first step—forgiveness. All its softness, all its nobility, all its serene and sanctified humanity, had been dead to him, rejected, scorned, destroyed:—and now it had risen and saved him, and in its light he saw the vastness of his own sin.

All his past life lived once more for him through those long and solitary hours: as men drowning in the great waste of the sea remember every face, every link, in the years that are ended for ever, so he saw all the forgotten things of his youth and of his manhood. He seemed to look back on his life as from the depths of a grave, and to behold it—proud, powerful, generous, honoured amongst men; but stained with error, wrecked by passion, riven at the core by the curse of one crime, and never reaching expiation because never bending to humiliation. For he had never forgiven!—he had never learned that frailty in his own life commanded from him pardon to others even for seventy times seven; he had never recognised that his own criminality forbade to him for ever the right of judgment, and enjoined on him to his grave the duty of an exhaustless clemency, unswerving, unweakened, whatever temptation might assail.

He had never forgiven!—there, worse than in the firstborn crime which had sprung from the blindness of his passions, lay the depth of his sin, the vainness of his atonement.

The night was very still.

There was no breath among the falling leaves, no movement except the ceaseless ebbing of the sea below. Countless stars shone without a floating cloud to veil them, and the long ivy coils over the lonely graves lay dark and stirless in the moonlight. There was not a sound borne on the air, not a shudder that stole through the autumnal forests; the silent hours swept on unmeasured and unbroken—for the night did not whisper the secrets it shrouded, the cold stars had no pity and uttered no warning, the world reeled on, and the innocent were unguarded, and the face of God was unseen.

Slowly and dully through the hush of the night there swung the midnight chimes of the abbey, iron strokes that dealt out the merciless passage of time, shadowy bells that echoed mournfully over the waters, wild beating cadences, now lost, now heard, dimly flung out in waves of sound upon the silence. Their melody fell upon his ear, and throbbed through his brain with a strange jarring echo, unreal and yet familiar; he rose slowly to his feet, and lifted his face to the coolness of the night. Beneath, stretched the silvered seas, where life and death had wrestled for him; around him was the deep and solemn tranquillity, when all things are at rest; above, the star-lighted vault that reached onward and upward to the infinite.

Mercy!—the whole night seemed to throb with that one word; the sea in its depths murmured it to him by whom it had been denied; the weary bells as they swung through the stillness bore it upon the wind. Mercy!—he had no right to it; no title to it; what his life had refused, his life could not claim. Mercy! Above, in the lustre of the skies, the light of Heaven seemed shining with the glory that is Forgiveness;—and below, in the black and endless waste of the ocean, lay the abyss into which his risen sin seemed to force the life that had been without compassion.

He stretched his arms out to the dark and fathomless gulf that had been his righteous doom, and upward to that cloudless light which never till now had shone for him, which now seemed dying from his sight ere he could reach it, or implore it to stay with him yet—yet to redeem him! That voiceless prayer went up to God in the silence of the night;—who shall say that it was lost?

He turned from the solitary shore, and took his homeward way through the shadows of the old monastic burial-place, where the sepulchres were made above the sounding of the sea, and were turned eastwards, that the light of early dawn, breaking on the world, might shine first upon them—the dead.

He reeled back, struck as with his death-thrust.

Between him and the twilight of the stars, standing out from the darkness of the ivied gloom, like a wraith from the tomb, rose the form of Marion Vavasour.

With her amber hair floating on the winds, with a wild beauty come back to her from that hour from her past, with the light of a merciless triumph, and the shadow of a deathless grace strangely blent with the soiled torn garments of an outcast, and the lost misery of one in whom shame had perished for ever, she rose in his path—now, as before, claiming him hers by right of that companionship in guilt, by title of their mutual bond of sin. Temptress, traitress, assassinatress, she returned to him after the long flight of years, holding him yet her own by the close tie of died-out passions and of buried sins; and behind the ruthless cruelty of the destroyer there looked the grand and austere justice of the Avenging Angel.

For her the sin had been sinned; by her came its retribution.

There, between the skies and him, she rose, hovering, as it seemed, upon the watery mists, the shining brilliance of the night;—and he gazed at her, filled with the speechless horror that had come on him when he had seen her face rise out of the depths of the sea in the white storm-flame.

A mocking mirth rang down the stillness of the night, vibrating through the chimes of midnight bells, echoing above the sounding of the seas:

"At last, Strathmore!—at last!"

"At last!"

The words broke from his lips in an unconscious echo, while the great dews gathered on his forehead, and in his eyes came the agony of the stag hunted to bay and caught within the toils. The supreme hour of his life, the supreme retribution of his sin had come. A shiver ran through his frame;—he had loved her! So well, so well! as never man loved woman, and even now the music that still lingered in her voice thrilled through him with its melody. It was the echo of his past; the echo of his youth.

Had that love ever wholly died, though hate had trodden it out and been greater than its greatest? Love is its own avenger.

"At last!" She seemed to float still before him on the shadowy luminance of the starry night, her hair flung out upon the winds, her wreck of broken and dishonoured loveliness a spectre risen from the buried years. "My lover, who lived but in my life, who saw no sun but in my eyes, who held crime sweet if I but bade it! did you think we were parted for ever? did you dream that the years could long sunder us? did you not know I should soon or late claim you my own? You are mine—you are mine! To-night I take back my empire!"

Mute, blind, paralysed, he stood and gazed at her, the sickness of horror on him; on the silvery mists of the night the words lingered; a strange triumph blent with the rich and thrilling melody of voice. Ghastlier than any curse of vengeance, more horrible than any dagger-stroke dealt him, were those words that spoke to him in the love-tones of old! —were those words which across the great chasm of crime and enmity floated to him and smote him with his past!

Her laugh rang down again, breaking the murmur of the seas.

"What! no word when I claim back my sovereignty? No vow, no kiss? You! my lost lover—who adored the very roses that my lips had pressed, who let honour drift away, a jeered and useless thing, to lie at my feet, to rest in my bosom, to gaze in my eyes; who wooed and courted guilt, as others glory, when *my* hand pointed, and *my* voice whispered it? What! no caress, no oath, no gratitude, when by our love I claim you, and own you, alone to-night? What! the roses are dead, is the love dead too? The murdered are buried, is the love buried too?"

"In mercy,—in pity,—be silent!"

The words broke, inarticulate, from his throat; he thought her senses gone, and in the chastened passions, and pride, the poignant remorse, and self-abasement of that hour, he knew himself too deeply guilty to have title to lift himself above her, or wreak his wrongs on his destroyer. The evil had gone from him, the hatred from his life: in his own sight his infamy was now so great that it lowered hers, and withheld her from his vengeance. The relentless and iron hate with which it had pursued her had died when the light of mercy had shone on his heart, and the appeal to Heaven been on his lips; if she had tempted, he had avenged; if she had murdered with her lie, he had slaughtered with his hand. What was he that he had title to condemn this woman, vast as were his wrongs, wide as were her crimes?

She drew nearer to him, leaning on the flickering brilliance of the night like a spirit borne upon the air; and as her eyes gazed closer into his, as her hair floated in the light, as nearer and nearer came that soiled, broken, ruined wreck of all that she had been, she saw him shudder and reel back, and close his eyes to shut out that mockery and resurrection of the past.

"Silent?—silent?" she echoed. "Why, the days were when the world had no music for you but my voice!—when but to hear me murmur those fool's words, 'I love you!' honour, duty, brotherhood, men's laws, and God's commands, were all thought worthless! 'Eternal love, eternal love!' that was what you vowed me: though the earth should be shattered, and the heavens should flame like a scroll, *we* were to love for ever! Heaven itself was not to sever *us!* Ah! and the love lasted but the life of the rose!"

"Oh God, cease!"

Her words as they lingered down the air with all the unforgotten melody of old, mocking, terrible, yet with a strange and bitter sadness sighing through them,—the lament of youth, the weariness of despair—pierced him to the quick, till the pent suffering of years broke out and poured itself before the woman by whom his youth had been destroyed, his life been wrecked.

"Love?—love? Dare you speak it to me?" he cried aloud. "Ay, I loved you, Heaven help me! I loved you, better than life, or guiltlessness, or brotherhood, or God; sorceress, temptress, traitress, that you were! You had my life, my heart, my honour, all that was mine on earth and in eternity. What were they to you? Toys that you played with, and hurled back into ruin: slaves that you dragged at your feet for the whole world to laugh at, then steeped in blood and hounded on to murder!"

A tearless sob caught his breath, and broke heavily on the silence of the night, then the loosened rush of words swept on again, all the silent reproach, all the crushed-out misery of so many years breaking their prison before the woman who had known his madness, made his doom, and suffered from his vengeance.

"Is there measurement for your sin to me? Guilty I was, but not to you; shame was glorious for you, death welcome for you, dishonour sweet for you! I gave you all the glory of my manhood, I gave you all the peace of my whole life, I gave you more—a devil's gift, yet given because I loved you —*his* blood!—sacrificed, guiltless—his blood, that is on me and mine for me! Your crime is without end to me; to my dying hour the guilt you scourged me to, is on me; it poisons every innocent thing, it curses every hope of peace; every year the roses bloom, I think of you; every summer sun that sets, I see his death-agony, I hear his dying words, —I know I slaughtered him as wild beasts kill what they hate. Oh, God! the vileness of your sin was never equalled upon earth—save—save by the vileness of my own."

Her eyes fastened on him with a strange look that seemed to burn through the misty brilliance round them, wildly mournful, cruelly triumphant; to-night, for one brief hour at least, she took back her empire, she ruled him, she tortured him, she shook his passions as the cycloon shakes the cedars; she alone was remembered by him. His proud and ice-cold life still was riven to its centre by her; in all its mailed and kingly power, within it had ever lived the agony of a cheated love, the torture of a deathless remorse; he had never forgotten the idolatry of his youth, he had never ceased to suffer! And the vain and evil triumph of her nature flashed out with exultation, even while her eyes dwelt on him with pain, which in her, too, wearied for the past—which in her, too, yearned towards all that was lost for ever!

"Vile as it was," she said, slowly, "you revenged it as brutally! Once you drove me out to what was worse than death, once you loosed me to death itself, and the storm and the waves knew more mercy than you!"

"Such mercy as you gave, I gave to you!" the words that he had spoken in the past, broke unconsciously once more from his lips, hoarse with anguish, pleading not with her, but with the condemnation of his conscience, the accusation of his past. "I pursued you, I destroyed you, I hunted you down to ruin, as you had hunted me to fratricide. I bade you die the death that you had dealt to him. I had no pity —*I*—who should have seen my brotherhood in the foulest criminals that taint the earth, who should have known that I had forfeited for ever my right to judgment! But it was not *my* wrongs that I revenged, it was not the curse on *my* life that I remembered when I smote you,—it was his! Guiltless, you slew him. Loyal, and just, and stainless, your lie hurled him to his grave. That was your crime—for that my vengeance. Answer me now, before God, you who made me his murderer, you who slew him without pity in his glory and his youth—answer me, was the vengeance greater than the crime?"

Where she stood before him, she to whom crime had been triumph and duty fable, who had been without pity and without remorse, shrank for one moment as though struck to the heart; then she raised herself slowly in the starlight, with something of the old grand grace and sovereign gesture of the past, while for once in her eyes there was no evil, for once on her lips no lie.

"Greater?—No! But it was not *your* hand which should have dealt it, Strathmore."

He bowed his head where he stood in the bright mist shining from the sea.

"I know it,—*now!* Your sin was mine, and mine was yours. *I* had no right to strike you,—*I!*—who was guiltier yet than you."

He had drunk the bitterest dregs in the cup of his chastisement; he had vanquished the darkest passion of his nature; he had taken submissively as his due the cruellest stripe of his scourge, now, when to the woman who had been his betrayer he spoke in peace, and accepting her sin as his own, laid down his rights of vengeance.

She was silent, in her eyes passionate hate and wild regret, love that seemed to live again, victory strange and nameless, passions dead, and conscience wakened, seemed to gleam, all mingled and in conflict, and burn through the floating shadows of the night; while on the stillness there only broke the sighing of the midnight seas, the echo of the midnight bells. She leaned nearer yet towards him, her hair driving backward in the wind, the ravages of time and shame fallen from her in the softened shade; and with that gesture both remembered how she had once pressed his hand against her bosom and bidden him go sin for her, when with tiger-thirst she panted for blood, for life!

"Strathmore! I wronged you once; I came to-night to wrong you more. I murdered once; I came to-night to slaughter yet again! Years ago, in my extremity, you said such mercy as I gave, you gave to me. Such mercy I came to-night to give to you—no more!"

She saw him stagger again, she heard one convulsed and tearless sob break again upon the stillness, she saw in his eyes gather the wild and hunted misery that she had known, —and in that moment the vile and cruel nature inborn in the traitress revived and ruled. He suffered!—he suffered! She had her triumph; she had her foot upon the haughty, humbled neck; she had her hand upon the proud, mailed heart, to wring it as she would. Through all the course of baffled years she had waited for that hour—and it was hers.

Her laugh, jeering, victorious, abhorrent in its melody, rang on the air.

"Ah! the love lived but the life of the rose—you have replaced it. Why leave what you cherish! We can strike you through her! While she sleeps in her innocence, and dreams of your kisses, the whisper can steal to her that will scarce sleep for ever, and tell her the life that her husband destroyed."

A cry from him broke her words—a cry so terrible, so heart-broken, that as it echoed down the lonely shore and far across the waves, those sleeping out at sea heard it, and woke and shuddered, thinking it the death-wail of some drowning man sinking, beyond help, in the solitude of the ocean. It silenced even her.

This had been her coveted lust; this had been the moment for which she had watched, and waited, and pursued, and endured the weary course of loathsome years. He suffered! where she hovered, shadow-like, before his aching sight, her eyes seemed to pierce through into his life, her laugh to echo with a devil's joy. His secret in *her* hands!—his darling's peace laid at her mercy!—than whom the panther were gentler to move, the vulture were more pitiful to spare! His lips parted, but formed no sound, the great drops stood like the sweat of death upon his brow, his limbs trembled, his eyes were fastened on her with a dumb, agonised appeal. If before that hour retribution had never overtaken him, in it retribution would have fallen on him vast as his dead crime.

"Your lips were mine!" she cried, laughing still in that mocking mirth; "their kisses must poison hers. Your hand slew him! its touch must pollute hers. Oh, lover, who lived but in my smile!—did you not know the dead passion would rise up and curse the new? Oh, lord of the iron will!—did you dream that you were stronger than fate, and vengeance, and a woman's hate, and think you could strangle your secret, and shelter your darling for ever? What! while the earth held your crime, and I still had life?—while the red grasses had once drunk his blood, and I lived to tell her the hidden sin of her husband? Strathmore, Strathmore! was *that* your wisdom, *that* your strength! Oh, fool, who thought yourself as deity! Oh, madman, who hoped that the past could ever be silenced!"

The words vibrated through the air, ringing high in cruel mockery, throbbing on the stillness with their irony, piercing him with iron thrust; and his agony broke out in a single prayer, not to her, never to her, but to the Eternity that shone above and gazed upon him through the calm eyes of the stars.

"Lucille!—Lucille! Oh, God of the guiltless, save her!"

The prayer rang through the silence as though pleading at the very throne of heaven, borne there by all the voices of the night; before its anguish her laugh died, the triumph faded from her eyes, a sigh ran through her.

"God of the guiltless!—he is not *our* God!"

In the words there were the wild regret, the passionate derision, of a life dimly waking to remorse, and struggling under the heavy, stifling burden of unrepented sins and of inexpiable crimes.

"But he is *here!*"

The answer was still a prayer, broken, hopeless, pleading; not to his torture, not to his destroyer, but to those serene and lustrous worlds in which were spoken the majesty and the pity of the Infinite. Could they look on and see the sinless perish? Would the God she worshipped in her childlike trust, with every sun that rose and every night that fell, desert her now? The night swam round him, the noise of the waves surged in his brain, his lips were white and cloven, his eyes saw nothing but the face of his destroyer, and the radiance of the heavens shining far away.

There was no thought of violence, no instinct to crime in him now, sin had lost its hold upon his soul, for belief in immortality had risen there; there was nothing but a stunned, dull despair, in which he saw his own deed recoil upon the innocent, and was powerless to shield or save her.

Marion Vavasour stood and gazed on him, and in her eyes there gleamed that strange and nameless blending of hate and love, of triumph and regret, of mocking victory and of futile pain, which had come there before; if ever in her life she had loved, she had loved him, and she thought of the glory of her womanhood, the splendour of her power, when his life had been hers, and her loveliness had bound him in its golden chains; she thought of the great passion that he had poured out at her feet, and that she had cheated, ruined, and driven to its guilt.

In his presence something of the brutality of hate perished; something of the memory of love revived.

She leaned nearer to him once more, with a relic of the proud and sovereign grace returned to the dark, dishonoured wretchedness of the Outcast.

"The God of the guiltless! We know no God, you and I. We know that if there be a God, he sends his sunlight on the criminal, and lets the sinless perish. You have lived in honour, and riches, and power, and men's esteem, and I in beggary, and misery, and shame. What justice is there *there?* Our sin was mutual! Since I am a wanderer and an outcast, so should you be; since I am homeless, and dishonoured, so should you be. Our guilt was equal, why not our punishments? If I deal you back your cruelty and your vengeance to-night; if I tell you such mercy as you gave I give to you;

if I smite you with your dead crime, what is it more than justice?"

His head sank; he knew it was no more. And a great darkness covered his sight, hiding the radiance of the stars; his life was held in the iron bonds of a pitiless retribution, and in his misery the voice of the woman who had been his temptress came to him like the voice of vengeance, inexorable but just.

"No more," she echoed, slowly. "No more—to you. Listen, Strathmore! Since the hour that we parted I have had but one aim, one toil, one thirst, one hope—to destroy you pitilessly as you destroyed me. To see you suffer, to see you fall, to wring your heart, to kill your pride, to make every breath a pang to you, to have you at my mercy and deny it you, to shame, dishonour, scourge you, curse you. I have only lived for that!"

The words had risen, hissing through the night like a snake's hiss, all the intensity of hate that she had cherished vibrating through them, and showing him the black and fathomless abyss on which he stood—one gesture of her hand, and he must fall, dragging downward the soilless life he loved, to perish in his guilt.

No word escaped him, no movement, his blood was ice, his breath crushed; all of life that was in him gazed out from the agony of his eyes;—it was the petrefaction of despair.

Yet—even now—even for the innocent—he would not plead to *her*. She might destroy—she could not abase him. She saw it;—and out of the poignant virulence of her hate, a kindred grandeur, a wild reverence, flashed from the proud instincts of Marion Vavasour's nature for this man, who even in crime, even in torture, never wholly lost his greatness.

"I came to destroy you! Why not! Why not! The tiger does not spare its fangs, nor the vulture its fury; while neither hate what they pursue as I have hated," she said slowly, while her voice sank lower and thrilled its rich music through the night. "I have your secret, Strathmore. I can slay what you love to-night. I can whisper to her what her husband is; and the day when it breaks will find her dead. Oh, Heaven! I have longed for it! I have only lived for that —to strike her in your arms, to rend her out of your honour and shelter, to crush her down where your love cannot shield her or reach her, to take her youth, her loveliness, her innocence, and make them vile as my life, to have no pity on her, and torture you through her, till in all your years you should have learnt no misery such as *that* love should bring you. I hated her—I cursed her!——"

He stayed her with a gesture, grand in its command, supreme in its agony:

"Peace! Slay her if you must with my guilt, but never dare to curse her—you!—her father's murderess."

Her eyes dwelt on him with a nameless pain, a softened light, in which their evil and their lust were quenched: she flung her arms up toward the skies, and raised her shameless and dishonoured brow to the pure cool of the autumnal skies.

"Oh, God! to-night I too remembered *that!* I had your secret; I panted to destroy her; the wind was not swifter than I as I went to my vengeance——"

Again over the seas rang the cry of a man in his extremity —it was *past* then—her vengeance! God had looked on and seen the guiltless perish!

"It was so sweet—so sweet, that death-blow to strike *both*," and her voice rose higher, piercing through the air, while still she raised her face upward—upward—to the light of the stars. "She was alone—your love, your strength, your power, could do nothing to shield her *then*. The night gave her to me, there where she leaned in its starlight, watching for *you*. There was no arm to protect her—no eye to behold us. She was mine! mine to crush with my hand like a bird or a flower—mine to kill with more torment still by your crime, and I could have stamped her life out as we tread out an insect's;—and I longed for it, hungered for it, pined for it. And yet—*is* there a God? Does he keep even *us* from the last depths of hell? Where I crouched in the darkness, I heard her pray, pray for all things that suffered, for all that were in sin and woe; in her joy, in her youth, she prayed for us—the guilty and the cursed! The light was on her—and I saw in hers her father's eyes, her father's smile; I remembered how I had murdered him! I could not slay her then—not *then*—even though you loved her. I could not touch her—look on her—breathe near her. Her prayer stood between us, her father's memory held her from me, the dead himself smote my vengeance from my hands. I spared her! *I*—the world must end to-night!"

Her laugh rang on the air in mockery of herself—then into her burning, weary eyes tears rushed for the first time since years of shame; she quivered from head to foot, and stood there, in the starlight, trembling and afraid. In fear of him? No; in fear of that long and shameless evil which was called her Life.

He heard her;—and on his face there shone a sudden light, pure, cloudless, glorified, like that of the planets above. In torture she had not abased him, in agony she had not humbled him, in vengeance she had not laid him suppliant; but now—in that hour of release, when into the darkness of his life the ransom of an unhoped mercy came—she had her victory. She saw him bow down before her, broken, blinded, voiceless, senseless, his haughty power smitten as a granite shaft is smitten by the lightning, his proud life pierced and shaken to the core, his soul laid bare and without shield, in the moment of his deliverance.

By her had come his guilt;—by her also came his retribution and his redemption.

The skies reeled round him in whirling circles of starry light; the silence of the night seemed filled with murmuring hosts of angel voices; the dead past seemed to fall from him for ever, and be swept away into those still and lustrous seas that echoed at his feet; and on the air, borne up on the winds and on the waves, he heard the dying words of the man whom he had loved and slain: "I forgive! Oh God! *I* forgive!"—as though by that forgiveness pleading there for the pardon of the guilty, for the safety of the sinless.

He had forgiven: who should avenge?

In the silence where they stood together, Strathmore lifted his head and looked on her, the vulture that had spared, the panther that had known some pang of pity at the last; and in her he saw, incarnated, his own merciless and brutal sin—saw it, loathsome as it was, denying the pardon which it lived to need, usurping the power and the judgment of deity to sate through them the vilest passions of mortality.

His limbs shook, his lips quivered, his forehead was wet with the dews of a great suffering, but on his face shone that light which once before had come there when he had stood on the wreck of the sinking ship with death upon him, and the mad waves leaping round; and in his eyes as they dwelt on her there was a profound anguish, gentle, fathomless, merciful, in the consciousness of his own weakness, giving forgiveness to her at the last, by whom his sin had come, by whom his years had been accursed.

It was the supreme expiation of his life.

He stretched his hands towards her where she stood, and his voice vibrated with an infinite pardon through the night:

"The mercy you remembered to her, be remembered to you at the last, by her God! We both murdered him with brutal guilt;—we have both striven to atone to him through the innocent. Let us part in peace to-night; let sin be dead in both our lives for ever."

She looked at him one moment, in one long, last, mute farewell;—then she bowed her head in silent acceptance of his words of peace, of his renunciation of the power of evil; and like a shadow on the air, a spirit on the wind, Marion Vavasour swept from him through the autumn night and through the white and wreathing mists that floated from the sea, and faded from his life for evermore.

And once again, like a man bruised and stunned by mortal blow, he sank down among the coiling ivy and the sea-splashed stones, his arms outstretched, his limbs shaken by a voiceless agony, alone in the silence of the night. For he had loved her; he had sinned for her, and all the irrevocable crime of those dead years was but the darker and more deeply damned in his own sight, because the pity of God had touched his life with an exhaustless and unutterable mercy, and had spared him the just harvest of his work when his guilt arose to destroy the innocent, and the strength of his own hand was stricken powerless.

## CHAPTER XXXI.

"E poi uscimmo a Riveder' le Stelle."

IN the still night Lucille lay sleeping, as the young flower sleeps, unconscious of the ruthless hand that has been stretched to break and to despoil it, and that has passed over it without harm because its loveliness brought back a pang of memory, an echo of lost youth. Through the lofty casement left open to the night there shone the tranquil and star-studded skies, there came the far melodious murmur of the seas; and straying through dark traceries of foliage and the deep hues of the painted panes, the light fell on her where she slept, and shed its halo round her.

Her hair swept backward in its golden masses, a dreaming smile was on her lips, a soft flush on her brow, on which the chastened brilliance of the moonlight fell, and in her sleep she murmured, as though her dreams were seraphs' whispers,

"God is Love!"

They were the last words of her evening prayer; the words that had stricken strengthless the hand which had been lifted to destroy her.

He heard them as, from the lonely shore, he came into her presence as to some divine and sacred thing, and stood to look on her in the repose of innocence and childhood, unconscious of the peril that had drawn near her in the silence and the solitude of the defenceless night, to strike her with his sin, and sacrifice her for his guilt—drawn so near! so near! He shuddered and sickened at its memory, gazing on her with bursting heart and yearning eyes, listening for every soft pulse of her young life, watching for every noiseless breath that passed her lips, for every smile that dreaming lent its light to sleep, as though she had been given back to him from the hideousness of death by storm, by flame, by poisoned steel, or by plague-tainted air. His dead sin had risen, and had crept to her to slay her with his past. And he had thought to bury sin and bid it keep its peace, and have no resurrection! Oh, fool! oh, fool!

"God is Love!"

Yes! God was Love, since he had saved her. He heard the words murmured in her happy rest, where she dreamed of angel voices and of lands beyond the sun; and the smile upon her lips, where she lay in the serene and silvered glory of the heavens, lulled to slumber by the gentle echoes of the distant seas, smiled on him with pardon from the dead, with mercy for the past, with promise for the future, with light from Him by whom no prayer remains unheard and no remorse denied.

Burning tears rose into his aching eyes, deep sobs shook his frame—it was the agony of gratitude, the delirium of release; and as he threw himself down beside her bed, his arms cast over her in her sleep, his head bowed upon the loose trail of her bright hair, Strathmore laid down for ever the sins and the passions of his past, and gave, as to the hand of God, his dedication to a life that should know no law save of mercy, no governance save of compassion, no pause in self-humiliation, no pity in self-sacrifice, no effort but for redemption, no travail but for expiation—a life that should hold its holiest as nothing worth, its best as nothing given.

And the tender chastened light of the morning stars, growing clearer and clearer to the dawn in which the shadows of the night were fading, shone on him where he knelt beside the deep pure sleep of innocence.

\* \* \* \* \*

Away in the deep heart of the great western forests, in the silence of the solitary swamps, where pestilence is abroad in the torrid noons, and miasma rises with every night that falls, where the dank leaves drop death, and the graves lie thick under the cypress-woods, a woman in the Order of St. Vincent de Paul lives ever among the poor, the suffering, the criminal, the shameless, sparing herself no task, fearing no death—dead to the world, as the world is dead to her. For the dying her voice has a strange rich music, far beyond all other; for the innocent her look has a nameless terror, it is often very evil still; for those who are in dishonour, or in danger, her lips have a wild, sweet eloquence that scares them back from their abyss, and leaves them saved but sore afraid; for none has she a history. Once, when in her path some summer roses bloomed, and in the sunlight threw their soft fragrance on the wind, they saw tears gather in her eyes, and fall, slowly, as though each tear were a pang; then alone did they ever see that she thought of her youth, that she remembered her past.

In the press of the great world, far sundered from her by whom his guilt came, through whom his guilt still pursues him, one man lives who joins to the life that is known of men, a life that is unknown by any. A life, in which those who weary and are heavy laden are aided by a hand that they never see; in which every shape of suffering is sought and succoured; in which all evil memories that tempt, are crushed out, as in a debt that is due; in which all deeds of sacrifice are done with a strength that is merciless only to itself; in which a sweet and sinless happiness sheds its radiance; yet in which the poignancy of one remorse, the memory of one crime, are never lulled to peace or to oblivion, but, following the appointed travail of a silent expiation offered only to the dead, and of a supreme duty rendered for conscience' sake alone, lay subject the stained greatness of a grand and guilty nature, and lift it upwards into holier light.

By passion his life fell, lost in darkness of the night, and sunk in lowest deeps; yet, though once fallen, who shall dare deny that, in the end, it shall not reach that atonement which unceasingly is besought, obedient to the law which lies on every human soul, seeking for purification, striving for immortality, rising nearer and higher towards the perfect day, onward to

<blockquote>Other heights, in other lives, God willing!</blockquote>

THE END.

www.ingramcontent.com/pod-product-compliance
Lightning Source LLC
Chambersburg PA
CBHW031855220426
43663CB00006B/632